MW00721106

MASTERS OF THE MARKET

SECRETS OF AUSTRALIA'S LEADING SHAREMARKET INVESTORS

ANTHONY HUGHES, GEOFF WILSON & MATTHEW KIDMAN

Wrightbooks

First published 2005 by Wrightbooks
an imprint of John Wiley & Sons Australia, Ltd
42 McDougall Street, Milton Qld 4064

Offices also in Sydney and Melbourne

Typeset in Charlotte Book 11/13.2 pt

© A. J. Hughes, G. J. Wilson and M. J. Kidman 2005

National Library of Australia
Cataloguing-in-Publication data:

Hughes, Anthony, 1974-

Masters of the market: secrets of Australia's leading sharemarket investors
2nd ed

Includes index
ISBN 0 7314 0294 4

1. Stocks - Australia. 2. Capitalists and financiers - Australia - Interviews.
3. Stockbrokers - Australia - Interviews.
I. Wilson, Geoff, 1958- . II. Kidman, Matthew, 1968- . III. Title.

332.6322

Cover design by Rob Cowpe

Cover photos reproduced with permission, courtesy of as follows. Sir Ron Brierley: © Fairfax Photos/Jane Dyson. Gary weiss: © Fairfax Photos/Jane Dyson. Geoff Wilson: © Newspix/Bob Finlayson. Erik Metanomski: MMC Asset Management Ltd. Robert Maple-Brown: Maple-Brown Abbott Limited. Alex Waislitz: Thorney Holdings. David paradice: David Paradice. Anton Tagliaferro: Investment Mutual Limited. Tim Hughes: R G Capital Holdings (Aust) Pty Ltd. Peter Hall: Hunter Hall Investment Management. Brian Price: Brian Price. Jim Millner: Washington H Soul Pattinson. Rob Millner: Washington H Soul Pattinson. Peter Guy: Peter Guy. Phil Mathews: Phil Mathews. Andrew Sisson: Andrew Sisson. Author photo: © Peter Morris.

Printed in Australia by Griffin Press

10 9 8 7 6 5 4 3 2 1

Disclaimer
The material in this publication is of the nature of general comment only, and does not represent professional advice. It is not intended to provide specific guidance for particular circumstances and it should not be relied on as the basis for any decision to take action or not take action on any matter which it covers. Readers should obtain professional advice where appropriate, before making any such decision. To the maximum extent permitted by law, the interviewees, authors and publisher disclaim all responsibility and liability to any person, arising directly or indirectly from any person taking or not taking action based upon the information in this publication.

Contents

Acknowledgments

The authors would like to thank the Masters old and new for generously offering their time to tell their stories. They would also like to acknowledge the efforts of the team at Wilson Asset Management: Zahidi Agar, Natasha Cuffe, Justin Braitling, Karl Siegling, Catriona Alford and Kate Thorley were always happy to lend a hand even when they were already flat out with their own work.

Matthew Kidman would like to thank his workplace for its flexibility and allowing him time to put together a second book in two years. He would also like to thank his colleagues Anthony Hughes and Geoff Wilson for their efforts, especially Anthony's tireless efforts before and after work. He would also like to thank his former boss Glenn Burge for writing the foreword to the book and supporting the cause at *The Australian Financial Review*. Finally, he would like to once again thank his family for their tolerance given the amount of time a book takes. When the first edition of *Masters of the Market* was written, Matthew had two children. This has now expanded to three. Thanks goes to his wife, Suzy, for her hours as a mother and wife and, of course, a big hug to Bella, Will and Max.

Geoff Wilson would like to thank two of Australia's great wordsmiths — co-authors Matthew and Anthony — for their amazing skill and tireless effort. Geoff would also like to thank his father, Bill, for introducing him to the sharemarket and his late mother, Quita. Geoff also thanks his wife, Karen, for supporting him while he spent too much time absorbed in the market and his daughter, Amelia, who is his most devoted stock market student.

Anthony Hughes would like to first thank his co-authors. Matthew showed he hasn't lost his journalistic skills despite seven years out of the industry and seemed the most focused on getting the job done. Geoff was always an inspiration and showed great skills in solving some of the problems that inevitably arise in the mad rush to meet deadlines. Anthony Hughes would also like to thank friends, colleagues and wiser heads at *AFR* for their support and sageful advice. In particular, Tracy Lee provided valuable assistance in transcribing interview tapes as the deadline loomed.

About the authors

Matthew Kidman is a former journalist with *The Sydney Morning Herald* who now works as a fund manager for Wilson Asset Management. He worked for *SMH* for four years, covering the media and telecommunications sector, and edited the commercial property section. In 1997, Matthew was appointed investment editor of *SMH*, with responsibility for the paper's sharemarket coverage. He has also been a feature writer for the paper. Before joining *SMH*, Matthew completed dual degrees in law and economics at Macquarie University.

Anthony Hughes is the editor of *The Australian Financial Review*'s 'Street Talk' column. Prior to this, he was at *The Sydney Morning Herald* for eight years, which included a stint as investment editor. He has covered most sectors of the market, including the financial services, media, telecommunications, commercial property and construction sectors. He has covered many of the top corporate stories and companies in Australia including all four big banks, Telstra, BHP Billiton, News Corp, Lend Lease, Woolworths, Macquarie Bank, Wesfarmers and AMP. Prior to the *SMH*, he worked at *Business Queensland/Business Sydney* newspapers for two years. He has a degree in journalism from the University of Queensland and is an affiliate of the Securities Institute of Australia.

Geoff Wilson is both a subject and a co-author of the book. He is the managing director of his own funds management business, Wilson Asset Management. Geoff has more than twenty-five years' experience in the securities industry, having worked in both stockbroking and funds management. His stockbroking career spans fifteen years and has included posts in the United Kingdom for Potter Partners, and in New York for McIntosh Hoare Govett. Geoff worked for Prudential-Bache Securities in Sydney between 1990 and 1997, where he was an executive director responsible for institutional stockbroking. During that time he provided corporate advice on equity-related transactions to a large number of Australian public companies. He is a fellow of the Securities Institute of Australia and has a bachelor of science degree from LaTrobe University.

Foreword

In 1985, NSW premier Neville Wran found himself facing off against Sir Ron Brierley, the New Zealand-born corporate raider who began his career running an investment newsletter analysing dozens of sharemarket listed companies and looking for opportunities to make money. Brierley's Industrial Equity had taken the extraordinary action of buying 41 per cent of Australian Gas Light Co — despite a government shareholding restriction that limited any individual shareholder to just 2 per cent.

It was as a young business reporter following this extraordinary battle on the now defunct *Sun Newspaper* that I first came across Brierley's legal whiz Gary Weiss. Weiss led the team that navigated the legal and commercial nuances of the AGL raid. In the often early morning telephone calls I made to Weiss, it became clear that Weiss was far from conventional.

His philosophy, honed by his exposure to Brierley and a small team of analysts, was quite simple — there were dozens of companies where management, usually led by a sleepy and often arrogant board, refused to make the decisions necessary to create shareholder wealth.

Through painstaking research, not just freely available information, Weiss would pull apart a company before making an investment decision. He would consider board members' corporate history and connections, rivals, suppliers — the forensic skills were extraordinary in their detail. Many of the 'targets' were unloved and low-profile sharemarket names — and the investment decision generally involved an 'exit' strategy, with the Brierley team often being the catalyst for many industry consolidation plays.

While Brierley and Weiss were at the centre of many high-profile corporate events in the 1980s, Paul Keating's introduction of compulsory superannuation accompanied by the rise of the funds management industry was also under way. Because of these changes, there were extraordinary opportunities for young fund managers to invest large sums of cash into the sharemarket, trawling the sharemarket lists for opportunities and taking strong positions to ensure that management and boards felt pressured to deliver returns.

The investment approaches may vary, but there are common traits in the most successful professional investors. They share a commitment to detail, a high level of healthy scepticism about the numbers, and the willingness to back their view with a significant investment. Many fund managers can work over an Excel spreadsheet and use various methodologies to work out the intrinsic value of a company. That is the easy part — understanding how to use that nous and having the skills to then successfully invest is more difficult.

Australia's best fund managers also show the ability to understand the intangible aspects of investing — when to make the right decision to buy or sell. Each year, the potential to make good and bad calls are numerous but an elite few have the ability to produce above average returns over the long term.

Over the years, I have listened to many professional sharemarket investors outline their views on dozens of Australian listed companies. The best are able to successfully take sizeable bets on stocks, pick the next takeover targets or sell a stock before trouble hits.

These successful investors also show a healthy scepticism towards the sell side of the market — the stockbrokers — preferring to do their own research to come to an investment decision rather than be 'sold a story'. Most impressively, some have played an important role in the market with their willingness — often publicly — to challenge management and company directors.

As for the authors, both Matthew Kidman and Anthony Hughes are former *SMH* business journalists (employed under my former editorship of the paper's business section) and have spent a considerable time following Australia's biggest corporate and sharemarket stories of the past decade or so. Mathew Kidman has now carved out a successful career as a fund manager at Geoff Wilson's Wilson Asset Management with Geoff Wilson, whose vision it was to create this book, while Anthony Hughes has since moved onto *The Australian Financial Review* as editor of the daily 'Street Talk' column.

For anyone who is serious about sharemarket investing, the insights of the likes of Weiss, Tagliaferro and the other subjects in the book make compelling reading.

Glenn Burge
Editor, *The Australian Financial Review*
August 2005

Introduction

As I sat down to write the introduction to the second edition of *Masters of the Market*, I looked back and read large sections of the original book to warm up my brain for the exercise. Quite regularly throughout the book we mentioned the possibility of writing a second edition — so I suppose it was always going to happen.

The consensus at the time was that maybe in five years (that is, 2008) we might all put our heads together again and have a go at writing ten or twelve new chapters. By that stage, there would be a new squad of gun professional investors who would have great track records worth recording.

When our publisher asked whether we could produce a new edition only after two years, the camp was split. Given this is only a side job for the three of us, the hard work of doing all those interviews and editing them into shape good enough for a book seemed like a lot of hard slog. But after a meeting or two between the three authors we actually realised that while the first book was tough work, it was also a fabulous experience.

More to the point, our egos got the better of us.

Strangely for Anthony and myself, despite being journalists and having our names in the newspaper on a daily basis, there was a tantalising attraction to writing a book. A man who lived across the street from me approached me at a kid's party one weekend and said, 'I know your face from somewhere. That's right! You're on the back of this book I'm reading ... What's it called? *Masters of the Market'*. At that stage, my ego went into overdrive.

For whatever reason, the kudos associated with writing a book far outweighs that of daily appearances in the newspaper or successfully managing money.

And so, in January 2005, we again met at the Grind Café in Sydney's Bligh Street to nut out our strategy for our next 500 pages. It was quickly concluded that picking a whole new batch of investors was near impossible given it was only two years since the last edition. It was also thought that we wanted to write a book only about the best investors to give further credence to the description 'Master'.

It was finally resolved that we would introduce only three new subjects. In that way, it could almost be a hall of fame instead of a hall of many. It was also decided very quickly that the authors would remove themselves as the judges for the new entries, killing any possible criticisms about the people we may have missed or simply not been aware of.

Instead, we left it in the hands of the original fifteen masters, who all voted on the people they thought deserved to be included in the book. We made it clear that they had to vote for people with outstanding long track records and people who concentrate on equities rather than alternative asset classes. Those with the most votes would be selected.

As authors, it was also a way of covering a question many people had asked — who do the Masters themselves rate as top-notch investors? Many names were thrown up but in the end only three investors got the votes. The result was a tremendous mix of styles and areas of expertise. Little known Melbourne-based small-company investor Peter Guy got the nod, as did long/short fund manager Phil Mathews. Our third nominee was Andrew Sisson from Balanced Equity Management. Sisson manages $8 billion in equities, focusing on the top fifty companies.

All three agreed to be interviewed, making the authors' jobs significantly easier. As one of the authors and a green professional investor, I believe the three new inductees were all insightful in their own way, the match of any we conducted as part of the first attempt in 2003. We hope you enjoy their insights as much as we did.

All three have differing styles and confirm our belief that there is no one path to success, and no secret formula. The new interviewees also confirm that investment styles in many ways reflect the individual's personality.

Once the 'new kids on the block' were sorted out, we then thought it appropriate to go back to our original Masters and see how they have fared since we interviewed them in 2003. We posed each of them a similar batch of questions along with a series of questions that were specific to each one's situations. Some of the masters have, like the Australian sharemarket, enjoyed tremendous success over the last two years; others have struggled to keep up with the 75 per cent return (at the time of writing) delivered by the market. It shouldn't be surprising that some underperformed, given a large group are classified as value investors and bull markets do not usually throw up a lot of value. Also, for many two years is a short investment horizon. Many of the investors, like Robert Maple-Brown and Erik Metanomski, mostly invest in companies based on a five- to ten-year view of value. Given their long-term success, they will continue to do this despite the short-term hurdles the market may throw up.

All of the old Masters agreed to participate again with the exception of Greg Perry and Peter Morgan. Perry, after more than two years out of the game, has recently set out on his new venture, QED, and was not ready to go into print. He said once QED's track record was established, he would be more than happy to be involved. Does that mean we have to write a third edition? We will jump that bridge when we come to it.

Matthew Kidman
September 2005

The idea is ... to own our best ideas and hold as much as we can of them, but make sure that we are right and they are liquid enough to sell if we have made a mistake.

Finding the theme
Phil Mathews

The first thing you notice about Phil Mathews is his intensity. He has a pleasant smile and a warm welcome but his eyes zero in on their target and don't relent. His conversation is considered and he seems to hang on every syllable of every word you say, as if hoping to extract the maximum amount of information possible.

His office on level 33 of Grosvenor Tower in Sydney's CBD is purpose-built for his personality. Even though the outlook is picturesque, with a direct view of the Sydney Harbour Bridge, the interior is compact. Mathews sits in his own, glass-wall office looking out at the Opera House and the Harbour Bridge, with his team of five organised behind him according to feng shui principles. They look as if they are in a rocket ship ready to blast off to the moon. The phones don't ring too often and there's minimal chat. Most of the team are happy to see us arrive to conduct this interview but, like Mathews, while the smiles are warm, the conversation is kept to an absolute minimum.

In many ways it felt like we were interrupting an exam that everyone had studied very hard for and wanted not just to pass, but to score top marks. Those first impressions linger. As we discovered in our interview, Mathews is indeed an intense individual and his staff are extremely focused on getting the best possible results out of each day at the office.

Mathews has a very similar background to many of the other Masters that we interviewed. He grew up on Sydney's affluent North Shore and attended Sydney Grammar School before heading off to study economics at Sydney University with a major in accounting. As seems to be the well-beaten path, Mathews did two years of accounting with a large chartered firm in Sydney before pursuing a more exciting and stimulating career in the sharemarket in London. Like many of his colleagues back in the late 1980s, he headed towards stockbroking to break into the market. In those days funds management was not flourishing like it is now in Australia and other parts of the world — then, the whole industry was lowly paid.

Mathews's success as an investor meant it was eventually not worthwhile for him to stick to the broking game. The monetary rewards from investing dwarfed any return he could possibly garner from broking, even to Australia's top fund managers. That is not to say Mathews was not a good broker — quite the contrary. He was one of the top commission writers in the country in the mid-1990s. In 2001, Mathews left broking to start his new career at Mathews Capital Partners. In June 2005, Bloomberg rated Mathews's Sabre Fund the best performing non-US equity long/short fund in the world over one and three years.

Like the person, his style of investing is equally focused and intense. His style was initially forged as a value investor, primarily a result of working for two years with fellow Master Erik Metanomski back in 1986 and 1987. But, as time passed, Mathews evolved differently, developing a brand of investing that very few people, if anyone at all, replicates in Australia.

At the centre of his investment philosophy is the identification of demographics, themes and trends. Once Mathews discerns a theme that can be expressed in sharemarket terms, he'll choose a few stocks and plough a significant proportion of his funds into these themes. He believes that maximum returns only eventuate if you back your best ideas to the hilt, and is perhaps the ultimate example of someone who invests with conviction. He believes that, through investing in his best ideas as opposed to spreading his resources over a more diversified portfolio of more average ideas, he has a lower risk profile.

Mathews does not stop at the big picture or 'top-down view', to use finance industry vernacular. Any stock that Mathews places a large bet upon is analysed from every possible angle and every relevant bit of information is gathered, consumed and digested.

While many fund managers are forced to conform closely to benchmark indices and are happy only to take overweight positions in stocks at the margin, Mathews is searching for sectors and stocks that he can pour a large percentage of his funds into. Just like the man, the portfolio is focused and intense. In the middle to late 1990s, he identified financial services, and in particular superannuation, as a highly positive trend. This led him to invest heavily in Lend Lease in 1996 and 1997, with its MLC funds management business as the jewel in the crown. He doubled his money and cashed in before Lend Lease hit hard times after 2000 (after selling MLC to National Australia Bank, no less). Buying Perpetual Trustees at $8 in 1997 (it is now $60+) was another example.

The proliferation of gambling was also a favoured theme that he capitalised on to make sizeable profits. His buying of just under 5 per cent of Aristocrat Leisure in March 2003, at an average price of around $1.80, was perhaps his best ever single trade, with the stock subsequently rising to over $13.50 (in August 2005). Between 2004 and 2006, the theme that dominates his stock selection is the rising oil price, fuelled by heightened demand, finite reserves and worldwide lack of exploration success.

Obviously, the reason why many investors refuse to follow Mathews's lead and focus a significant proportion of their funds on one investment is that the risks are significant if something goes wrong. Mathews is well aware of this. When he eventually officially quit stockbroking in 2001 to establish his Sabre Fund in 2002, Mathews watched his initial capital shrink by 50 per cent in the first six months. He calls the period the 'perfect storm' — where anything that could go wrong did go wrong — and the memories still haunt him today. At the time, he was investing in demutualising financial exchanges worldwide. Although the trends were positive for exchanges, a worldwide stock market meltdown caught his new fund in the slipstream.

By early 2003, markets had turned and he was again achieving high returns, with the Sabre Fund accumulated unit price (including distributions) reaching $588 by August 2005 from a $100 issue price in April 2002. His good, and bad, performances have been magnified by the use of leverage (or the use of borrowed money). He also utilises futures, commodities and options to both maximise upside and help protect downside.

For most, that kind of rollercoaster ride leaves a giddy feeling in the stomach. Mathews would not have it any other way. He sees no reason why he would change his style and conform to the way things are done by institutions. In modern parlance, Mathews operates a long/short fund, but to him it is the only way to invest.

He does not shy away from that image either. His earliest fund is simply named the Focus Fund, and no doubt there is plenty of focus from Mathews and his team.

We interviewed Mathews at his office in Sydney on a Tuesday afternoon after trading on the sharemarket had finished for the day. Mathews preferred being interviewed earlier in the week because he gets quite tired by Friday — such is the nature of his personality.

Can you give us some background on where you were born and where you went to school?

I grew up in Killara on Sydney's North Shore and went to Sydney Grammar School, graduating in 1977. I was a solid student at school and went onto study economics at Sydney University, which at the time was the launch pad for a number of successful finance careers.

So why economics? What was your interest there?

Economics was what I was most suited to. Without a great deal of effort, I scored highly in the school exams. As I believe in playing to your strengths, it was a natural choice to gravitate towards.

Who were some of the people you went to university with?

There was the stockbroker Ian Simmons and also David Paradice, who is one of the subjects of your book, Rodney Payne and several other guys who ended up in the BT brains factory back in the 1980s and 1990s.

I didn't have a great first year at uni. I'd split up with my girlfriend and was very unfocused. The unstructured nature of university was initially quite daunting. I went from having a full day's organised curriculum at school to having only twelve contact hours a week. I was also living out of home at the time and was quite broke. At eighteen, in my first year of university, I slept on a mattress on the floor and my shared rented apartment had the bare minimum of furniture. My car, an old Mini Moke that cost more to keep it on the road than to buy it, was constantly breaking down.

I managed to get through that first year and finished with a very basic degree three years later. My aim at university was to do no better than pass, because I theorised that I was putting in way too much work if I did better than pass. I felt university was my time to have fun. I didn't want to do any more work than I had to, because I believed even then that later in life, I would be working much harder. So while I was young and healthy, I wanted to be as carefree as possible.

What happened after uni?

I worked for three years as a chartered accountant in Sydney and London and completed my professional year, which was a character building experience.

Why do you say it was 'character building'?

I felt unsuited to being a chartered accountant. It is essentially all about learning procedures with little scope for imaginative thinking. However, the professional year provided a good education and it's certainly helped me in my later stock market career (which I had planned from the beginning). Looking back the professional year was character building as it taught me how to problem-solve by finding and applying information.

What sort of accounting were you initially doing?

I was doing auditing. Auditing is a good background as you get to see first-hand many different industries from the ground up. An example was working in an engineering factory in Blacktown [in Sydney's western suburbs]. We were auditing Demag, a crane company. My boss insisted I work a twelve-hour day, no matter what, and then I would drive the one-hour trip home to central Sydney. Working twelve hours was like a badge of honour to him. However, I managed to get through those two years of auditing in Australia before applying for an opening in London. I think I was the second choice for them, but I got the job after someone else pulled out.

While you were working as an accountant, did you have an interest in the sharemarket?

I had a lot of interest in the sharemarket. My first trade was around the time that the Private Blood Bank saga was taking place. The first stock I invested in at the time was called Vapocure. It had a process for instantly curing paint on cars. I think the stock went from $1 to $14 and then back again to $1. So while I was counting cranes, I was also trading some Vapocure shares from the boardroom of Demag in Sydney's Blacktown.

> *The main driver behind my interest in the stock market was that I could make money with little actual elbow grease. I could think up a profit.*

What got you interested in the sharemarket at that time?

I really liked the idea of theorising and mentally making money, as opposed to physically making things. A lot of people like making things. I prefer to think about ideas and apply concepts; share trading fitted the bill for me. So the main driver behind my interest in the stock market was that I could make money with little actual elbow grease. I could think up a profit. That was my main driver. At university I never had any cash so I couldn't get involved in the market at that time. I had to wait until I had some seed capital.

Was there one person in particular who got you interested in the sharemarket?

There was no one person who got me interested. I've found often through my life that you just have to pioneer a path yourself, and then other people join the journey as you go.

And what about your parents, what did they do?

My father was a merchant banker and he wanted me to be in merchant banking, specialising in corporate mergers and acquisitions. I tried that profession for six months, but felt totally unsuited to it. The job again required incredibly detailed work and very long hours, whereas I wanted to think more conceptually and be able to apply those concepts as a principle.

As a merchant banker, your father was close to the sharemarket. Did that mean the sharemarket was already part of your life?

Yes, it was in my life but it wasn't like some people — who might have had their father give them a share portfolio when they were fifteen, might have made some money and then realised that here's the magic pudding. I never had that. If you haven't anyone to learn from in close detail, like a stock trading father, you just don't have that input in your life. You have to actually discover it through your own trial and error, by trying different things.

Can you tell us what you bought and sold the Vapocure shares for?

I think I paid $11 and they went to $13 and I was really excited about it. I was getting hourly price updates in the Demag boardroom via the automated telephone recorded price system (which was the only way at the time — no mobile phones or internet!).

So you made 20 per cent on the trade?

Yes.

When you first bought it, did it worry you the stock had already gone up something like 1100 per cent?

I wasn't really aware of what the price had already done, due to my inexperience. I just liked the concept after reading about it in the newspaper. Another trade I remember was in a tannery. I thought it was a cheap buy because it was trading on seven times earnings, but it went to five times earnings after that. As I had borrowed the money on my credit card, it was an uncomfortable experience. I learnt that cheap companies can get cheaper!

What did that teach you?

It taught me that I should do much more homework and try to understand what I was doing! I still liked the idea of thinking up a profit from an intellectual perspective and then investing in a situation but, of course, I had no background in the market. I had no understanding whatsoever. I was just grasping in the dark the whole time, just hungrily trying to learn anything new I could. I remember being very clear, though, that this was my future.

So you went to London after you finished your two years of chartered accounting in Australia. Did you work as an accountant in London?

Yes. It was 1983 and I finished my third year of chartered accounting there before joining a merchant bank.

Which merchant bank was it?

County Natwest. I was working up to fourteen hours a day in the job. As the junior, you might have to go down to the printer in the middle of the night to make sure that everything was being printed off accurately for a particular deal. You could find yourself somewhere in London at the printers at 4 am in the morning and be expected to be back at work at 7 am. None of the staff had any outside interests whatsoever. Often they would go to lunch, drink four or five gin and tonics and come back to the office and work until 8 pm. Such was the culture of the city at the time. No-one did any exercise as it was not 'de rigueur'. I decided to escape that life and was successful in getting a job at top ranking stockbrokers Ord Minnett. Merchant banking was a tough six months, as I wasn't interested in the job. I was always more interested in trading shares — something you can't do in corporate finance, as everything's on the banned list!

Did you get run down?

At the merchant bank I became run down and ended up with a mild case of chronic fatigue syndrome. Eventually I had to take a month off work.

When I joined Ords in 1985, I was ecstatic. I wanted to be a broker. I loved the idea of being close to the market and being paid for it! As soon as I was following my passion, my career seemed to take off like never before. At the time, Ord was also Australia's top broker.

What were your thoughts before joining Ords?

Before joining, I remember being warned that it was 'last on, first off' in the event of a downturn, but I just didn't care. It was my opportunity! There was a great bunch of guys there and it was an extremely good introduction to the sharemarket for me. I'll never forget getting my first IPO allocation as an employee. I made $1500. That was the world to me at the time.

Do you remember which stock that was?

Imagineering. I just took it because it was offered. It was a placement and hard to get, so we took it. I didn't really understand the investment. Some time later the company fell into receivership, I think.

Imagineering was Jodee Rich's first foray into a publicly listed company.

Yes — he had been at Sydney University a year or two ahead of me.

How long were you at Ords and where were your clients from?

For two years. We had UK and Australian clients and the market was roaring. At the time, all the emerging Australian and New Zealand so called entrepreneurs were coming to London. It was 1985 to 1986 and they came to London in search of cash boxes [see glossary]. Dewey Warren was Holmes à Court's UK vehicle (stock tripled), Tozer Kemsley was Brierley's (quadrupled), Brint Investments was Garnet Harrison's (tripled) and Charterhall was Russell Goward's. As soon as someone announced they had acquired control of a cash box, all you had to do was buy because the stock would soar. It was an amazing time to be in the market.

We also had Larry Adler coming to London to take a stake in Hill Samuel [the major shareholder in Macquarie Bank], which seems extraordinary now. I mean, you can just imagine how in 2005 APRA would feel about an insurance company investing all the policyholders' money in one large investment. It would almost be impossible to do now. The scale of the hype was breathtaking but, of course, our level of experience did not allow us to put any of it in context.

Where were you at the time of the 1987 sharemarket crash?

Before the crash I'd been lured away from Ord Minnett to a funds management vehicle in the UK by Erik Metanomski. Stephen Sedgeman had started an outfit called SPAL, which was based in Melbourne. Erik was running the London office.

Why did you switch to the 'buy' side?

Erik and I got on like a house on fire. At the time, Erik was a young fellow with a lot of responsibility that he applied himself wholeheartedly to. For me, it was an amazing opportunity to work with someone who was open-minded and in control of his destiny. He made me an offer that I just jumped at. Together what we lacked in experience, we more than made up for in enthusiasm!

How much money were you managing?

I was managing a small fund and helping Erik on his funds. What was memorable about the relationship was that we continually scaled new frontiers, often by trial and error. I always think back to this time as a period that gave me a level of confidence on which I was to rely from then on. I have

The secret is to make sure that your learning experience never stalls. In order to do this you need to continually push your knowledge boundaries.

a saying now that after one year in the market, you think you know everything; after two years, you realise you knew nothing after year one; after five years, you knew nothing after two, three or four years! Now after nineteen years, I realise I knew comparatively little after ten years. The secret is to make sure that your learning experience never stalls. In order to do this you need to continually push your knowledge boundaries.

Sometimes it's better to be naive.

I believe it is important to make mistakes, because through our (hopefully small) mistakes, our biggest profits often eventuate; however, the point is not to repeat the same mistake and to keep losses small. When you first come into the market you can easily think you know everything. You're a young gun and nothing can stop you. You're fired up. Your early enthusiasm helps to overcome the daunting learning curve.

What did Erik teach you about investing?

We found a book on Warren Buffett and we both read it avidly. Erik's still very much of that style, whereas my style's changed a lot from then. It's evolved in a very different way to his.

Your style back then was picking deep-value stocks?

My style was just to learn whatever I could. At that stage, we found this guy called Warren Buffett, who for Australians was unknown, and we read the book. We both got hooked, and we tried to apply whatever we could learn from the book, even back then.

Would that be to value a company and buy it if it is below what you think it is worth?

Correct. At the time, Erik was very keen on the stocks trading on low price/earnings multiples, so we applied that as much as possible. After a while we learned to value management more highly, as we hadn't fully realised that management had to have a strong track record. We were like fledgling birds emerging from the nest at that stage — I was twenty-six and Erik was almost thirty. Having only a small amount of experience between us, we had to basically learn everything the hard way.

By experience?

We learnt to research management and we learnt to check industries. We basically learnt everything from the ground up. The pillars of what I know today were formed in those years.

When did you come back to Australia?

I came back after the 1987 stockmarket crash. I ended up getting a job with fund managers Armstrong Jones. Graham Lenzner was in charge of the operation and Paul Jenkins (now Jenkins Asset Management) was running the investment side of things.

What was your role?

Bank analyst, although initially I knew nothing about banks.

What else did you learn working at Armstrong Jones?

You learn something from everywhere you work. I learnt to do much more detailed analysis than what we had done in London. Although it was less of a transformational time, it did help develop my analytical skills.

They had a different investing style to you?

They had a completely different style to what I'd developed in London, and I initially found it hard to fit in.

What was their style?

It was very systemised and, although I learnt things there, I felt constrained in how much I moved forward in my learning.

Did you learn anything about banks?

I did learn about banks and also basic industrials.

Did you find that period dull in that you weren't buying and selling shares?

I had no authority to directly buy and sell shares. I would turn up at the morning meeting and make recommendations to the team and try to convince them to buy my ideas. I left Armstrong Jones and took six months off at a time that was an absolute nadir [1991] in the market, a time when everybody was getting retrenched. Today, it is hard to imagine how tough it was both in the economy and the stock market. The property market had crashed and it is almost impossible now to visualise how depressing the environment was at that time.

What did you do when you took the six months off?

A lot of training, physical fitness work and had a great time. When I did decide to get back into the market, I was lucky enough to get a job at Jardine Fleming in Sydney.

On the funds management side of things?

No, on the stockbroking side. I was their only research analyst as they had retrenched about twenty-five analysts in the previous year or so. It was a job that really suited me, because I could basically research any company I wanted. As long as the investment made money, the team was happy. Being part of one of Asia's blue chip franchises helped me to become acquainted with the number one investors in Asia at the time, Jardine Fleming Asset Management.

And it was then that I met Jonny Boyer, who eventually left to start a super-successful hedge fund based in London [Boyer Allen]. When I was trying to get up the courage to start my fund, I kept asking him what I needed to do. All he would say is, 'The only way to do it, is to do it' — advice which I have found to be correct, but not always easy to follow!

He was the only hedge fund manager I had ever met and he was a great investor. What intrigued me about Jonny was that he always seemed very relaxed. He focused on picking sectors rather than just stocks. So if you could pick a sector correctly, most of the stocks in that sector would go up. You were never privy to the information he received but he was very good at picking sectors and that had a big influence on the way I began to think about investing.

Then Jardine Fleming Stockbrokers closed in Australia and I joined stockbroker Bells in 1993.

What did your stint at Jardine Fleming teach you?

At Jardine you had the opportunity to develop in the way you wanted as long as it was profitable for the group. What I enjoyed most about it was that I was able to use my own initiative to work out how to make money for other people. I had the freedom to do exactly what I wanted to do and that's what I thrive on most. I like to have no constraints on my thinking and to be able to apply time as I deem fit.

At Jardine Fleming I'd sit in a little back room where people rarely bothered me. My main daily responsibility was to address the morning meeting. As long as I recommended good ideas, the team were happy.

Do you remember some of the successful stock calls you made at the time?

I recommended [gas company] AGL at $1.50 (in 1992) and it was a big success.

Why did you recommend it?

It was a very complicated story. Sir Ron Brierley was on the register at the time [see chapter on Sir Ron Brierley and Gary Weiss] and it had a monopoly on NSW gas distribution. You could see demand for natural gas was increasing as AGL sold more and more gas appliances to a growing New South Wales population. It just seemed to have a great growth profile and a low price/earnings multiple. So it suited all the things that I'd been brought up to look for back in London.

So the recommendation was value based with a view that it had a good future?

Correct. Another stock that performed well back then was Lion Nathan, which had bought Alan Bond's brewery assets on a highly geared basis.

How long were you at Bells?

I was there from 1993 till 2001, so quite a big stint. At Bells I was essentially a salesman thinking up money-making ideas for the clients. At the time, the company was a very small operation with a futures arm.

And what were you doing there?

It was similar to what I did at Jardine except I wasn't paid a salary.

Were you selling your own ideas to clients?

Yes, just broking my own ideas.

Was it about this time that you started managing money as well?

In 1992 we set up a private company with a number of individual investors. We set it up with $54 000 in capital, and I put in $10 000 of that.

Who else was in there?

Close friends and relatives were the main contributors.

How has it performed?

The fund's returns would rank in the top 1 per cent of hedge funds worldwide over a fourteen-year period, with a 38.5 per cent per annum compound return for the period until June 2005.

That is spectacular. Have any of your investors wanted to sell out along the way?

Everybody wants to sell when things go bad, and everyone wants to buy in when things go well. So when people sold out, existing investors would just accumulate their shares. 1995 was a bad year and everyone was quite down but that was actually a great time to buy in. 2002 was another tough year and everyone was down again but that year was also a great year to invest.

So over fourteen years?

It's something like a 12 800 per cent total return.

How did you combine being a stockbroker and managing money for people?

It was like having a stockbroker's managed fund account.

Do you still look after the fund directly?

Yes — although now it is invested in the Sabre Fund that we set up in April 2002 to begin managing money full-time.

When did you officially leave broking?

Officially in 2001, but mentally a long time before that as we had stopped ringing any clients some time before.

The fund had become significant enough that the broking was less relevant. We decided that our time was best spent looking for investment opportunities.

You were totally focusing?

We adopted the view that we had to cut out all distractions — no clients, no lunches, no superfluous phone calls, nothing except factual information.

Could you short stocks back then?

We didn't know about shorting back then.

Okay. Can you tell us some of the stocks that contributed to your performance in that period?

Basically, we ran the fund like it was private money. We used leveraged equity accounts, so we could maximise our exposure to a smaller number of our best ideas and hold them for a long period of time. There wasn't much trading, it was all about longer term investment.

Can you describe some of your thinking here?

We seek to envisage a valuation of a stock at some twelve to eighteen months in the future. If we think it could be worth $100 and it is trading at $50, we would consider this a great buy. Eventually, we realised that if we had one good idea for every ten or twenty research situations, our upside percentages would improve if we could cover over a hundred opportunities and garner ten to twenty great ideas from that. As usual, we would seek to own as much as possible of our best ideas.

How concentrated is the fund? You were saying you were running it a bit like individuals run their own money, and they can tend to have quite a concentrated portfolio.

It's quite concentrated. With a smaller amount of money there's even less stocks, but as the size of the fund increases you have to increase the number of stocks that you own. Also, we generally like to invest in large-capitalisation stocks so as to increase our liquidity.

What were some of your big wins back then?

Well, Lend Lease was a big win, it doubled. Colonial was another.

And what percentage of the fund would you have had in Lend Lease?

We would have had 35 per cent of the fund in Lend Lease, but again it was a much smaller fund. We liked bigger cap stocks.

> *The idea is ... to own our best ideas and hold as much as we can of them, but make sure that we are right and they are liquid enough to sell if we have made a mistake.*

Fauldings was a very large win for us as well. The company got taken over and we doubled our money. Colonial also doubled and was taken over.

Would you gear the fund for a dollar of equity to a dollar of debt?

At that stage we would gear it as much as possible, but we'd always have some room left over, so up to 100 per cent. There is no fixed percentage.

The idea is, as I discussed, to own our best ideas and hold as much as we can of them, but make sure that we are right and they are liquid enough to sell if we have made a mistake.

How do you do that, if you're going to be that concentrated?

What you do is you start trusting yourself. If you haven't got the knowledge and the ability to do it after ten or fifteen years of painstaking stock market investment research and training, you never will. You've really just got to start believing in yourself.

*Let's talk about Lend Lease, which is one of Australia's best known
organisations. What made you think of it and how did you go about
researching it?*

What I really liked about Lend Lease at the time was that they owned
MLC, and we liked investing in trends. Superannuation is one such
government-mandated trend. Contributions grow a set percentage
each year. I saw that MLC was linked to this superannuation trend.
I also really liked the hidden assets, which weren't valued in the
stock price. It had a number of assets that were in there for free,
and when I stripped all the assets out I found the stock was on a
very low price/earnings multiple.

And then a number of positive things happened, which often
happens when you invest in a strong trend. Good things happen
because you've got the trend behind you, not in front of you. I like
to know the wind is at our back and not in our face.

*When you talk about trends you're not talking about the share price,
you're talking about the business fundamentals and the industry.*

Yes. When we 'discovered' Lend Lease, we were looking for a stock
that fitted a theme and a trend and was cheaply priced. Now, at that
stage we loved financial services, so I investigated all the significant
listed financial services companies, one of which was Lend Lease.
Another was Perpetual Trustees, at $8 in 1998 (now $60).

Industry trends triggered the interest in these companies. More
diligent company research is done later.

You're looking for industry trends.

Industry trends, demographic trends, government-spending trends
and government growth. Anything interesting and sustainable.

*Can you give another example of a stock that was enjoying a
positive trend?*

Faulding [now part of Mayne] was a good one. I identified generic
drugs as a trend in health care. At the time, a lot of drugs were
coming out of patent and Fauldings had this great generic business.
I thought the company was attractively priced. I thought the generic
drug companies were going to eat the big pharma companies for
breakfast as their patents ended. So Faulding, which was right in
our backyard, fitted that trend. Mayne came along and made a bid,
so we doubled our money on that. These are big-cap stocks; they're

not small backyard stocks where, you know, you're hoping for some story to push the price up. We love investing in big, liquid stocks, that's what we do.

Why do they have to be big and liquid?

If you're going to put a lot of money into a stock, you have to have liquidity so you can get out. I learnt from the Clayton Robard's[1] experience back in the 1980s. When the market went bad in 1987, the fund manager couldn't sell much of their portfolio, except at steeply discounted prices, because they owned many third-line stocks with poor liquidity and trends. I never wanted to be in that situation. So we may have some smaller cap stocks, but we love big-cap stocks, particularly if we're going to use gearing.

> *There's trend and there's valuation, and you've got to have both in your favour. You can't be overpaying and expect to make money.*

Once you've identified a trend or a theme, how important is it to analyse the fundamentals of the individual companies you invest in? Say, for instance, a trend was positive and the best company in the sector was trading at a massive multiple like forty times cash flow, do you still buy it?

Well, there's trend and there's valuation, and you've got to have both in your favour. You can't be overpaying and expect to make money. I mean, the greatest recent example of that was the tech boom in 2000, when stocks were trading on revenue multiples instead of earnings multiples.

It's easier to make money if you can pick the trend right and buy the stock at the right price. So if you can pick the trend, you simply have a smaller universe of stocks to pick from. Like right now [April 2005], we love oil stocks.

What's so good about oil at the moment?

There have been virtually no new major oil discoveries for over thirty years! 20 per cent of the global supply comes from only fourteen giant oil fields, which were mostly discovered over fifty years ago; the biggest one, Gharwah in Saudi Arabia, was discovered seventy years ago. Oil is a depleting resource and, as a real estate agent would say, 'No-one is making any more'. I still think most people are of the view

---

1   Clayton Robard was a fund manager in the 1980s that later became Tyndall.

that global oil is never really going to run out. But look at the North Sea of the UK, or Bass Strait in Australia. Both of them are declining fields. So let me tell you, it does run out and all the countries that have had their reserves run low or run out are now paying big prices for import bills. I mean, Indonesia, which is a member of OPEC, is actually an importer this year. Gas prices in the US recently reached highs of $US7 [now over US$10], and who would have thought that three years ago when they were around $1?

What is your prognosis on oil?

Our basic point is that world energy markets will only add 300 000 net barrels of production a day between now and 2010, and yet demand is projected to grow from eighty-four million barrels a day now to 125 million barrels a day by 2025. So you're going to have a 50 per cent increase in demand and there's been almost no significant, major new discoveries for thirty years!

Santos did discover a new field ...

The Santos one is thought to be 250 million barrels, which is only three days' world supply, if it indeed lives up to early expectations.

It was so small it didn't matter.

Yes. The world is using eighty-four million barrels a day, and it is difficult to think of the last billion-barrel oil discovery either locally or anywhere in the region. You can just imagine what the outlook for the oil price is.

That is a trend?

That's a trend that we've identified and we've backed. Our funds are committed to that trend.

What does that mean? What percentage of your funds would be in oil?

We've put over 60 per cent of our net assets into oil, oil-related stocks or any energy related theme that fits the trend.

And gas?

Yes, gas as well, because we see it as energy, as opposed to just oil. Anything energy related that we can find — whether it be gas, whether it be uranium, whether it be wind power — anything that provides energy to the world is interesting to us.

You said before you liked to set a price for what a stock might be worth. Did you do the same for a barrel of oil?

Yes.

And what do you think that price is?

Well, it's hard to forecast what the price will be. We keep re-evaluating by setting an achievable price and then re-analysing the situation when it gets there.

What does that mean?

We started by using $40; when it got there we used $50, then $55 and so on. Eventually, though, I expect it could go over $100. However, we are not modelling this scenario yet. As a consequence, it's made us cut back on our leverage in the rest of the portfolio and invest more in our oil investments.

So you've reduced your gearing?

We've reduced our gearing. In fact, we've gone from having a 200 per cent long position in the last three years to a net 70 per cent invested position at the moment.

70 per cent invested in equities and 30 per cent cash?

Say the fund is $200 million net. We could have $300 million worth of longs and $130 million of net shorts, including futures and options. That way we could still hold all our best stocks and be short the index and certain selected sectors that didn't fit our current parameters.

Given that you've got such a big sector view, do you invest globally or do you invest primarily in Australian stocks?

If we can't get the exposure locally, we'll go global. First stop's local. We've learnt to go local, because the information is more easily available locally. Global's harder, because the information is more difficult to get. However, if we have to, we'll go global.

Of your funds invested in oil stocks, what would be the biggest holding at the moment?

Woodside Petroleum, but we own all the top eight Australian oil stocks.

Do you hold Woodside because it's the biggest pure energy stock on the market?

Yes — because it's the biggest stock, we had to have most of our money in it, plus the fundamentals really stack up for it. Basically, here's a company with production almost tripling by 2012 and when you combine that with an oil price potentially doubling or trebling, it is easy to understand the upside.

So what is your valuation on Woodside?

I'd see Woodside going beyond $50 a share or possibly $60.[2]

Does that assume the oil price gets to $US70 a barrel or higher?

We think there will be peaks and troughs in the oil price, and we don't expect it to go in a straight line — maybe it goes lower first — but very clearly the trend is that it's going to go up a lot, and we want to be there. The last major oil bull market was in 1972–73, and it was quite a different situation. There is very little understanding on oil stocks below the top four or five now and it's one of the few under-researched sectors in our market. When you talk about oil stocks to other investors, we often find the level of knowledge is low, which is rare in the highly researched Australian market. We must all agree the Australian market is very extensively researched, but oil stocks, who knows about them? I mean, who owns Santos? Nobody I know seems to own Santos except for index funds.[3]

Perhaps many institutional investors don't own Santos because they believe that the oil price is unsustainable at these levels.

They don't have our macro view. We have spent a year researching the emerging trends. We've come from a standing start, and are very confident in our analysis. Of course, you can always be wrong.

---

2   On the day we interviewed Mathews, Woodside closed the trading day at $24.24. By September, it had surged to over $32.00 a share.

3   Santos is Australia's second-largest oil and gas company with a market capitalisation of $6.8 billion as at June 2005.

It's a probability thing. We think the high probability is that we're right, and that's what we do — we weigh up the probabilities and we place our bets.

Is the energy strategy the most committed you have been, in terms of money, to any theme?

We are always strongly committed to our sector views. It's just that this happens to be the latest sector view. I guess our most phenomenal success was Aristocrat back in 2003. We bought nearly 5 per cent of the company at under $2, and we have realised $80 million in profit and we still have almost half our stock [Aristocrat's share price as at 8 September was $12.37].

Of course, you can always be wrong. It's a probability thing. We think the high probability is that we're right, and that's what we do — we weigh up the probabilities and we place our bets.

How did Aristocrat fit into a theme or a sector view?

We realised governments around the world needed to consistently raise money to pay health and other costs for ageing populations (another trend) and we therefore concluded that the easiest way for them to raise money is to issue poker machine licences. For instance, in the US if one state has poker machines and the next state doesn't, the people simply migrate to play the machines in the next state. So there's a very strong compulsion for all the states that don't have them to introduce them.

Likewise in other countries around the world such as in Asia. If Macau has gambling, Singapore will want gambling as they are losing revenue to Macau. And so it goes. Aristocrat satisfied a number of different trends, which were really attractive to us, and topping all of that was that there was only three or four of these international companies in the world that we could find. To be able to buy into the Australian icon at a big discount was a great opportunity.

The poker machine manufacturing business has very high barriers to entry as a business, due to the licensing regime. Aristocrat has over 170 licences globally. The Japanese licence alone took fifteen years to get; the Nevada licence took fifteen years to get. These are high barriers to entry for such a high cash flow business. The company ran into some management and earnings problems in early 2003 and we were set to pounce. We'd really done our original foundation homework for the investment in 1999.

You were buying it on the way down?

We started buying it around about 90¢. We bought it near the absolute bottom, which was probably a bit of luck; however, we bought it all the way up to $2.25 as we don't mind increasing our position if the fundamentals are getting stronger, and that's what we found in that situation.

Was that your biggest ever position?

Well, it was the biggest dollarwise, but they're always getting bigger as the funds grow. At the time, Lend Lease was a big position; at the time, Fauldings was a big position. Perpetual the same.

In percentage terms was it the biggest?

It was around 20 per cent of our net funds at cost prices but, as the price rose, so did it as a percentage of our fund.

As we have shorts and longs in our portfolio, a stock might be a bigger part of our net position but a smaller part of our gross position.

Okay. Let's concentrate on the establishment of the Sabre fund. You left Bells and stockbroking in which year?

Officially in 2001, but in my mind, much earlier. We had really wound down our stockbroking to a maintenance situation only; however, we completed the transformation in 2001 by setting up Mathews Capital Partners.

Tell us about the early days and the first year or so.

We launched the Sabre fund with $9 million. We invested some of our first money into Germany, following our stock exchange theme of the time. The German market proceeded to fall from 5000 to 2800 over the next five months. We thought it was a reasonable place to invest the money, given the market had already fallen from 7000 points, but it just kept crashing and eventually bottomed near 2000. An enormous percentage fall from 7000.

What attracted you to the German market?

We'd identified demutualising stock exchanges, financial exchanges, as a trend at the time, and we were looking for exchanges all over the world. Because there were only two in Australia, we went to

Europe and invested in all the European ones, because we thought they were cheaper. We were also on an international trip mentally at the time and we wanted to try new things. So we invested in the European exchanges; unfortunately, the markets got crushed and our investments got crushed with them. Although we were right in the long term (these investments have now doubled from our purchase price), we got hurt in the short term.

How much did the unit price of the Sabre Fund fall by?

The unit price probably halved over the first six months.

How did that feel?

It was a crushing experience for me.

Although we were right in the long term, we had to be able to hang on for the short term, and by using gearing it amplified the positions. We couldn't imagine the market falling 40 per cent or so over five months. Sitting here in Australia, investing in the Australian market you can't imagine it either. You cannot imagine how fast and furiously markets can crash. It was another great lesson for us.

When you say crushing, can you tell us how you were thinking?

It was extremely stressful. If you believe that something is worth $100 and you pay $50 for it, that's normally a good investment. But if it goes to $40 first, what do you do? Do you sell, because it's going down, or do you buy more? We believed our original research was correct, so we put in more of our remaining capital. And it went from $40 to $30 and then we thought, 'Well, what do we do here? It's now $30 and we think the stock's worth double or triple that price'.

> *It's an agonising thing to do, to hang on, but you have to do everything in your power to do what you believe is right.*

So we had to grin and bear it. There's nothing more you can do, because if you sell out, you may not be able to buy back in if the market rises quickly from such an oversold position. You may find the first move up will be a 20 per cent to 25 per cent move, and then you'll be wondering what to do, because it's gone up. So it's an agonising thing to do, to hang on, but you have to do everything in your power to do what you believe is right.

Were you getting pressure from any of the people who had put money into the fund?

We explained to all our investors that this was what we had to do and that's what we were going to do and, thankfully, everyone was supportive. We had no redemptions.

Given it was your first year for the new fund, what was the personal impact?

Personally it was exhausting. I'd be up at night trading, and we kept wondering what we had to do to turn the situation around. We went through that for over a year, and the team — they're all still with me today — went through it with me. But, personally, it pushed me to my limits and I don't want to go back there. I remember at the time thinking that I was totally, mentally and physically, going to do everything in my power to make back the loss.

Were there any lasting side effects?

I think I stopped sleeping as well. I don't think I've ever slept as well again — my sleeping patterns were disturbed forever after that.

People need sleep. If you don't sleep, you make poor decisions.

So, given you went through that, what's your working day like now? Long days or shorter days to preserve yourself?

Yesterday we got in here at 6.45 am and we left at 7 pm. We do that regularly. The team works extremely hard and they're all motivated by having their wealth in the fund.

In the Sabre fund?

Yes. Everyone's motivated by having their money, bonuses — everything — paid on the performance of the fund.

Talk us through what happened after that first tough year.

In December 2002 I'd been reading *Market Wizards* and I remembered one of them saying that the 1991 Gulf War was the pivotal point for the market to turn. I thought, 'That's what is going to happen this time as well, as uncertainty would be removed'. As it happened that was the bottom of the market. From there the market went up in a straight line. Many of the overseas markets were up 40 per cent in a very short space of time, and if you'd sold hoping to buy back, you may have completely missed making the money back. Luckily, not only did we make all of our money back very quickly, but since then the fund has now more than quintupled.

So the original unit price in the Sabre Fund was $100 and it went to around $50 in the first six to twelve months. Where is it now?

It has risen to $424 [in May 2005].

From that bottom, investors have made eight times their money, while the original investors are up four times in about three years and one month.[4]

When people think it's the end of the world, it's often the best opportunity to invest. We pride ourselves on taking advantage of turning points. It's what we do well.

Why is that? Because you get fully invested on the way down like in Germany?

No. Because we are on the lookout for pivotal inflection points that may make the difference. We're prepared to hang on and grin and bear the volatility in the meantime.

What about other aspects of investing? For instance, when you look to invest in a company, is management still important like it was with Erik back in London during the 1980s?

Yes, management's the key, but often a rising tide will lift all managements! You can try to get rid of the companies that have bad management teams later if you don't know those management teams, but the thing is to invest first in the trend. Shoot first, ask questions later if you really believe you're right, because by owning a stock you learn about the stock. Once you own it, you become emotionally involved in it and you tend to do more work on it, whereas if you don't own it, you don't follow it. Once it's in your portfolio, you look very closely at it. That's what we try to do.

We like to own little bits of things as well as the bigger positions. For instance, in the fund we have an incubation section, where we incubate ideas. We put them all in there and we have a small position and if we find out later that it stacks up, we double, triple, quadruple its size in the portfolio. Alternatively, we'll just simply

---

4   In June 2005, after we conducted our interview, the Sabre Fund rose 30 per cent and the unit price soared to $494 as the oil price leapt to new highs. By August, the unit price for the fund was $588 including distributions.

cut the position. It makes you very focused on selecting the wheat from the chaff.

How many stocks would you hold in your fund at any given time?

Currently, we probably have about seventy ideas.

Seventy investments?

Seventy positions, and as we discussed, currently a big oil position. Conceptualising the 'macro' trend alone has taken a year of painstaking research. From there, the company research was also very time consuming. It's taken a long time, but we've now got down to what we want to own, and we've interviewed management from each investment extensively a number of times and feel very comfortable with what we own. In the incubation section of the fund, we might have emerging ideas that we think can double or triple as well.

How many stocks would you have incubating?

It could easily be thirty to fifty. At any given time, we might have ten to fifty in the incubation section.

Would they be half a per cent of the fund or even less?

A quarter per cent each maybe. The point is to own the position, so you have an 'at risk' situation.

On that basis do you spend your whole time in front of the screen and reading information, or do you spend a lot of time on the road visiting companies?

Well, technology's a great thing. You can now do a lot of your work simply by listening to recorded interviews and conference calls. Just about everything can be done by phone and internet so, fortunately, you don't always need to leave your office. You can cover a lot of ground simply by sitting in the one place. Generally, however, we like to do 450 to 500 company contacts a year through various methods, such as conferences, earnings season and meetings.

Taking Woodside, for example, did you get on a plane and see them in their offices in Perth before you invested?

Mostly, but with bigger companies we have generally always seen them present before. On this occasion, we purchased a small holding and chipped away at the company's reports for a good three or four months before buying more stock. The more work we did, the more comfortable we got, because we think Woodside is an under-researched situation — strangely for a big Australian company. We believe the company has significant hidden value. It's got three billion barrels of uncontracted gas reserves, and the gas only becomes a reserve once it's got a gas contract next to it. If you believe the gas could become contracted and you put a value of US$10 a barrel on that, that's US$30 billion. The stock's capped at US$12 billion or US$13 billion, and that's US$30 billion of additional value that could be incremental to the price of Woodside.

Do you think Treasurer Costello did the right thing when he stopped Shell taking over Woodside?

Well, whether he did the right thing or not, it's been good for us, because we had the investment opportunity available. It's one of the few growth oil or gas investments available in the world today, and we've looked at a lot of oil and gas stocks. Most oil stocks have declining or flat production. Woodside's production is going to double or triple by 2012.

Continuing the oil theme, you mentioned briefly before what happens when oil gets to US$70 a barrel or US$80. Can you just elaborate what that means for sharemarket investors? Obviously, oil stocks and gas stocks are the beneficiaries, because they've got a price for their product?

Unfortunately, it's very bearish for the rest of the market. We don't know when it's going to happen, so we're not slitting our wrists now, but we're certainly conscious of it, and we're monitoring it closely.

Up until now, oil has been up to US$55 or US$56 a barrel.[5]

It hasn't affected anything.

It hasn't impacted too much on the growth of western economies.

Quite honestly, that's very bullish for the price of oil stocks, because once it starts affecting the economy, the whole thing goes down. But if the economy can stand US$55 oil, well, imagine what the oil stock earnings are going to be when it goes to US$65 — you know, it's all margin.

---

5   The oil price rose to more than US$70 a barrel in August–September 2005.

Are you bearish on global sharemarkets?

We're longer term bearish for the market, but we're not slitting our wrists over the market at this stage, we're going to stay with it. We like to stay with things until things turn, until the trend changes, and right now we think there's still a positive bias to the trend.

For the overall market?

For the overall market. We could be waiting a long time for the end of the world, so I'm not betting on that. But in the meantime the oil sector's cheap and it fits what we're looking for.

What are the other themes you are interested in right now?

Well, that's the major theme right now. The gambling theme is still there. We like medical devices, we love airports, we love financial exchanges still.

Financial services?

Yes, also financial services. Although, if we are right on oil, financial services will not perform so well. Demographics is perhaps the daddy of all trends and Japan's a great example of that. If you go to Japan, it's got zero population growth, so there's no demand for new housing. Therefore, there are all these empty houses around the place and there's no new building. In Australia the building sector drives the market. There's no doubt that the housing sector and the infrastructure sector is a massive driver in Australia, because we don't manufacture much here. We rely on commodity exports.

What does that mean, though, for Australia? Are our demographics good?

Australia has good demographics. China's a great example of demographics. It's got 1.3 billion people and a large section of the population is becoming middle class. At the moment there could be 100 million people who are middle class and that could grow to 200 million soon. So it's like a massive push in demand, and that's affecting the whole of Asia. Australia's got a moderately increasing population due to migration so it looks okay. The key trend underpinning growth in China is the closure of high-cost western manufacturing bases and the opening of low-cost Chinese ones.

Do you worry about the fact that we're getting older?

I worry about that, but we can all work harder — we could all work longer and harder, unfortunately. But working keeps us young. Doesn't it?

That's what they say. Can you share with us your worst trades?

The worst trades I guess are where we had incorrect facts and where management snowed us with misleading information.

I think maybe Look Smart was a good example in the tech area. We like to hire consultants, and we hired this consultant in the tech boom. I think we paid him something like $200 or $300 to come and talk to us. At the time he was running a consultancy practice and he was doing metrics for the internet, where he would measure how many hits a particular site would get and he'd report it. He came in and started telling us how this particular company was a washing machine, where it would wash the revenue around. We had never properly realised that they were reporting their gross revenue as opposed to the net revenue. It's like the old travel agent trick, reporting gross ticket sales as opposed to the net commission. No analyst in Australia had really focused on it, but the consultant said the company was a washing machine.

Back then, internet and tech companies were getting valued on revenue multiples so it was to the company's advantage to report the highest revenue possible.

Then he proceeded to tell us that valuations were all getting very high and he was selling his internet company to sell pizzas! This was in 2000. So we all stood up and went out and sold a fair few of our investments after that. We love to hire consultants.

At the moment, we have been trying to get a guy who has advised President Bush, who is predicting oil shortages. We would love to speak with that guy. But it could be anything. It could be a telco consultant, or anyone who can give us an external view.

Other worse trades? I think our worst trade was investing in the German stock market just before it crashed, as opposed to a particular stock.

How much of your portfolio do you usually have short?

Well, for instance, right now — say the fund is worth $200 million [in April 2005], we've got gross assets of $280 million (including debt) and $140 million of shorts plus futures and options. It's a true hedge fund, it's not a pretend hedge fund. It's what we believe a long/short fund does. It's been very hard getting established in the hedge fund industry, because there's been no-one to tell us what to do. There's no book here, you know, there's no recipe; you just have to go out and find the way to do it, and that's what we've done.

Do you have any mentors or books that have guided you over the years?

> *I don't care what we spend on books, because if I spend $150 on a book that gives me one idea, I think that's a great buy.*

Books have been more influential than mentors. At home I have a wall full of books that I've bought. I don't care what we spend on books, because if I spend $150 on a book that gives me one idea, I think that's a great buy. So we'll send all over the world for books, and Amazon delivers!

As a broker, do you learn much from speaking to professional investors?

I actually think you do. But normally the way it works is that you give 90 per cent and they may give you 10 per cent back if you're lucky. So you can learn, but you're really giving nine times more than you get, and they'll let you know what they want you to know and that's it. Because, clearly, why would anyone give away their secrets!

What are the best investment books you've read and would you recommend any?

Currently I'm reading *Return to Go*, by Jim Slater, which we bought on eBay. It went out of print over twenty years ago, and we're reading it because that was the last time we had an oil boom, in 1973, when oil prices went through the roof. We're trying to learn what happened to the market at the time.

What we found was that it was highly correlated with strong inflation and high interest rates, both of which are usually extremely negative for the market. High oil prices created an economy with no growth because interest rates were too high and stifled all demand. So we're aware of that situation, but we're not going to predict it until it happens. But when and if it does happen, we want to be ready to act.

You're on alert.

We're always on alert.

But you won't change your course until you see valid signs of it happening?

There's no point in changing tactics until you can sort of see the whites of the eyes of what's coming at you, because you may well be too early and miss the last 50 per cent. It could be any amount you miss, but a lot of people have gone down waiting for the end of the world.

That strategy of waiting for the end of the world usually has proven to be the wrong one.

Correct. But if you can react quickly because you're organised, which is what we pride ourselves on, you can still make money.

But in many ways this potential oil spike is different to the one in the 1970s. Back then OPEC deliberately reduced supply. This time there is just too much demand.

Correct. In the seventies there was a withdrawal of supply by the major producers, Arabian major producers. That's what it was. What we think is coming is not a withdrawal of supply, but a 50 per cent increase in demand over the next twenty years, with no new supply, which is a completely different scenario, one which I'm not sure what the answer to is.

Do you believe the US Government and its people, who are the biggest guzzlers of oil and its by-products, are ready for the worst outcome or are they unaware of the situation?

Everyone wants to gloss over the problem because it is such a big hurdle, but the US is currently using thirty barrels per person per year, China is using 1.7 and Mexico is using seven. If China simply goes to Mexico's level, world demand goes up 30 per cent. And China is quickly industrialising as we speak. So we're expecting a big increase in demand and we just don't know where the supply is going to come from.

And then I presume you've got India as well.

There's India. In fact, we call it Chindia — the China and India effect.

So while it is nice to have strong world growth, it could be a major negative in the years to come?

Yes, from an energy on commodity point of view.

Once again we have digressed. Are there any books you would recommend?

Market Wizards is good; books about Warren Buffett — just anything you can find that looks interesting.

How much of your day would you spend reading?

We spend all our day reading. That's what the job is, reading, interviewing and interpreting.

Do you do financial models on individual companies, or is that a waste of time?

We don't do a lot of modelling, although we do back-of-the-envelope work. We find back-of-the-envelope profit and loss calculations are often more accurate than the models out there in the market, and we can do them quite quickly because we have over fifty years of experience within the group.

If you work between ten and twelve hours a day, what do you do if you are not building financial models?

What we're doing is checking facts. We want to make sure that we have the right facts and we want unfiltered information. So we will go to source magazines, we will listen to internet interviews recorded around the world, we will subscribe to trade magazines and have consultants come in to see us. We'll go to conferences, we'll listen to conference calls on company results. We'll do anything that increases our knowledge, but the basic point of it is to check facts and continue checking facts.

And how long, on average, do you hold individual stocks for?

We like holding stocks until the fundamentals change.

Until the theme changes?

Either it's fully priced, at which point we probably still won't sell it, because often prices go way beyond what you think the full valuation is. But until something changes that causes a complete rethink of the investment. Quite often it is obvious in the market when these trend changes occur. Out of nowhere, you'll get a sudden movement against the trend of 10 to 15 per cent and everybody will be wondering what's happened, but looking back on it you can quite often see that it was a turning point for that industry or stock.

What is your usual time frame for holding a stock?

It could be three years, it could be three months, or it could be one week. We prefer to hold for at least three years.

It's much easier to hold the stock you know, as opposed to finding new ones to replace it.

That's a nice situation, when you get your thinking right and it plays out.

We love to buy and hold and we do not see ourselves as traders.

So, fundamentally, you're looking for multiple gains over a number of years.

It's much easier to hold the stock you know, as opposed to finding new ones to replace it. The stock you know is way better than the one you buy that you know nothing about or you don't know the management team's background or the industry.

Earlier you said what led you to the sharemarket was your ability to use your mind as opposed to your hands. What drives you and what do you think makes a good investor? Is it the desire to make money or the desire to be mentally stimulated?

My motivation originally was financial freedom. I had no money at university. I wanted to improve my lifestyle by finding something I was good at and at which I could leverage my attributes. I wanted to achieve in something I felt suited my strengths, and the stock market suits all my strengths, as opposed to my weaknesses. I think everyone should play to their strengths and they should find the vocation that suits them. So the stock market suits me but it could easily be something else for somebody else.

What's your strength?

To be a successful investor I think you have to have a number of strengths. You have to have an ability to read emotional situations as well as financial situations. That is, you have to understand what people are really saying when you interview them. And you have to be able to take a lot of knocks, because out of every down time is born the next great up time. We've often found that our mistakes can lead to our greatest future successes. In fact, without our mistakes we could never have had our successes. It's by learning from our losses that we are what we are today. We don't like making losses, but by having a loss you learn your best lessons.

But that doesn't tell me what you're good at.

We're good at learning our lessons. That's what I'm trying to say. We learn our lessons. I don't think I have significantly greater smarts than the next person. I'm just more willing to take the losses that other people aren't in order to learn. By taking the loss I learn more than the other person, even though they might have greater ability. We also believe in not repeating our mistakes.

Do you keep a book on your lessons, or anything like that? Or just keep a mental note?

No, we go over our losses and look back over the year and we do an attribution analysis for those losses, where we see where we made them and why we made them. Losses are always very hard at the time, there's no two ways about it. We always find them very difficult.

However, we like to learn from our mistakes. This is the key.

What is the advantage of running an aggressive long/short fund over a standard institutional fund?

I think we have an advantage over other funds because we can own our best ideas in size, and that's what, from what I have read, all the great investors in the world do. They own their best ideas in as big a quantity as they can possibly buy them without risking the fund.

But are you a high-risk person?

No, I'm a low-risk person. We believe it's a lower risk to invest in our best ideas, not higher risk. It's actually lower risk. That is the common misconception of it all.

But all your own money is in your funds?

Yes. Most of my money is in the funds.

Right. But people would perceive that as risky — that you've got all your money tied up in a smaller number of stocks.

I can't think of a better place to be, because we've researched those stocks and we know them backwards. Isn't that safe, if you understand the situation backwards, and you've got nineteen years of experience and you've got another forty years of research talent in your team to draw upon?

And given that you made quite a lot of money from investing, is it best to plough your money back in or do you like to take money off the table?

There is a price for everything, but we are looking for trend changes.

You've got no other interests?

Well, we have no other financial interests. We're only interested in the stock market.

You are not interested in maybe buying a boat or buying a series of houses or something else?

I'm happy to have one or two houses and a car. You don't really need much more than that.

And you haven't changed that philosophy since the early days, given you personal wealth has increased considerably?

No. I've got a bigger, faster car and a bigger house, but I'd be just as happy having an average house and an average car. We just like investing in the sharemarket.

That's the thrill?

Yes.

Finally, do you have a target size for funds under management that will still allow you to perform?

Our strategy allows us to easily support $2 billion plus, because we can invest around the world in a range of products. For example, I could buy any energy-related stock around the world and I would be happy with that at the moment.

As we left the interview at about 6.15 pm on the Tuesday we jokingly suggested to the Mathews Capital staff that they should all pack up and go home for the night. Once again we received warm smiles, but not one person suggested that they were just finishing up. When individuals are making 100 per cent plus returns per annum, it becomes addictive.

Interviewing Mathews was a great learning experience. While his intensity verged on distracting, it was fascinating to talk to someone who had formulated his own style without having to conform to any outsiders. Basically, his style was find a growth theme, find the best stocks benefiting from that theme and then place large bets. Terminologies like valuation styles, following benchmarks, tracking errors and market risk are virtually non-existent. To most professional managers, Mathews's approach is just too left field. It would be like wearing a green or purple suit to a black tie party — a big risk, but something a few people can pull off. Over the last fourteen or fifteen years, for the most part, Mathews has pulled it off. Maybe that is why many of our Masters voted for Mathews this time around. They find his style unusual and would love to find out how he makes it work.

You can educate yourself and push the boundaries out, but first
and foremost know where the boundaries are, and only invest in
what you understand. If you invest in what you don't understand,
you speculate.

2

The ruminator
Peter Guy

When we mentioned to those who asked that we were planning to include Peter Guy in the second edition of *Masters of the Market*, the response, almost without exception, was, 'Peter who?' They might have been borrowing the famous comment from legendary cricket commentator Richie Benaud but, like Benaud, they were genuinely unaware of Peter Guy. When Benaud asked the question, he was commenting on the selection of little known off-spinner Peter Taylor in the Australian team in 1987. Like Taylor, Guy has never let down the faith of his selectors (or investors), despite his low profile in the game. In keeping with the comparisons with Taylor, Guy is not flashy and in some quarters might even be considered slightly daggy. But don't be fooled. He is a tenacious character and a meticulous researcher of stocks. He has a slightly nervous manner, but when discussing a topic that relates to the sharemarket, he becomes quite outspoken and even aggressive.

Guy, who runs his funds from Melbourne, could be labelled an accidental fund manager. He studied and worked as an accountant but quickly turned to stockbroking. Unlike many of the Masters who followed a similar career path, he then stumbled into funds management — he didn't set out with the intention of managing other people's money. Guy was merely happy to invest his own money in his pet area of small capitalisation stocks, scouring the market for his so-called little gems.

However, circumstances in the late 1980s saw him also managing money for others through his work for Warakirri Asset Management and a large Victorian industry superannuation fund Equipsuper (the old State Electricity Commission Superannuation Fund of Victoria). Since then, Guy has gained a reputation as one of the smartest small-cap investors in the market. Guy was an early investor in several of the current market darlings well before they hit the sights of other investors, including child-care group ABC Learning Centres, Chris Corrigan's transport group Lang Corporation (later to become Patrick), and radiology and aged care company DCA Group.

A voracious reader of the investment classics, Guy is unashamedly an acolyte of the Benjamin Graham/Warren Buffett school of value investing. He is arguably the most enthusiastic Buffett exponent of any of the Masters.

As one who religiously applies Graham's fundamental analysis to find value others can't see, Guy is critical of the superficial research reports produced by many broking firms. He argues they often fail to look much beyond the profit and loss statement to determine a company's prospects and value. Guy certainly takes a more detailed approach to examining accounts than many of his peers. This is undoubtedly also a reflection of the extensive financial training (including full accounting qualifications and an MBA) he received before joining the industry.

Interestingly, however, Guy has not been bogged down by pure value-based investing. He is a firm believer in buying stocks for the right value. His career, not unlike Buffett's, has seen him use Graham's analysis and apply it to companies that are going to grow at a pace well above average in the medium to long term. The key to picking these stocks, according to Guy, is trying to work out where a company sits in its life cycle. If a company has managed to establish itself and is ready to enjoy a long period of organic growth, Guy will be extremely interested in investing at the right price.

In our interview, Guy also provides insights into one of the most important developments in the Australian funds management industry — the spawning of influential asset consultants that advise fund trustees on which fund managers to use.

As a founding shareholder, Guy was there at the birth of asset consultant John Nolan & Associates, now the National Australia Bank–owned JANA Investment Advisers. The little-understood role and influence of asset consultants is helpfully explained by Guy, who counts friend and business partner John Nolan as one of the people he admires most.

Asset consultants have partly been blamed for the rise and rise of index-based investing. But at the same time, the support of consultants like JANA has been crucial in enabling the boutique funds management sector to flourish as it has in recent years, providing investors with an alternative to the faceless large institutions and access to some of Australia's best individual stock-picking talent.

We interviewed Guy in April 2005 in Melbourne. Because Warakirri's Queen Street offices were going through a much-need renovation, the interview was held in his lawyer's offices, a short stroll down the street. Guy begins by explaining why he's not your typical fund manager, having only ever made three so-called marketing presentations to sell his funds management expertise.

———————●———————

How long have you been in the funds management industry?

I got into stockbroking in 1972 and became involved in funds management in the late 1980s. I basically make my money as an investor [rather than a manager of money]. I've never solicited funds in my life, but over the years, I've been asked to manage other people's money. If I was just a pure contractor and wanted to make money as a fund manager, I would have marketed my record and solicited funds. If I'd done that, I'd be managing a lot more money than I am managing, but then I'd be wrenched out of the micro-cap area where I really want to be. It's where I make money for myself.

Just so we're clear, you earn money by investing your money alongside that of your clients?

What I'm saying is, I make my money primarily as an investor. For example, one of the funds that I manage is a small-cap fund set up within Warakirri ten years ago. I put $500 000 into the fund on the basis that it was briefly marketed to a dozen people or so and that I'd be managing my money alongside theirs. They also knew that apart from the $500 000 I'd put into this particular trust, I'd be owning the same stocks outside the trust and 100 per cent of my investment exposure wasn't going to be in this trust. I would own the same stocks in my super fund and in my family company outside the trust.

I also manage money for a large institution here in Victoria and they know that what I buy for them I'll buy for myself.

For years, I was just investing in the market and then on a number of occasions I was asked to manage money. I was hardly going to abandon what I was doing for a living, which was investing for me. So professional funds management to me is like an adjunct. It's leveraging off the work I'd be doing anyway.

So your focus has never been on accumulating a large pool of funds to manage.

My funds have been closed for years. I mean I've really got more money than I can manage anyway.

I've been absolutely dedicated to staying at the micro end of the market. I knew that if I went out there and solicited money and if I ended up managing $800 million or $1 billion, I couldn't focus on stocks with market capitalisations of as little as $10 million or $20 million — the little gems.[1]

Do you see enormous opportunities in the micro companies?

I would say the smaller the better. For some fund managers, a company must be of a minimum size but I don't have a minimum size requirement. A stock I bought yesterday has a market cap of just over $3 million, and that is really about as small as they get.

---

1   The micro-cap sector of the Australian stock market is regarded as those stocks listed in Australia excluding the stocks that comprise the S&P/ASX 300 Index. There are about 1000 micro-caps on the Australian sharemarket. Small-cap companies are generally considered to be those outside the S&P/ASX 100.

Peter, can you tell us a little about your background?

I was born in Bendigo and I came down to Melbourne to boarding school at Melbourne Grammar when I was ten. I've never been back. I still have family in Bendigo. In fact my brother Richard is chairman of Bendigo Bank. I was on the board years ago. Both of my parents were born in Bendigo and now live in Melbourne.

We had two family businesses. One was cold storage and ice manufacture, and the other was an egg-grading floor. The egg-grading business finally closed its doors about six or seven years ago. It didn't have a poultry farm. It was just an agent of the Victorian Egg Board and it packed eggs. The ice business was founded by my grandfather in Bendigo in 1928. I wouldn't say that that ever had an influence on me.

I did a commerce degree at Melbourne University. I graduated in 1966 and then I got a full-time job with a precursor to Ernst & Young, Edwin V. Nixon and Partners. But then I went back to university as a part-time student to complete my accountancy subjects so that I could become a member of the Australian Society of Accountants. I decided that, while I basically specialised in economics in my commerce degree, I really should have done accountancy.

I didn't particularly like it in the first year, but I forced myself to do it and to study it properly, and I got a job in an accountancy firm initially as an auditor. I then did the university accounting subjects, and then the taxation exam set by the Australian Society of Accountants.

Why did you do something you didn't really enjoy?

I realised that was a huge gap in my armour. I don't know whether I knew at that stage I was going to end up in investment markets, but I sure as hell knew I wasn't going to be an accountant. It was only ever a means to an end. I've got a son who's doing first year commerce at Melbourne University this year and, believe me, he's doing accountancy, and I'm going to make sure, to the extent that I can influence him, that he does it all the way through.

For me, if you understand accountancy really well, you have a huge advantage as a financial analyst over other people. At the same time I was doing accountancy, I actually became a qualified chartered secretary as well. I just decided to do that, and then I did an MBA [master of business administration]. So I pretty much got all the financial qualifications you could do at that time. This was in the 1960s. There wasn't a CFA [chartered financial analyst] course or the Securities Institute. I went to America and did an MBA.

At Edwin V. Nixon, it was standard practice for someone coming from university into the accounting firm to be an auditor. I left them and I joined a small suburban practice, where my job was to do all accounts for small businesses. A small businessman would bring in his cheque butts and his bank statements and then my job would be to literally write up the books, do the trial balance, prepare the income statement, prepare the balance sheet and do the tax return.

That was a fantastic experience because you really understand accounting when you have to actually build a complete set of books for a business. So I did that for a number of months and then I left Australia and went to America.

So where did you go to do your MBA?

The University of Virginia.

It would have been unusual then, and expensive, for someone to do an MBA in America. Was it a big investment for you?

Well, I didn't have any dough, but my father could afford it.

Why did you do it?

Really it was the culmination. When I was doing commerce at Melbourne University in the 1960s, the first MBA graduates were coming back from America. It wasn't really a qualification that was widely recognised, and so some of them were going into academia. Some of the Harvard MBAs, for example, were at University of Melbourne as lecturers, strange as that may seem. I was impressed by those people. To me, it was really a matter of just finishing a business study program and then working out what I was going to do.

Were you perhaps buying a bit of time?

I just wanted to become as fully qualified as I could be in the areas of management and accounting and finance, and then find a career. I finished my MBA in 1971, and then I was offered a job by a large mining company. At the university, companies came down to recruit people for summer jobs, and I was offered a job by American Metal

Climax, or AMAX as it was called. This was a time when mining was booming, so the mining sector was very much on my mind.

They offered me a summer job in New York, which was fantastic. When I graduated they offered me a job in their aluminium division, based in San Francisco. They were going to build what in those days was going to be a $400-million project, a bauxite-alumina project in the Kimberleys in WA. Like a lot of those mining projects, it was going to be a consortium of companies, not just AMAX.

It didn't take very many months for me to realise that the feasibility studies weren't stacking up and the project was not going to proceed. So one day I said, 'This thing is not going to get off the ground. The project's dead and you're asking me to hang around for the burial. I'm going home'. They couldn't argue, because in their hearts they knew that the numbers weren't stacking up and it wasn't going to go ahead, and of course it never went ahead.

I came back to Australia and my choice was between going into what was called merchant banking in those days and stockbroking. I was hired by Charles Goode, and I joined the research department of stockbrokers Potters in 1972. I realised very early on two things. One was that I loved research and two was that I liked researching small stocks. It was just right from the word go. That's what I enjoyed doing.

And what did you love about research, or researching stocks?

I realised that I like investing for myself. I also realised that I didn't particularly like broking, and I was no good as a broker. My heart wasn't in broking. I just loved delving into financial statements, beavering away, working out what the value was, and discovering something that was really cheap. To me the icing on the cake was to put some of my own money into it and make a quid.

Right from the word go I realised that I wasn't interested in the resource sector, and in due course I came to realise I wasn't really interested in the technology sector, so pretty much forever I have defined my universe as small-cap industrial companies that are easy to understand.

So how many people were there in the research department at Potters in 1972?

From memory about six people. John Bartley ran the research department in those days. He was a good person. He was smart and competent. In those days people tended to stay in research for experience and training and then progress to what was called the underwriting department, which was run by Gordon Stuckey and Charles Goode. This department engaged in fund raising and corporate advice. But I didn't want to do that. My heart was really in research.

What do you remember about those days in the research department at Potters?

Charles Goode had done his MBA at Columbia University, the intellectual home of Benjamin Graham. Just before Benjamin Graham's death [in 1976], he was interviewed and an article appeared in a financial journal about his favourite criteria for analysing stocks. One of his two favourite criteria was what was called net net working capital or net current assets.

Just as a matter of clarification, what is net net working capital?

It's basically current assets minus all liabilities per share, or putting it another way, it's NTA [net tangible assets per share] but applies a zero value to fixed assets per share, including a company's plant, machinery and its land and buildings. You're just looking at the value of stock, debtors [receivables] and cash. If you pay out all liabilities and the residual per share is greater than the share price, you've met your net net working capital test.

So it's not just shares selling less than NTA. It's less than NTA after ascribing a nil value to fixed assets. When you think about the asset base, you're focusing on your cash, stock and debtors. The higher the cash the better, then the next best quality asset would be debtors and then the third best quality asset would be stock.

If you found that you had a carpet manufacturer that might qualify, and 90 per cent of its assets are unsold carpet stocks, you might think it's not a very high quality net net, but if it was a net net and had high cash backing per share, you might have struck gold. Of course, the days of Benjamin Graham were in an era prior to computers. These days computers can calculate net nets in the blink of an eyelid, but back in those days there was lots of number crunching underneath these things.

So Benjamin Graham's statistical cheapness approach to the market was really a big thing for its time, but now with the computer and databases he'd find it a lot tougher going.

The net nets were screened out years ago, and no-one ever talks about them these days. You might occasionally find some.

But it's unusual.

Very unusual. So no-one could make a living out of it any more. No-one ever talks about it any more, because it's almost dead as a criterion, but it made Ben Graham famous.[2]

It was one of Benjamin Graham's favourite criterion for finding bargains. He talked about this in his interview and Charles asked me to see if there were any Australian stocks that met this particular criterion.

In those days the only real database for Australian stocks was Statex, which was owned by the Sydney Stock Exchange. I went to Statex and they just wrote a program that incorporated the formula for net net working capital. We came up with a list of six, seven or eight stocks that qualified. About eight or nine months later, the market had gone up about 10 per cent and this basket of stocks had gone up around 70 per cent. It was absolutely dramatic.

When Graham died another article appeared. He'd retired to California, and he'd done a lot of work with a fellow called James Rea. Rea had written an article basically saying that Ben Graham really had ten favourite criteria, while in that previous article he'd referred to only two. Because that first computer run had been so

---

2   More specifically, the concept of net net working capital values a company based on the liquid components of working capital, net of all its liabilities. Specifically, the NNWC formula is: NNWC = (cash & investments × 100 per cent) + (accounts receivable × 75 per cent) + (inventory × 50 per cent) – total liabilities. The formula values cash at 100 per cent, receivables at 75 cents on the dollar (because some of them might not be collectable), inventory at 50 cents on the dollar (because of likely discounting when sold at fire sale prices). After subtracting all the liabilities, what's left is the company's net net working capital. NNWC is really a conservative estimate of what a company might be worth if it shut its doors, sold everything, paid off its creditors, and returned all the money to shareholders. (Source: Motley Fool.) Companies that might be worth buying are trading with a market capitalisation less than their NNWC.

successful, it was just natural then to take the ten criteria and do a real job on it, and that was probably the most comprehensive piece of research I ever did while I was at Potters.

It was an enormous amount of work, because we ran the Statex database against the ten criteria and I did a very large research report identifying the top twenty stocks using these Benjamin Graham criteria. In fact, we published a more comprehensive list to see how other stocks in the Statex database rated on this Benjamin Graham analytical approach. There was an enormous amount of calculations. Initially the calculations were done by the computer but, of course, I then had to go and check every single one of them. It was an enormous amount of work but, I tell you what, if you bought that list of twenty stocks you would have absolutely cleaned up. Fair dinkum. I remember Laurie Cox [then a partner of Potters] telling me one day that he bought the whole twenty. I'll just sound like I'm boasting, but it was very high quality research.

What that did for me was totally inculcate into me the concept of value investing with a Benjamin Graham approach. He was the Rosetta Stone. But there was a second Rosetta Stone and that was Warren Buffett. Buffett really was the intellectual successor to Benjamin Graham.

Buffett always gives Benjamin Graham a lot of credit.

He does and to me that is my ideology. I absolutely follow the principle of value investing a la Benjamin Graham and Warren Buffett. I mean, it sounds almost superficial to say that, but it's the truth.

Benjamin Graham was very much a quantitative person, and he looked for statistical cheapness. It was all about PEs, debt and equity ratios, compound earnings per share growth rates and net net working capital. He wasn't much into company visits or the qualitative aspects of business. That, of course, was the great thing that Warren Buffett brought to value investing. Warren Buffett has described himself as a business analyst, rather than a financial analyst. Buffett repeatedly advises people to identify their 'circle of competence' — what businesses they understand — and to confine their investments within this boundary of understanding. You can educate yourself and push the boundaries out, but first and foremost know where the boundaries are, and only invest in

> *You can educate yourself and push the boundaries out, but first and foremost know where the boundaries are, and only invest in what you understand. If you invest in what you don't understand, you speculate.*

what you understand. If you invest in what you don't understand, you speculate.

I mean, when you think about it, ABC Learning Centres is a pretty simple business; Baxter Group is in the rubbish tip business. You don't have to be a rocket scientist to understand businesses like that. But when you start getting into laser technology and biotechnology, you have to ask yourself, do I really understand those businesses? And I don't, so I don't go there.

Buffett talks about an enduring competitive advantage, business franchises, barriers to entry and pricing power. To me, anybody wanting to learn about investing should first of all study Ben Graham and then they should study Warren Buffett.

Whenever Warren Buffett refers to Graham's book *The Intelligent Investor*, he always says read two chapters. He says read the last chapter, which is called 'Margin of safety', and which basically says two things. It says you calculate intrinsic value and buy a stock where there is a significant margin of safety between share price and intrinsic value. The second thing it says you need to do is diversify. This gives you two safety nets.

Those three words, 'margin of safety', encapsulate in three words Graham's philosophy of value investing. The other chapter is the one with the 'Mr Market' metaphor. This is a brilliant explanation of how stocks can be mispriced.

Getting back to Buffett, there is a question he asks that I think is a brilliantly articulated business quality test — how much damage can a competitor do if he is stupid about returns? Buffett likes metaphors and he frequently refers to the size of the 'moat'. Commodity businesses don't have a moat.

How can the lessons of Warren Buffett be applied to the Australian stock market?

Well, you're not going to find counterparts to stocks he is famous for owning, such as Coca-Cola, Disney, American Express and Gillette. But in looking for companies with great moats, a good starting point is to look at the natural monopolies — companies like ASX, IRESS,

Cabcharge and, of course, the tollroad operators like Transurban. To apply Buffett's lessons, you need to constantly think about the quality of a company's business in terms of the concepts Buffett talks about — does the company have an enduring competitive advantage (a moat)? is the moat contracting or expanding? what are the barriers to entry for competitors or barriers to exit for customers? what is the pricing power? and so on.

When you started, do you think that investing wasn't very sophisticated, in the sense that you just went and applied Graham's ten criteria? Now you've got hundreds of people scouring over stocks with various valuation methods. Do you think 'Mr Market' is still around in a holistic sense? In those days when very few people were buying stocks, it was much more of an emotional ride.

First of all, the markets were much less efficient than they are now. I don't think many people followed Benjamin Graham at all. It was almost virgin territory back in the 1970s when I was doing what I was doing.

But that's not to say that there weren't other investors around who didn't have disciplined value investing approaches. They certainly did. I can give you a classic example of someone who did, because he was a client of Potters, and that was John Templeton. He was very much a value investor.

And incredibly successful.

Phenomenally successful.

Many readers of the first edition of Masters of the Market *have suggested that professional investors had a big advantage in that they can visit a company and talk to management. But why can't anybody off the street who has a basic understanding of accounting, read chapter 8 and chapter 20 of* The Intelligent Investor *and become a great Investor?*

They can. And in terms of the advantage the institutions hold, there's been a great levelling of the playing field. There are investor briefings that companies invite us to but they have to lodge their presentation material instantly on the internet [on the ASX website]. Anyone, with today's technology, can get the same information as a fund manager.

But, if the information is there, why aren't there hundreds of great investors? Is it a discipline thing?

It takes a lot of hard work and dedication to be a really good investor. Most people are probably just part-timers, aren't they? You can't expect the average person in the street to put in the hard yards that we put into unearthing bargains and staying knowledgeably on top of the stocks that we own. It is a full-time exercise, isn't it?

How long did you stay at Potters?

I left Potters in 1981 and joined broker Cortis & Carr. The reason I did that is that the culture in Potters really was pretty much against personal investing. They were brokers first and foremost.

I wasn't precluded from buying shares myself, but it wasn't something that was encouraged. They didn't even like the partners investing.

Cortis & Carr was a a broking firm that specialised in small-cap stocks. It was a firm, and the partners of the firm made a lot of money as investors, not just as brokers, so the whole culture was different.

> *It takes a lot of hard work and dedication to be a really good investor. Most people are probably just part-timers.*

I became a member of the stock exchange, and I stayed there until Prudential-Bache took it over.

Cortis & Carr had very little institutional capacity. It was a private client firm with a small-cap focus. Pru Bache, which was looking to build an institutional platform in Australia, bought it and had to change the whole structure.

What did you do after Cortis & Carr?

With John Nolan, I co-founded John Nolan & Associates, which was then located at 401 Collins Street [in the Melbourne CBD]. That business was founded very close to the crash in 1987. There were people at Cortis & Carr I was very close to and I was saying to them this was not the place for us any more [after Pru Bache took control]. They took a long time to move. I rang up John one day and just said, 'John, I can't stand it here. I'm coming and moving in with you'.

So that would have been about 1988 I think, and [since then] John's office has been ten or twenty yards from mine.

John's really been responsible for me getting into funds management. But, life is so circumstantial, and I've had a big influence on John and he's had a big influence on me.

John used to work for National Mutual. Then he worked for the State Electricity Commission of Victoria (SEC). In short order he became chief financial officer, but also chairman of their superannuation fund. I told John he should set up an asset consulting business and become a consultant to superannuation fund trustees. I told him if he decided to do that I would back him — put money into the business and fund it. And that's what he did.

The reason why I said that is because every year I went back to America and talked to fund managers. I went to Boston and talked to Peter Lynch. I met some really great fund managers, because I was a student of investing. My hobby has always been reading investment books. I have read every good investment book I've ever been able to put my hands on, and if you can recommend something I haven't read I'll buy it and I'll read it. I mean I have literally read hundreds.

So what's the best thing you've read, besides the Benjamin Graham books?

If someone asked me what books to read, I would say, well, start with this [holds up *The Intelligent Investor*], then go and buy Lawrence Cunningham's *The Essays of Warren Buffett*. He put together the essays of Warren Buffett, but then also get the Berkshire Hathaway [Buffett's company] annual reports. And read all the Buffett books, and probably the best one is *The Making of an American Capitalist*, by a fellow called Roger Lowenstein. It's a good book. Probably the best of them, but a lot of them are very good.

Robert Hagstrom's books are excellent. He's written a number of books on Buffett. Pretty much all of his books are very good. He wrote a book years ago, *Latticework*, which was really picking up an idea from Charles Munger, Warren Buffett's deputy chairman. That's an outstanding book. I recommend everyone read that. Benjamin Graham, Warren Buffett, Peter Lynch, John Train, David Dreman, Robert Hagstrom; I mean, all their books are excellent

Another good one is a book by Ralph Wanger [and Everett Mattlin], who used to run the Acorn Fund in America. He wrote a book called *A Zebra in Lion Country* [about investing in small-cap stocks]. There's also a book called *Margin of Safety*, written by a fund manager called

Seth Klarman. That was very good. Ned Davis has written a couple of books [*Being Right or Making Money* and *The Triumph of Contrarian Investing*], they're very good. And then you've got your classics like *Extraordinary Popular Delusions and the Madness of Crowds* and Le Bon's *The Crowd*. They're the classics. I think everyone should have a copy of the classics. If you read all that stuff with an emphasis on Graham and Buffett, I reckon that's the guts of it.

So tell us more about your visits to America.

I used to interview fund managers. One day I visited a fund manager in New York called Ron Haave, and he said he was in Budge Collins's top ten. I said, 'Who is Budge Collins?' Collins was a consultant to pension funds, helping them with manager selection. And the thing you have to realise is that in Australia in those days funds management was very concentrated in that there was only about two dozen or three dozen fund managers and they were all in Sydney or Melbourne. There were no boutiques, or virtually no boutiques, whereas in America you had thousands of boutiques. It was very, very fragmented over there, quite different to Australia. Budge Collins had clients like Safeway stores, Champion Spark Plugs, the Coors Foundation — you know, that make the beer — and University of Texas super fund. They were his clients and he would literally go around America interviewing hundreds and hundreds of fund managers and then recommend them to his client base. I hadn't met him, but I thought, 'Wow, what a great job and what a great business'. So, getting back to John, when he told me that he was going to leave the SEC, I said, 'Why don't you do this? This is what's needed, and Australia tends to go the American way'.

So no-one would have been doing that in Australia at that time?

Well the superannuation fund trustees all needed to have a liability consultant, or an actuary, but they were asking the actuary to leap over to the other side of the balance sheet and give them advice on asset consulting. When I suggested this to John he went to talk to Bruce Cook [head of the biggest actuary firm at the time]. Cook said he was getting into asset consulting because there was a demand for it from his clients, but if John set up a business, he'd like to have a piece of it.

So John Nolan & Associates was born [with Mercer Campbell Cook & Knight a minor shareholder]. Then Mercer's boss came out from America and said, 'What have we got here? You know it's not company policy to have minority interests in what we believe to be core businesses. Get rid of it'. And they were forced to divest. Well, the rest is history. It is by far the biggest asset consulting firm in Australia, and we sold it to the National Australia Bank in 2004.[3] By then we had thirty clients and $30 billion under consultancy in round numbers. It was hugely successful and an enormous tribute to John.

My relationship with John is important because it really explains how I got involved in funds management. Getting back to John's work with the SEC super fund, the typical super fund has its trustees and puts all of its assets out for external management. Not many super funds manage money internally. The old SEC super fund was different. It did both. It managed money internally and it put money out to external managers as well. And the trustees appointed a sub-committee to manage the fund — $1.5 billion in the mid-1980s was a lot of money. It was a big fund. The committee that managed the money comprised two or three of the trustees and one or two members of the staff of the fund, but they had three external consultants. They had a property consultant, a fixed-interest consultant and an equities consultant — three outsiders. Some time in the late 1980s I got invited to be the equities consultant to the SEC super fund. To some extent I was a misfit, because all I was interested in was the smaller, micro-cap segment of the market. But it was an interesting experience to sit on an investment committee that managed $1.5 billion, owned shopping centres, had fixed-interest portfolios, managed money internally and used external managers, and was big cap as well as small cap. It gave me a real introduction into the institutional mindset, because there's a huge difference between what I call absolute return investing and relative return investing. Most fund managers and most institutions are into relative return investing, whereas I'm an absolute return investor. Warren Buffett is an absolute return investor.

With relative return investing, if the market's down 30 per cent and the fund manager's down 20 per cent …

He's done great.

---

3   John Nolan & Associates, founded in 1987, has since become JANA Investment Advisers but is run as a stand-alone entity with the National Australia Bank. Nolan continues to be the firm's chair of research, although in a scaled back role.

… and he's very happy.

Yes.

Whereas to the absolute return investor, that's a major failure.

It's a disaster. But it's more than that. I am stating the obvious here but if you are a funds manager appointed by an institution and your mandate is to beat the 50 Leaders index and only invest in stocks included in this index, the whole concept of being overweight and underweight [in those stocks] becomes relevant. If you went to Warren Buffett and said, 'Warren, you're overweight Coca-Cola and American Express, and you're underweight General Motors, IBM and Microsoft', you'd get laughed out of the room. It's chalk and cheese. People really have to understand how it affects the behaviour of institutions or fund managers. They talk about the risk of not owning something. Remember some years ago when News Corp's share price suddenly went haywire [that is, up].

Many fund managers who were underweight News Corp were getting bloody slaughtered because they were underperforming the benchmark. There were some fund managers out there who couldn't stand the pain any more. They didn't want to buy News shares before they had risen, but they ended up buying them after they had gone way up, because they couldn't stand the pain of not owning them. It's an absolute perversion of the investment process if you're an absolute return investor to behave that way, and to talk about the risk of not owning something. You read all the [stockbroking] research reports these days and it's all 'overweight' and 'underweight'. They even talk about the risk being on the upside when referring to an earnings per share forecast. The concept of risk in today's investment industry has been absolutely bastardised. It's been made absurd.

> It's an absolute perversion of the investment process if you're an absolute return investor … to talk about the risk of not owning something … The concept of risk in today's investment industry has been … made absurd.

So the SEC introduced you to the concept of managing institutional money?

That's right. What happened was the SEC appointed an external small-cap funds manager, and he was given about $20 million in funds to manage. About eight months later, the $20 million was worth $13 million and they were in an absolute state of shock. So he was fired and then they shifted the portfolio to the internal funds management team to manage. They asked me to help manage this portfolio, because the internal bloke was a big-cap stock investor called Stephen Thompson (who now works with Paradice Cooper in Melbourne). He is a good fund manager; however, they knew that my speciality was in small stocks.

So the SEC put $7 million into the fund to bring it back to $20 million. Five years later, the $20 million was worth $50 million.

Stephen got headhunted to work in Sydney and so they needed someone to manage their small-company fund. They asked me to manage it — remember, I was sitting on the investment committee. I said it wasn't what I wanted to do and it was too much money for me anyway. By that stage [1997], John Nolan & Associates had started and the SEC had become one of its first clients, and I was a director of John Nolan & Associates and the second largest shareholder after John. So I had a strong reason for not getting the SEC offside. Anyway, after a lot of discussion, eventually I ended up agreeing to do it. And the moment I did that I had to resign from the investment committee, because I became a hired hand. Some stocks were taken out of the fund I had helped Stephen manage and I started managing a $27 million portfolio for them in May 1997. The portfolio today is around $64 million, but they have withdrawn $33 million over time. It's done over 20 per cent compound.

[Prior to this] John Nolan & Associates had been set up targeting the biggest superannuation funds in Australia. As I said, it had thirty clients and $30 billion under assets. It had the likes of Wesfarmers, Southcorp, National Bank, Commonwealth Bank, Mayne, Orica, Lion Nathan [as corporate super clients]. It also targeted the biggest super funds, the industry funds, as clients. But John was a very religious person and in the early days of the firm he started getting approaches from religious bodies and charities, and he couldn't say no. If someone had walked in with a $50 million super fund he would have said, 'No, you're too small for our fee structure'. But if someone walked in with a $30 million charity like the William Buckland Foundation here in Melbourne, for example, John couldn't say no. He just couldn't.

So, we ended up in the early days of John Nolan & Associates having some small clients, but they really wanted direct investment advice. For a time, we gave individual investment advice to a number of charitable trusts and religious bodies, but then it started to grow and become too important. We decided we couldn't give individual investment advice to these entities and created a common pool. We said to these clients that if they really wanted us to manage their money, they were just going to have to put it into this pot.

We called it our charities trust, but in those days there was stamp duty on shares and, in fact, it was an entity that was open for investment by stamp duty–exempt entities. That encompassed religious bodies, registered charities and school endowment funds.

In due course, we decided that John Nolan & Associates was an evaluator of fund managers and it shouldn't be one [a fund manager], so Warakirri Asset Management was formed. Whereas John Nolan & Associates was in William Street [Melbourne], Warakirri was initially set up in Queen Street. It was something that John wanted to do, but we realised that it compromised the nature of the business of John Nolan & Associates, which was to be an evaluator of fund managers.

So you had to separate them.

Initially the share registers of both companies were identical, but that changed over time.

So that's one of the pools.

Today, we [Warakirri] manage over $300 million for charities and religious bodies and school endowment funds. That goes back to the 1990s. I used to do the small-cap part of it, and Andrew Sisson used to do the big-cap part of it.

Then as it got bigger and bigger, we decided that we needed to have a third manager and Peter Wetherall joined us. Peter Wetherall tends to do the mid-cap area. Once a month we meet — John Nolan chairs the meeting — so Andrew and Peter handle the big and the mid and I do the small stocks. Our main trust, which we closed off at $100 million, is now over $200 million, because it's grown organically [without inflows].

Which means the value of the assets has gone up.

Absolutely. I think we've done 18 per cent compound, something like that, since it started. That's the overall performance [rather than just small cap], and I know that people have tried to segregate the difference, but what's the point?

How much of the $300 million do you manage in the small/micro cap area?

It's very hard for me to say, because some of my smalls have become big. Like one of my big stocks, one of my great picks in the early days, was Lang Corporation [now transport and logistics group Patrick Corporation]. We bought Lang when it had a market cap of around $100 million. Today Lang Corp is valued at $4.1 billion. [Diagnostics and aged care company] DCA Group is one of the largest holdings in our portfolio. When we bought in it had a market cap of $50 million. We've sold a lot of our shares as it's gone up and it's still a large holding for us.

So when John Nolan & Associates was established in 1987, there was no thought whatsoever of getting into funds management. We first got into it because John couldn't say no. Warakirri has $2.6 billion or so under management today and it is a very successful business.

Right. So there was other money that came in?

We have a number of funds other than the funds we manage for the charities and religious bodies.

And they came in subsequent to setting up those funds?

Yes. When we decided that we would segregate it and have a separate company, obviously, the aim of the business was to make a profit and to grow. We moved into 53 Queen Street because it was cheap. It's a terrible building, but we moved there because it was cheap. It took some years before we actually made a profit, but it's grown substantially now.

So Warakirri was set up in the mid-1990s?

Initially funds management for the charities was housed in a wholly owned subsidiary of John Nolan & Associates; then Warakirri was formed as a separate company. Once Warakirri got going, John Nolan said to me, 'Come on, Peter, start up a dedicated small companies trust'. Eventually I agreed to do it and the Warakirri Small Company Value Trust was formed on 1 February 1995. It was very small and I put in $500 000 and about ten other investors put in money so all up I'd say there was about $3 million.

$3 million. And what would that be worth now?

$25 million. This is something I'm quite proud of. The $500 000 I put in was just left there and on 1 February 2005 — the tenth year — my $500 000 was worth $5.2 million, so it went up, in gross terms, over ten times.

What's that in compound terms?

It's 26.5 per cent.

Compound?

Yes, average compound — but not for investors, because there is a 20 per cent profit share [fee] there too. Investors made just under seven times their money if they put money in and stayed for the full ten years.

So, in chronological order, I started managing money through Warakirri for the charities in the early 1990s, the Warakirri Small Company Value Trust was set up on 1 February 1995, and on 1 May 1997, I started managing money for the SEC super fund.

Can we get onto your investing style? When you were an analyst at Potters, you didn't necessarily look at micro caps or small caps versus big caps. Why did you end up specialising in micro caps?

I think for a number of reasons. One was because they are simpler than looking at a company like Pacific Dunlop [since split up] or Amcor, with multiple divisions. Secondly, you're more likely to get bargains at the small end. There's no question it's less efficient at the bottom end, and it's simpler. A third reason is that at the small end you can occasionally find companies at the early stages of their life cycles that have a period of major growth ahead of them.

There's a fourth aspect too — it can be more fun, more interesting. If you are investing in BHP Billiton or National Australia Bank, what access do you as a fund manager get to the managing director? I mean Eddy Groves [founder of child-care operator ABC Learning Centres] has been to my house for dinner, for example. The chairman of DCA is coming to my house for dinner tonight. When you're investing in smalls, you just get to know the entrepreneurs.

It's not difficult in smalls to get to know the people who run the companies. That's one of the delights of what I do. I got to know Chris Corrigan pretty well back in the early days and, of course, I met David Vaux [the chief executive of DCA] then, because he used to be number two to Chris Corrigan. You get to meet some really fantastic entrepreneurs.

Do you see management as crucially important for the small-cap company?

Yes and it's not just management ability that is important. It's also attitude towards minority shareholders. Most small companies are proprietorships, where there's one individual who owns 25, 35, 55 per cent of the capital. The question that I always ask myself is whether that proprietor wants me to make money as an investor in his business and what's his attitude towards me. That's critically important.

Would you elaborate on the growth appeal of small-cap stocks?

It is useful to consider their life cycle graph. Basically, whenever I look at a company I ask, where is it in its life cycle? In the graph of the classic pattern of a company life cycle, if the curve started off on the X line it would be a start up [point 'a' on figure 3.1]. Investing in the start-up phase is venture capital investing and I rarely do that. What I do could be described as development capital investing. The ideal time to invest in a company is at the inflection point [point 'b'], when it's sort of established and it's fairly developed and it's raising capital and about to enter into a period of sustained growth.

Figure 3.1: Company value life cycle

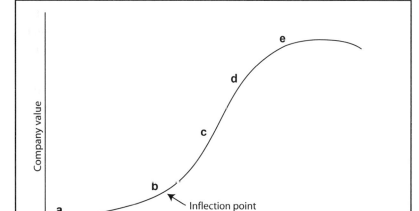

At the inflection point?

Yes. ABC was at the inflection point when it went public. It started in 1988 with one centre and when it went public in 2001 it had thirty-four centres. Today, they are heading towards 1000 centres. They've just taken off.

———————— I would say the Holy Grail of investing is to find

I would say the Holy Grail of investing is to find growth.

growth. I'm after growth stocks. I want to find stocks that will go up six-, seven-, eight-, tenfold. I'm not trying to find a stock that is selling at 70¢ to go up to $1 — where all I'm going to get is another 40 to 50 per cent gain. I mean I do a bit of turnaround investing and try what Warren Buffett refers to as 'cigar-butt' investing.[4]

I do a little bit of that, but really, I'm after the big ride. You are going to find the big ride at the inflection point. So how do you find growth? Well, I differentiate growth. There are growth companies like Austrim or Ariadne — companies that are making takeovers all the time. Their PEs rise and they start issuing paper. I'm not interested in that kind of acquired growth.

I'm interested in organic growth, and organic growth starts with sales. Ultimately with growth, you're talking about growth in earnings per share. That's the bottom line. I'm looking to get growth in the bottom line. But I'm also looking for growth in the top line, which is revenue growth — not growth acquired by leveraging up or by an Alan Jackson [former Austrim boss] getting on the takeover trail. That's one way to manufacture growth, but that's not what I'm trying to find.

How do you find companies that are going to have sustained periods of sales growth? Peter Lynch used to find regional success stories like Dunkin' Donuts, which was succeeding in New England, and rolled out across America. Take Baker's Delight [bakery business]. Baker's Delight started here in Victoria. I know they're now moving into Canada, but if it came to me as an IPO I would ask, 'How many stores do you think can be accommodated and how far have you gone?'

---

4   Cigar-butt investing, a term coined by Buffett, refers to investing in stocks that have sunk to the bottom but still have a bounce in them (even if they remain bad businesses). The analogy refers to a discarded cigar butt that has one puff left in it. It may not provide much of a smoke but perhaps enough to produce a good profit.

Look at Freedom Furniture [the now unlisted furniture retailer]. You can think about companies like that in terms of Peter Lynch, where he looks for a formula that could be rolled out nationally. But when you see Gerry Harvey opening up stores in Singapore, that tells me he could be up there.

That's 'e' on the chart.

The 'e' on the chart. I reckon when Just Jeans floated for the first time it was around about 'c' on the chart and then it got taken over when it was beyond 'd'. Now it's come back to market [as Just Group]. When Freedom Furniture floated, I reckon it was around 'c'. It had a lot more franchising opportunities and company-owned store opportunities to expand. I think that's a really useful way to think of companies.

So one area of growth is finding a regional success story that can be rolled out nationally. Another area to look for growth is industry aggregations, industry consolidations. I tend to find more growth opportunities in this area than in the first area. If I see a cottage industry that's starting to aggregate, I am seriously interested.

It doesn't mean that all industry consolidations work and all industry consolidations are of interest, so whether I ultimately decide to invest in them depends on whether I like what they're doing.

Can you give some examples?

The best and perhaps simplest example I can give was one that I essentially missed — [pathology operator] Sonic Healthcare. It was the first to do a consolidation in the pathology area. When you think of a pathology business, it consists of a lab, depots where people go to have their blood or tissue sampled, and it consists of transport infrastructure that takes the tissue sample from the depot back to the lab. Of course, once the lab's done the analysis, they then communicate the results back to the referring doctor.

If you put two pathology businesses together, you can close down a lab and restructure the depots and the transport infrastructure. The benefits of scale are just absolutely fantastic.

Sonic started doing that and taking over other pathology businesses and it just took off. I bought $1000 worth of shares back in the early days. I sat in on a couple of presentations and I didn't buy more because it was, like, twelve or thirteen times earnings. I thought I wanted to buy it at nine times earnings or something, but I didn't understand. If I had thought in life cycle terms and the opportunities that it had before it, I would have paid up because it was a really good risk and they had so much growth in front of them. I didn't see it clearly enough in life cycle terms. Pathology I think was a great example, but there have been lots of examples now.

If you look at my portfolio, I've really honed in on a lot of companies that were fairly cottage. DCA Group is in two industries — one of which is in the late stages of industry consolidation, with the other in the early stages of industry consolidation. Radiology was an industry consolidation, but that's pretty much fully consolidated now. Its other business is in nursing homes, and nursing homes are very cottage.

The reason I invested in ABC is I met Eddy Groves at a presentation at the time of the float, and he said, 'We've got thirty centres, we're going to forty and there's 4500 centres in Australia'. I said, 'Where are you?' And he said, 'We're number two'. I thought, wow, he's got less than 1 per cent of the market and he's number two in the industry. What a cottage industry. Boy. The bell rang for me and I was the biggest investor in ABC when it floated.

_____ And that's gone up how many times?

The first principle of investing is you've got to be rigorous on price. About fourteenfold. 40¢ was the float price and it's risen to $5.50 — just sensational.

[Financial planning and accounting group] Investor Group is another one that is interesting. I've sold out of Investor Group now. Harts and Stockford and Garrisons tried to do it and failed. But Investor Group got it to work, and I think the history of that industry is that the model is so important.

It took Investor Group a while though, didn't it? They've had their ups and downs but they've basically got it right over time.

The first principle of investing is you've got to be rigorous on price, and I bought in when the shares collapsed. I bought in at $1.50 and the shares had gone up to $4.00 before they came down. I sold out because I thought the shares became too expensive having regard to where they had got to on the life cycle curve. I should make the point that in an industry aggregation a public company as the acquirer is likely to have a PE multiple well in excess of the earnings multiple it is paying to acquire private companies. There is a significant element of PE arbitrage for the benefit of the public acquirer. But I don't just want to play the PE private-to-public arbitrage game. On top of that I want to see true integrations, true synergies and scale benefits from putting the businesses together. And, of course, most of my investments are service companies. I very rarely invest in manufacturers.

Is that because the returns are so much higher and you don't have to have the massive capital expenditure outlay?

I think the cash flow characteristics by and large are far superior. It's hard to find manufacturing businesses that have got really strong franchises.

In Australia, yes.

But I have invested in some and I'm currently trying to buy a lot of shares in one manufacturing business. Gale Pacific is one of my investments, and it's a manufacturer.

How do you apply your life cycle thinking to the decision to sell?

If you look at my second graph [figure 3.2], you will see I have shown intrinsic value increasing in a linear way — which, of course, doesn't happen — but it is drawn that way to illustrate how growth stocks might sell below and above intrinsic value at different points in time.

The share price can get ahead of intrinsic value. Sometimes, the biggest mistake investors make is selling too early, and it was a mistake I made early in my career. I'd buy a stock at $2 and it would go to $5 and I'd say, wow, you know, I've made two and a half times my dough and cash in my chips, but now I resist that. Sometimes I can see that the share price might get ahead of fundamentals — say, point (i) on the graph. But provided the distance between point (i) and (ii) is not too far in time, I'll stay with it. Point (iii) corresponds with the company getting closer to its mature phase, and here it makes sense to consider selling. You'd only want to sell a stock down around point (i) if the share price got way ahead of itself. Way, way ahead of itself.

Figure 3.2: Share price life cycle

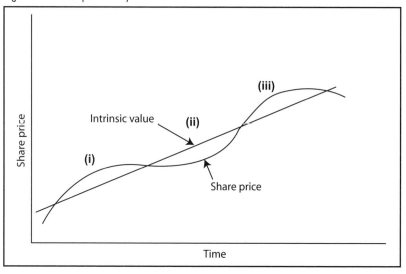

And in that scenario would you look to sell and then buy back when
you thought it was cheaper?

No, I tend not to do that. I mean I've done that with Gale. I've
actually sold it and bought back. And I did that with Tempo too — I
sold out in 2001, I think, and made four times my money and I did
buy back into it, but my second trip has been pretty rugged.

So can you explain intrinsic value? What does it actually mean and
how do you get the intrinsic value on a stock?

Well, you go to Warren Buffett and he will tell you it's easy to define
but hard to calculate.

So does that mean it's like the missing link?

It's the net present value of all the money you're ever going to take
out of the business, that's what it is.

So you can work out a company's net present value, but you've got
to have a view on how much it can grow and what kind of cash they
can produce over time?

Theoretically, it is the net present value of future cash that will be
generated by the business from now to the hereafter. But if you
factor into your assumptions, for example, a growth rate higher than

the discount rate, you'll come up with a value of infinity so, I mean, you come up with absurd numbers doing that. That's why a lot of investors don't calculate it, and they use simple measures like PE or price to book or something like that. To me, that's oversimplifying things at the other end of the spectrum, if you know what I mean.

You can number crunch till the cows come home and do twenty intrinsic value calculations doing all sorts of sensitivity analysis varying assumptions, but people who do that tend to kid themselves because the future is so hard to estimate and you can delude yourself with a false sense of precision. But then using a single valuation metric like a PE is oversimplifying it.

I'm always looking forward about three years, trying to work out what this company can earn in three years' time and, based on what it will earn in three years' time, how do I think the market will value it in three years' time? A useful shortcut technique is to think in terms of PEG [price to earnings growth] ratios — that is, to compare the PE multiple with the forward three-year growth rate in earnings per share. For example, if a stock is selling at ten times current year's earnings and you think it can grow its earnings per share over the next three years at more than 20 per cent compound, the stock is worth more detailed analysis because it looks to be cheap having regard to its growth outlook.

And do you hold stocks on average for three years?

My average holding period would be probably five. I've still got ABC. I've owned DCA for ten years, and I still like it. I think my main success as an investor is not selling too early. I mean, if you sell a stock at $8 and it goes to $10, well, that's okay, but if you sell a stock at $2 and it goes to $10, you've made a terrible mistake, haven't you? A terrible mistake.

If you thought a stock was heading towards the mature end of its life cycle and if its price was significantly above your perception of intrinsic value, it makes sense to consider selling — point (iii) on the second graph. But a stock can go from being fully priced to overpriced to way overpriced. To finetune the selling decision, you might consider such issues as momentum, insider buying, insider selling, institutional buying and selling.

By insider buying and selling, you mean directors buying and selling?

Yeah. Looking at just who is really buying and selling. I mean if a stock's about to join an index because it's got to a certain market cap and you're going to get a new universe of institutional investors buying the stock, well, you'd hold off selling, wouldn't you? So in looking at that aspect, you'd be recognising what I'd call technical analysis, rather than fundamental analysis.

People always talk about when to buy, but when to sell is as big a decision.

Well, as for when to buy, if you determine that intrinsic value is $1 and the share price is 50¢, it's not a very difficult decision. You know you're getting a bargain. And while 50¢ might become 40¢ — suggesting you bought too early — you still feel pretty comfortable because you bought cheaply.

> *A stock can go from being undervalued to overvalued to enormously overvalued, so when to sell is a more difficult decision than when to buy ... I think in terms of life cycles, share price and intrinsic value.*

But a stock can go from being undervalued to overvalued to enormously overvalued, so when to sell is a more difficult decision than when to buy. So how do you apply a bit of science to this tricky question of when to sell? This is how I do it [pointing to the two graphs]. I think in terms of life cycles, share price and intrinsic value. And if I finally come to the conclusion that I am going to sell, I might try to finetune it by taking into account the factors I mentioned.

Getting back to investing in the stock market, what was the first stock you ever bought?

The first stock I ever bought was Calsil. It's still listed on the stock exchange, but under the name of [auto products group] Schaffer Corporation. Calsil made calcium silicon bricks in Perth. It was a brick company and, ultimately, they sold the brick business and it became an investment company. They changed the name to Schaffer Corporation, because it was always controlled by the Schaffer family.

When did you buy it?

I probably bought in 1972.

Was it a good performer?

Yes, I got to know George Schaffer, the current chairman's father, who was a wonderful man, but there was no science to my investing in those days.

I think all of the research that I did in applying Benjamin Graham to the Australian stock market in the mid-1970s made me very value orientated. The first big quid that I made in the market was with a company called Watkins Consolidated. Nominally, it was a building company based in Brisbane, but they had a habit of keeping assets and they owned a lot of land at Surfers Paradise, an office building in Brisbane and drive-in picture theatres in New Guinea. It was actually a treasure trove of assets, but the share price traded as a function of their reported earnings and their dividend. And they didn't revalue their assets so it was just misunderstood in the marketplace.

At what price did you buy into the company?

I think I probably started buying it — this was a long time ago — at 75¢, 80¢, and I probably bought it up to $1.40 or $1.45. It ended up getting taken over at a price well over $10.00.

What did you learn from Peter Lynch, who used to talk about five-and ten-baggers?

That was his expression. Peter Lynch was the one who talked about life cycles. I remember him saying the first thing he considered when he looked at a new company was where it was in its life cycle. Peter Lynch was always trying to find baggers — three-baggers, four-baggers — so his Holy Grail was growth, as is mine. He would try to find regional success stories that could roll out across America.

You can try to do that in Australia, but you don't find many Noni Bs or Fantastic Furnitures or Freedoms where you can apply that kind of analysis. That's why in looking for growth I tend to find more opportunities in industry aggregations, in the cottage industries that are being consolidated. But I look at both, and ABC was really both. I mean in ABC you've got a regional success story in Queensland rolling out across Australia, but also it was an industry consolidation story.

Can you tell us about your biggest winners and bigger losers in terms of stock picks?

Lang Corporation was a big winner for us and Tempo was a big winner for me.

On Lang, how many times your money did you make?

The highest price I paid was probably $2.50 and it ended up going to $16.00. My average entry price would have been below $1.00 and I sold out north of $9.00. The shares have since split.

When I sold out of Lang, I rang Chris Corrigan. Chris had always been very co-operative and communicative. He was accessible, he was a good proprietor in my book and I felt he'd done a sensational job with that company. What he did in winning the waterfront battle was quite awesome, and he created an enormous amount of value for his shareholders. When I told him I had sold and rang almost to apologise, his response was that he could understand why I was selling, given the multiple the shares were trading at. But he said he believed he could take the company to a new level of profitability — which, of course, he did.

And I'm applying the same thing to ABC. When they get to 1000 centres, one might say that they've gone a fair way up between 'd' and 'e' on the growth cycle curve. But I think Eddy Groves is so dynamic, he'll get a second wind through schools.

That's not a forecast, but I truly think that you could apply what Chris said to what Eddy will do, because he's very young, extraordinarily ambitious and just immensely competent, and he's already earmarked schools and is going into schools. The education sector is just so vast. Eddy's already got a toehold and I think his toehold is going to be the thin edge of the wedge.

Gale Pacific was a big winner for me. In terms of current stocks, Baxter Group has been very successful.

You've done incredibly well there, haven't you? How many times your money have you made?

The shares were floated at $1.00 a share, but they're $5.50 now, and they've only been listed for a couple of years.

That's five and a half times.

It's been a very good stock for us. With Gale Pacific I didn't buy it in the float, but I bought at 55¢. They floated at $1.00 and then went to $3.00. I did sell a lot of our shares, but I bought back into it more recently, because I think the market did get overpriced. Then earnings disappointment saw the shares halve, and I think that they went from being overpriced to being significantly underpriced, and in the meantime I think management continued to improve the business, so the intrinsic value kept going up.

And what about your worst calls? Or have you still got a few more big wins?

I have probably had six or seven stocks in my career where I have lost 100 cents in the dollar, the most recent ones being Reynolds Wines and Nautilus. It's why you diversify. But you can only lose 100 cents in the dollar on the downside, whereas on the upside you can get 1000 per cent. One that I have done very well out of in my portfolio is Concept Hire, a scaffolding hire company based here in Melbourne. That's been a very good company for me, and I think there's a lot more in it.

I bought in at 80¢ and the shares are now $1.90. I've only owned them for about a year. But it was a company that had a very good business in scaffolding hire. They're number one in Victoria. They compete with Boral and Waco, but they are bigger than both Boral and Waco in Victoria, although smaller in New South Wales and Queensland. But they were hamstrung, because the company had another business that was in property development, and it was losing money hand over fist. So you had a property development division that was haemorrhaging and, of course, that was depressing the share price because it was affecting the group's profits, but they closed that down. That just left their scaffolding hire business, which was a very good business. And by taking the monkey off their back, they've been liberated. They're using their cash flow now to expand into New South Wales and Queensland and they're very good at what they do.

To me that's almost a perfect small-cap stock, because it's a single business, it's fairly easy to understand, you've got a family with control, and the family is a good entrepreneurial family and committed shareholder. As I said before, the first thing I ask, because most small stocks are proprietorships, is, 'Does the proprietor want me to make money?' And if he doesn't pass that test, no matter how good the business, you just don't want to be there.

How do you tell that he doesn't want you to make money? Things like paying himself too much and taking too much out of the business?

That's right. Also disclosure. But general attitude. I mean normally you can tell, can't you?

That's why the man on the street should go to the annual meeting. You pick up on the vibes. You can pick up on some vibes by reading the annual report, but if you go to the annual meeting and you look at their eyes, you'll pick up the vibes.

> I think face to face is terribly important, and for individual investors ... [to] go to the annual meeting.

You can ask them a question, see how they react.

Before Baxter floated, Polly Mazaris, who's the managing director, drove me over to one of their tips and she looked at me and said, 'Peter, that is a goldmine'. The way she said it ...

You can tell.

If I'd read that on a piece of paper, I wouldn't have picked up on the vibes.

Body language is important?

I think face to face is terribly important, and for individual investors who don't get institutional-type briefings, they can go to the annual meeting and they ought to do so.

You talked earlier about Benjamin Graham and Warren Buffett. Do you have other mentors?

Benjamin Graham and Warren Buffett are the two geniuses of our industry, and they both were or are extraordinarily articulate and generous in wanting to teach. What they have to teach is so profoundly wise. It's not that complicated. People wanting to learn to invest should study those people and when they invest they should keep reading. Whatever you're reading you always apply to your investment portfolio. If you read about this concept or that concept, apply it to your portfolio and think all the time. My other mentor you might say is Humphrey B. Neill. He was known as the

Vermont Ruminator. It always intrigued me that Benjamin Graham used to write under the by-line Cogitator. Cogitator and ruminator are synonyms. My family company is Ruminator Pty Ltd.

Who was Humphrey Neill?

He was really the father of contrarian thinking and contrarian investing. He wrote *The Art of Contrary Thinking*. He died some years ago, but he's got a lot of followers in America. It's a wonderful book. There's no formal, official definition of contrarian investing, but to me it's not identifying what the crowd is doing and doing the opposite — that could be just plain stupid. As Humphrey Neill says, the crowd gets it right during the trends, but wrong at both ends. So the crowd is right most of the time, but they're wrong at the critical junctions, at the turning points. What Humphrey Neill teaches is just to always question conventional wisdoms and always consider the other side.

In the category of 'mentor', I also would include Buffett's partner Charlie Munger. The book *Poor Charlie's Almanack* compiles all of his speeches. Munger advises investors to draw on multiple disciplines, in particular psychology, in the investment decision-making process. What he has to say is quite profound.

Who else do you admire?

Two people I admire are John Nolan and Ian Rohde, who's the managing director of Warakirri.

JANA has been very successful for two reasons. There are plenty of people who hold themselves out to be equity experts; there are a number of people who would hold themselves out to be experts on the fixed-interest market; and probably a lot of people who reckon they're experts on the property market. I don't really like the word expert, but there are very few who you could say are expert in all three categories, and John's one.

He really is intensely interested in all asset categories, whereas if you put me in a meeting where they're discussing bond duration, you know, I'll go to sleep. It's as boring as hell. John is intellectually fascinated by all asset categories, and he's good at it. If you think about asset allocation, to be good at anything you've got to like it and John actually likes all asset classes.

And the second reason is that he is just scrupulously honest. When you're sitting astride an asset consulting firm that advises many billions of dollars, you have to be utterly dispassionate in selection. I walked into John's office one day and someone had sent him a Christmas hamper. He was looking at it like someone had soiled the carpet. His attitude was how could somebody think they could influence me by sending me something. People learnt over time you don't send John a diary, you don't invite him to the footy, you don't ask him to go down the pub and have a few beers. John doesn't want to become emotionally involved with people he may have to fire. So he's totally honest and his personality and character is such that he is very good at that job, quite apart from his expertise in all the asset classes.

And Ken Marshman, who's his successor at JANA, has grown the business from $30 billion to $83 billion. Few have heard of Ken, and yet he's probably more powerful in funds management than anyone in Australia. Quite simply he is formidably intelligent. So I admire him.

Of the people who do what I do, I admire David Paradice, Peter Hall and Jack Lowenstein. I've got a good relationship with Alex Waislitz, and I admire Robert Fraser too. Fraser is head of corporate finance at Taylor Collison.

Now there are a few other issues that are close to your heart — one being the quality of today's research by broking firms, and the other being whether the investment game's getting easier or harder. Can you tell us a bit about these issues?

When you look at today's research, in one sense you've got more and smarter people doing it — you're getting some very intelligent, well-trained people coming in, becoming analysts at broking firms and putting out research — but a lot of their research is quite poor.

One of the reasons for it is what I'd call homogenisation. They all have their standard formats with their bullet points, and then they've got their standard classification of balance sheets, but there's no detail at all. The word processor requires that maybe they have stock and maybe they have debtors, but there's no tie-in to the individual business of the company. Whenever I look at a company, I look at the balance sheet and I comb through it very carefully, and I restructure it so that the assets that I list are the assets that tell me what the company does. Whereas you look at a broker's research report and it's all bundled and aggregated into homogenous classifications.

Can you give an example?

In Baxter Group's case, it's airspace. With Concept Hire, it's essentially their fleet of scaffolding, their inventory of scaffolding. With ABC Learning Centres, the biggest asset on its balance sheet is goodwill or child-care licences as it calls it. You really need to look at balance sheets, because if a company is going to cheat on their accounting, it will show up in the balance sheet. If they're capitalising expenses and drawing on provision accounts, you're only going to pick that up by poring through the balance sheet in great detail. When I set out a balance sheet I always separately itemise those areas where I think I can uncover accounting irregularities.

So how much time do you spend looking at the balance sheet?

Far more than current analysts do. I reckon balance sheets are almost becoming ignored. That's probably silly for me to say that, but I look at today's research reports and they're very focused on the profit and loss statement. There's very little mention of the balance sheet. There's so much you can uncover in the balance sheet. If you do a company visit and you pore through the balance sheet, questions will come out about what the company is doing. If you don't read it in the narrative in the annual report, you'll spot it in the notes to the accounts. You'll spot it popping up in the balance sheet.

One other thing that makes you think is that the disclosure rules keep changing and you have things like IFRS coming in — you know, my God. It's almost as if the accounting authorities have a mandate of obfuscation. Really, I think that disclosure is becoming worse, not better, in terms of the rules. But to some extent that's an advantage to me, because I'll put in the hard yards and run it through analysis.

So you start off with the annual report?

Pore over it.

And do you go back a couple of years?

Many years. Much more than a couple of years. I go back at least five years. I like to look at five years. Work out from whence they came.

Accounting is quite complicated, but if you understand how the books are prepared, you are better able to read the end product.

Your other pet issue is whether the market is becoming tougher and is more efficient than, say, twenty years ago.

There are three answers to that question. We've been in a bit of a bull market for two years so, clearly, things are a lot more expensive today. In that sense, it is tougher to find value.

There's been a spawning of boutiques. And to a significant extent, it is because of the asset consultants like JANA.

[The growth of boutiques] is a recognition that individual investors are key, and if a star leaves one of the big managers, the company will say we've still got our processes and we've got a team of people. They have to say that, but it's rubbish really. If a star leaves a manager, that manager's hurt.

Anyway, whatever the reason it's happened, there has been a spawning of boutiques and, of course, a lot of the boutiques are gravitating to the small end of the market. It's becoming very crowded and very competitive. It's really only been in the last three or four years that I've found there's a cavalry behind or in front of me, and I worry about that.

About seven or eight years ago we identified Hamilton Island as a buy. BT had made a takeover bid — they owned 62 per cent or thereabouts and the rest was pretty widely held. I rang the leading institutional broker up in Queensland at Morgan Stockbroking. I rang him up specifically to ask about Hamilton Island, but I slipped the question in halfway through the conversation, because I didn't want him to know that was the reason why I rang. He said, 'Oh, don't BT own that?'

What that told me was that if the biggest stockbroking firm in Queensland didn't cover it and weren't even looking at it, it really was off everybody's radar screen. That pleased me, because we went into the market and I suppose we picked up about 8 per cent of Hamilton Island over a two-year period with virtually no competition. I don't think we could do that today, because all these boutiques have been spawned.[5]

---

5   The Oatley family and management bought Hamilton Island in late 2003/ early 2004 for $3.32 a share or $199 million after a protracted takeover battle for the resort group.

I used to have the luxury of looking at a stock knowing that no-one else would look at it. I think those Robinson Crusoe days are over now. With the spawning of the boutiques there is an advantage in that there's more liquidity and it's easier to sell when you want to sell, but essentially for me it's a negative.

Has that prompted you to look at even smaller companies?

No, I've always looked at real micro.

There are more investors in the micro-cap sector?

I am trying to beat the competition by seeing things that others don't see. You look at an ABC and actually look at it in a way that other people aren't, and you've perhaps got a bigger picture.

I've never been frightened about being Robinson Crusoe. Essentially I am a loner. While I do a little bit of networking with Alex Waislitz and Jack Lowenstein and David Paradice occasionally, I don't do a lot of that sort of thing.

David Dreman used to write a column called 'The Contrarian' in *Forbes* magazine. He used to talk about peer sanction. A lot of fund managers need peer sanction. They're only happy if they see that Geoff Wilson's buying it and David Paradice is buying it and Alex is buying it. They think it must be good. As long as they get the peer sanction, they get the warm and fuzzies. I couldn't give a stuff about that. I make up my own mind and if they agree, they agree; if they don't agree, they don't. David Paradice was in Melbourne a few months ago and popped into my office, and I said to him, 'I just bought a stock from you, David'. He'd just turfed out one of his stocks and I was the one who bought it. He couldn't have cared less, and neither did I. He might be wrong, I might be wrong, but that's not what we're buying. Neither of us are tailgaters.

> *I couldn't give a stuff about [peer sanction]. I make up my own mind and if they agree, they agree; if they don't agree, they don't.*

I'm a one-man band. To me investing is a do-it-yourself business. A number of people have said to me, 'Why don't you hire an assistant?' But I read the annual reports myself. I can't hire someone to do it and tell me what they've analysed.

You feel it's really important to do it all yourself.

I think it is important. That's very limiting for me and it's one of the reasons why my funds have been closed. Even with the Warakirri Small Company Value Trust, I've had existing investors wanting to put more money in and I've just said no. I'm preserving their interests best by keeping it small.

Are there other trends in the market you think are important?

The third thing that really fascinates me intellectually is the effect of technology, which is making the game real hard.

Back in the early 1980s, I sat on five or six public company boards. By investing in small caps, I got invited to sit on boards. I was on the board of a computer software company called Paxus Corporation and Rob Ferguson invited me on the Board of BT Innovation, which was a listed investment company of Bankers Trust. Those experiences hardened my aversion to technology and just proved to me that it was an area to stay away from.

In terms of it being a high-risk sector to invest in?

I'm not going to invest in an aquaculture company or a biotech. By and large, I'll invest in simple businesses that aren't going to get blown out of the water by technology. But things have changed. I may not like it, but things have changed, and I can give some examples. I was once on the board of Ausdoc. Ausdoc was in document storage and it was also in courier services. It never occurred to me that these businesses could be affected by technology. Then the fax machine was invented but, funnily enough, the amount of documents couriered — transported by Ausdoc — kept going up. The manager, when asked about this, said, 'Well, the fax machine has hurt our business, but the word processor means that people are producing more documents, making multiple copies and overall the total quantity of documents being transported has increased'.

But then the internet came along. I don't receive a research report now through the mail. I receive it all by email. Printers are higher quality and copies are so easy to produce at the click of a mouse. I'm long gone from Ausdoc. Ausdoc was floated and then subsequently taken over[6], but I wonder how their courier business was affected

---

6   Ausdoc was taken over by ABN AMRO Capital in 2002.

by the internet and how their document storage business is being affected by today's technology — digitisation, electronic storage.

I think twenty years ago, you could say I'm going to invest in simple businesses that aren't affected by technology. But I think all businesses today are affected by technology.

I read a book the other day — *The New Normal*. It was written by a venture capitalist out of Silicon Valley, Roger McNamee. One of the comments he made (it was just a throwaway line, but I thought it was a good one) was that technology has moved from the back office to the front office. What he means is that twenty years ago people used computers for their payroll and for preparing the accounts, but all it did was streamline the back office. But now with the internet, digitisation and globalisation, companies that you would think wouldn't be affected by technology suddenly can be hugely affected by it.

How does that affect how you invest or look at companies?

It means that you've just got to read, read, read, read and stay plugged in, and keep your antenna out. Those technology changes can be threats, but they can be opportunities. A fantastic example to me in terms of opportunity is DCA, because digitisation is going to transform radiology. If you think of the radiology business in the old days, radiologists would have film developed and then stick it up on a board with a light behind it. Now the radiologist can be in London looking at a perfect image on his screen and the photo was taken two seconds ago in Melbourne. So it's going to dramatically affect the productivity of radiologists and have a dramatic impact on the costs of their business. If you go back ten years before the pathology and radiology industries aggregated, before both went through a sustained period of consolidation, I think pathology was the better industry to invest in because the scale benefits were superior. But now that both industries have largely consolidated, I think radiology is the better business to be in because technology, so it seems to me, is offering greater benefits.

Warren Buffett says that he is a business analyst rather than a financial analyst. But to be a business analyst today, you must pay heed to the internet and to digitisation and to globalisation. It's much more complicated today, much more bloody complicated. And I'm fifty-eight and I'm not sure that I can keep up with the game, you know, because in my heart of hearts, I like investing in simple businesses. I'm well aware that I can invest in a business that I think is simple, and suddenly find out two or three years later that something totally unforseen has come along that's transformed the nature of the industry. You have to plug into it. You can't be close-minded and believe someone has a fantastic, bullet-proof business franchise. Franchises are being depleted in value all over the place. You have to keep your eye on the width of the moat.

Another point to make about being a business analyst is the need to think about business models. If I can use the example of Forest Place Group — which is a retirement village company in Queensland that I was the third largest shareholder in. I thought retirement villages were simple businesses, but probably two or three years after I bought in I realised I didn't understand it. I woke up one day and realised that I did not understand that business. It's very, very complicated, and there are different business models. You really need to pay heed to the business models and the business models of competitors, and to understand what they're doing. You can have an industry that's very attractive, but you can have one business model that is unattractive and another business model that is attractive.

Forest Place did not have a good business model. It had enormous cash flow drawback, but I didn't appreciate it until I'd owned the stock for two years.[7] I think other people had different business models and did very well out of it. In child care, you had Eddy Groves with his business model, and Peppercorn with their business model. What Eddy did and what Peppercorn did [ABC took over Peppercorn last year] were chalk and cheese. As it turned out, both were exceptionally profitable. But I think I would be much more appreciative today than I was five or ten years ago of the point that you have to look very closely at business models and recognise the different approaches.

---

7   Forest Place is now 85 per cent owned by Brisbane property developer FKP.

In Guy, we found a true disciple of the Buffett/Graham school of investing. For him and his investors, the discipline he has shown has been extremely rewarding. He is a committed value investor but he confines his investing to the small-cap end of the market where he searches for companies in a relatively early stage of development. Guy overlays his search for value with an assessment of the merits of the business or industry he is investing in and an in-depth analysis of company accounts.

But rather than assume there is a 'black box' to investing, Guy acknowledges that markets change and that investing has probably got harder with time and with the increased sophistication of markets. That has not diminished the opportunity to make big gains from investing in shares. However, Guy clearly understands the limitations of investing in some market sectors. He sticks to simple companies he can understand and with a growth path ahead of them that he can see.

You have to buy value because it will recover. If value gets bashed down, ultimately it will recover. If other stocks get knocked down, they might never recover. It [working in a bear market] instils a desire to own assets where, ultimately, the underlying value will be preserved.

3

Calculated risk

Andrew Sisson

At first observation there are no obvious signs Andrew Sisson is a big risk taker. In fact, everything about the man suggests he is one of the conservative set that has inhabited the Collins Street business precinct for the past fifty or so years. His hair is neat, his suit is pressed and his accent is verging on proper English, despite being born and bred in Australia. Even the name of his business, Balanced Equity Management, has overtones of the very conservative — as one might expect if your office is at 101 Collins Street Melbourne.

That said, our interview with Sisson, a virtual unknown even to his peers, revealed a string of calculated risks that over thirty-one years have seen the trained actuary develop one of Australia's largest and most successful privately owned funds management businesses.

Sisson began his sharemarket investing career with a fourteen-year stint at life insurance giant National Mutual (these days known as AXA Asia Pacific Holdings). It was in that period that Sisson first revealed his capacity to handle calculated risks. He was at the centre of what was then Australia's largest takeover bid in 1979, when National Mutual made a surprising move on BH South. Life insurance companies rarely, if ever, aggressively make takeover offers for listed companies. Sisson and his colleagues thought that BH South was asset rich and that the only way to extract that value was to own the business 100 per cent. The move stirred the infamous Collins House group into action. Collins House, once an actual building at 360 Collins Street, was a name given to the bevy of big conservative mining groups that resided there. Collins House, while not publicly admitting it, did not want an outsider like National Mutual becoming a major player in the mining industry. Within months, both Western Mining (recently taken over by BHP) and CRA (now known as Rio Tinto) launched their own takeover offers for BH South. National Mutual, which had already accumulated a 34 per cent stake in the company, almost doubled its money before selling out to Western Mining. The move put the life insurance company on the map as an innovative player in the then stodgy industry. Moreover, the experience planted the seeds of Sisson's later refined long-term investment philosophy — that of buying undervalued assets in the belief that full or fair value would be realised at some time in the future.

During the heady days of the 1980s, Sisson duelled with the likes of Alan Bond and Robert Holmes à Court as National Mutual became the powerhouse of Melbourne institutional investing. After a stint in London, where Sisson worked as a corporate adviser, he came back to Australia in the mid-1980s and eventually took the bold step of accepting a job with Holmes à Court at Bell Group. Holmes à Court was sufficiently impressed with Sisson's financial intellect to think he could be a major asset to his burgeoning empire. Sisson accepted the job just before the 1987 stock market crash, when the market fell 25 per cent in one day. By the time he arrived at Bell Group, the crash had sent Holmes à Court into survival mode. Within six months there was no job for Sisson and it was decision time again.

With some guidance and encouragement from his long-term colleague, John Nolan, Sisson decided not to go back to the comforts of working for a large institutional investor. Instead, he took the plunge into his own business and, in July 1988, founded Balanced Equity Management. Besides the Sydney-based Robert Maple-Brown, there were virtually no boutique fund managers in Australia at that time. It was a difficult start. Sisson could not afford to pay himself a salary for the first year or so.

In seventeen years, BEM has grown from managing just a few million dollars to managing $8.3 billion. During that time BEM has been able to beat the benchmark Fifty Leaders Index on average by about 2.5 per cent a year net to investors. Other than Maple-Brown, few could boast such a long and distinguished record. These days that extra 2.5 per cent represents another $200 million a year for his investors.

Unlike most of the other Masters, Sisson has very precise means of picking stocks. For most of the seventeen years at BEM, he has concentrated solely on the top fifty companies in Australia. The firm is always fully invested (that is, no cash holding) and has funds in at least forty-five of the top fifty companies at any given time. To deliver outperformance, Sisson either takes an overweight or underweight position in each stock relative to their weighting in the sharemarket indices, based on BEM's view of each stock's value at the time. While Sisson doesn't subscribe to the more brazen stockpicking style of Phil Mathews or Peter Guy, his approach seems to work.

One of Sisson's important lessons for investors is, 'Do not pay for blue sky'. This is something some investors may have forgotten in the heady bull run that began in March 2003. For Sisson, though, this probably reflects that as he has grown older he has realised that risk taking on a large scale is not necessarily the best way to achieve long-term success.

Andrew, can you tell us how you become interested in the stock market?

I finished my university degree in maths and statistics in 1973. There was no particular career path leading from that so I thought I'd be an actuary. National Mutual [now AXA Asia Pacific] was the biggest insurance company in Melbourne at the time. I did a one-week induction course. On the Thursday we each spent an hour with four or five people from different areas of the organisation. They were all dead boring, except the guy from investments. I thought that sounded like the most interesting area that I could work in while I was studying to be an actuary. I joined the investment department in January 1974 and never ended up working in the actuarial area at all.

Before that did you own any shares? Or did your parents own shares?

My mother was fairly interested in the sharemarket. While I was at uni I saved up a few hundred dollars. I walked into work on day one with $200 looking for ideas about where I should put the money. It was 1974, which was, of course, the worst bear market since the depression, and it was just beginning. Someone suggested that I put my money into [mining company] MIM. Six months later, MIM was about a third of the price I paid. My $240 had turned into $80.

So your mother had a portfolio of shares?

Dad wasn't the least bit interested but my mother always followed the sharemarket, buying the *Financial Review* back in the 1960s, and it rubbed off a little bit. My father was a doctor and my mother ran the non-medical part of the practice.

Did you finish your actuarial studies?

I became an associate of the Institute of Actuaries on passing the first set of exams. After that you had to do three final exams. One was about investments, which I took and passed; the others were life insurance and pensions, which were problematic unless you've worked in the actuarial area. So I only ever became an associate.

You started at National Mutual in 1974 during one of the worst bear markets. Who were you working with and what was it like in the first couple of years?

It was a great learning environment. Some of the people there included John Nolan [see chapter on Peter Guy] and Bruce Parncutt who went onto become managing director of McIntosh/Merrill Lynch. There were only seven of us. There were a couple of people there who had a lot of years' experience in the market, so it was a good group to work with.

What amount of money were you managing?

I thought you were going to ask what I was earning. It wasn't much — $5550 was the annual salary.

National Mutual had about $2 billion under management at the time. While not large by today's standards, it was very big at the time

— we were second to AMP in Australia. 1974 was one of those sorts of years where you would be tracking a stock, you'd say this is the _____ price I'd like to buy it at, it would get there, you would buy it and then the next day it would be down 10 per cent. The day after that it would be down another 5 per cent. It was a real learning experience. Nothing ever went up — things only ever went down. It lasted like that for nine months. The market just went down in a straight line — it was down 42 per cent in the first nine months of my employment.

> *You have to buy value because it will recover. If value gets bashed down, ultimately it will recover. If other stocks get knocked down, they might never recover.*

What did that teach you about markets?

You have to buy value because it will recover. If value gets bashed down, ultimately it will recover. If other stocks get knocked down, they might never recover. It instils a desire to own assets where, ultimately, the underlying value will be preserved.

I was the only person in the department without an economics degree and so they asked me to do the interest rate forecast. Interest rates started the year at around 9 per cent and by May had reached 21 per cent. It was a real experience — saying that we think they should go to X and they went there and kept on going.

I worked in Melbourne for two years, doing economic and sharemarket analysis. Then I worked for National Mutual in London for another two years. I wanted to get some international experience. I guess it was an invaluable period. We were over most of the bear market by then, but the sharemarket globally was still pretty volatile and uncertain. Working over there for a couple of years, I learnt a lot about the ways the different markets worked.

In terms of valuing stocks?

That's right — visiting companies, valuing stocks. I was developing an investment philosophy as much as anything else.

Was there anyone in the London office who had a big influence?

It was a department of about six or seven people in total. It wasn't, I guess, as much of an intellectual firmament as the Collins Street office was. But there were still a lot of people you'd come into contact with who offered insights that you wouldn't get elsewhere. But I really wouldn't put it down to anyone in particular.

After two years you came back to Melbourne?

I came back to Melbourne in early 1978. I was given charge of the share portfolio of National Mutual Fire. All the life insurance companies at the time had general insurance subsidiaries and National Mutual Fire was a small portfolio.

National Mutual then took over a company called Commonwealth Mining Investments, which was a subsidiary of Consolidated Goldfields. At the time, Australian investment institutions were only allowed to move $1 million each year out of Australia for investment — these restrictions were abolished by treasurer Keating in 1983. It didn't matter whether you had $50 million in assets or a couple of billion in assets, you could only take $1 million a year out of Australia. The reason we took over Commonwealth Mining Investments was that it had already had about $20 million invested outside the country.

Laurence Freedman was the portfolio manager of CMI, and Pat Elliott and Ray Soper were the investment analysts. I went up to Sydney to collect the company's records and then ran the Australian component of that portfolio for a while. We brought in Iain Mason from Hong Kong to manage the international portfolio.

Then one of the senior portfolio managers, Frank Buckle, left the company [National Mutual] and I was handed management of the big superannuation fund, which I ran for a couple of years. The most interesting experience in the role involved a takeover bid for BH South, formerly Broken Hill South.

BH South owned an 8.1 per cent holding in Alcoa of Australia. It was an ideal asset for a life company, a world-class producer of alumina. BH South had been poorly run and had lost a lot of money on a phosphate mine up in Queensland. The sharemarket had absolutely hammered it and its shares had fallen well below intrinsic value. We identified it as a cheap way into Alcoa of Australia and started buying shares in the market through JB Were & Son [now Goldman Sachs JBWere] at $2.50 a share against a previous price of $2.10. At the time, there was no 5 per cent substantial shareholding disclosure limit and the boys from Colonial rang up Were and said they'd like to sell into this buying, but not if it was a corporate player [who was subsequently likely to bid for BH South]. They wanted to be assured it was another investment institution. Were said it was just another investment institution, and Colonial sold into it.

We reached 15 per cent of the company fairly quickly, but we knew that North Broken Hill owned 18 per cent, and if we were going to have the ability to have any influence on BH South, we needed to build at least the same holding as North. Once it became obvious that we were a buyer, North came to see us. We thought they were not going to be very happy, but they walked in the door and asked whether we would buy their stake as well. So we bought theirs and that brought us up to 33 per cent and we made a takeover bid for the whole company. It was biggest bid that Australia had seen up to that date — there were 54 million shares in BH South and we were bidding $2.50 each, or $135 million.

When was that?

1979. BH South started a political campaign, arguing a life insurance company — a mutual, which can't be taken over — shouldn't be allowed to take over other companies. It became quite political at the end. The other big holder was Warren McCullagh from the Commonwealth Bank. He was a value investor as well, and had identified it as a cheap entry into Alcoa of Australia. He had about 15 per cent and wouldn't sell his shares to us.

In the end, the Collins House companies closed ranks with Western Mining in bidding for the company. They had done the same arithmetic as us and thought it was a cheap way to increase their holding in Alcoa. Then CRA came in over the top of Western Mining and Western Mining came in over the top of them and there was a real ding-dong war going on. The share price was going up, so we ended up getting over $5.00 a share for our holdings, which we had bought for $2.50 a few months earlier.

So that was very novel — a takeover bid from an institution or life insurance company. AMP has done that a little bit, but it doesn't happen very often.

That's right — it was very controversial at the time.

Back in the early 1980s, the view was that Australia's resource sector had fantastic growth prospects and National Mutual had a pile of cash sitting in the fund from where BH South was taken out. So the company set up a fund to invest directly in the resources sector, which they asked me to manage from its inception in 1981. Unfortunately, all of the resources stocks were extraordinarily expensive, which made it difficult to get the funds invested.

How did you know they were expensive?

We couldn't make them stack up on a NPV [net present value[1]] calculation.

Was it uncommon then for investors to do such valuations?

There was a program you could buy to do the calculations — which, really, you could do on a simple spreadsheet these days — and it could work out an NPV for you.

Our first investment was in the Cooper Basin. Bondy [failed 1980s entrepreneur Alan Bond] had control of Reef Oil and Basin Oil, as well as owning a big chunk of Santos. Reef Oil and Basin Oil were very small companies but they were the only things we could find that were cheap. We said to Bond that we would like to buy them, but he, of course, was only interested in borrowing money. He said he was not prepared to sell them, but if we would lend him money we could have them as security.

We lent him some money, using Reef Oil and Basin Oil as security, hoping he would default. We were then quite excited to receive notice that Bond was in default on his loan, with seven days to rectify before we would pay the money and get the shares. We got our money ready to buy Reef Oil and Basin Oil [and then to make takeover bids for the parts that Bond didn't own]; National Mutual's money market people raised $50 million and we were all ready to go. But, of course, on the very last day Bond Corporation was back in compliance. This happened about three times.

Eventually the money market boys got sick of being told to put all this money together and then not being asked to use it. In the end, Bond said he'd sell Reef Oil and Basin Oil if we bought 15 per cent of Santos as part of a trade. We did that, and stepped into the market with a view to buying 100 per cent of both companies. Unfortunately, on the day we went into the market to buy them, Schroders and BT came into the market and bought against us. They both ended up with close to 20 per cent. The day before our

---

1   NPV is still the favoured method of valuing resources companies to capture the present value of cash flows from a mine with a finite life.

formal takeover offer closed, Schroders sold out to us but BT didn't so we ended up with around 70 per cent of both companies.

Reef and Basin had interests in the Cooper Basin in South Australia?

They both had oil reserves and we had bought at the right price so it was a pretty low-risk investment from our point of view.

We also bought an interest in a coalmine up in Queensland called German Creek. Shell was the prime mover behind that. If you go back and look at that time, projections for coal were for an increase in production volumes and an increase in price and therefore very high profitability. The volume projections proved to be spot on, but the price fell well short of expectations. We thought at the time that we had paid too much for German Creek and we had.

How long did you run the resources fund for?

I was running that for a couple of years — 1981 and 1982. Then I was seconded to the London merchant bank Samuel Montagu. National Mutual had just taken over T&G, which, together with Samuel Montagu, owned the Australian merchant bank Capel Court. The job in London involved providing corporate advice to companies over there and it was very stimulating and enjoyable.

Can you name some of the companies you were advising?

One of the big clients was Safeway. We were acting for Safeway in the takeover of another supermarket chain. That was a really big deal that took a lot of effort. We spent a whole weekend arguing over the words of a 100-page purchase and sale agreement. The very next day, another bidder added £10 million to the price and adopted our document word for word. There were three or four counterbids and they kept topping us every time. In the end, we didn't get it and they did. It was really interesting being in the middle of that cut and thrust.

And you came back after that to National Mutual? Why didn't you stay in corporate advice?

I was on secondment. They asked me whether I would resign from National Mutual and stay over there and work for them, but National Mutual was keen to have me back and there were good opportunities here.

So you came back in 1985?

Back then, BT had been stealing the lunch of the life insurance companies with individually managed portfolios. Previously, the life companies had superannuation funds managed through their statutory funds. BT's investors didn't have to hold their super through a pooled fund in a life company — BT offered an individually managed share portfolio and that way investors could have a lot more flexibility. National Mutual, AMP and all the life companies were losing clients. BT was the leader, but others like Schroders were following pretty closely behind.

In response, National Mutual set up its own subsidiary called National Mutual Portfolio Management. National Mutual could then say that if clients wanted an individually managed portfolio, they didn't have to leave National Mutual and didn't have to go to BT. Unfortunately, the systems weren't there to support the product. For instance, the final reports for the September quarter of 1984 weren't out until the day before Christmas. My first job on coming back was to put the system back on the rails. Among the portfolio managers working with me were David Slack [who later co-founded Portfolio Partners] and Margie Waller. The portfolio managers were fine but the systems supporting them weren't there. It took six months to make sure we could actually deliver what we were meant to be delivering. Then I resumed management of the statutory superannuation fund in July 1985.

One of the things we identified was that the futures market — which was then at an embryonic stage — was mispriced. It was seriously undervalued — so much so that it made sense to switch our funds out of physical shares into futures.

Why was it underpriced?

I really don't know why they were selling as cheaply as they were. We put more and more of our money into futures. We could roll it from one quarter to the next cheaply and lock in certain outperformance.

That worked fine until March 1986. Our position was very big by that stage. We had more than $200 million in futures, which by the standards of 1986 was a lot of money. But then we couldn't roll it. The roll from March to June was expensive, more expensive than it should have been, so we had to move back to physical stock. Moving $200 million into physical stock was very difficult.

The turnover of the market was less than $50 million? What level was the All Ordinaries Index?

It was below 1100 when we started and above 1200 when we finished two weeks later.

Clearly, we had to start investing the money ahead of time; we could not leave it until the last minute, to the expiry of the futures. So we started buying two weeks prior to expiry. We were buying very aggressively for two weeks continuously, and the impact of that was that the market went up very sharply in that period.

By the afternoon of the futures expiry, we made sure we had all our money back in the market. The way futures work is that, effectively, you sell your futures at the closing price on the expiry date. The closing price on the expiry date was a lot higher than it had been when we'd been buying the physical stock, so it was a very profitable exercise for us. But, of course, as soon as the futures had expired we didn't need to buy any more. The market fell by 4 per cent the next morning — a very major drop.

Inevitably, the NCSC [National Companies and Securities Commission and predecessor to the Australian Securities and Investments Commission] launched an investigation into it but, in the end, we could show that everything we did was with a view to achieving a legitimate objective. It hadn't been market manipulation, as some had claimed.

Was it a highly stressful period?

It was a highly exciting period. It was a bit like the BH South takeover and buying those companies off Bondy. This was the third case where — even though there was quite a lot of criticism at the time, such as that this was not what a life company should be doing — it put National Mutual up there as innovative and successful. In all three cases, we made money. I think it did a lot to break the image of NM as a stodgy life company.

For how long were you running the pooled superannuation fund?

I ran that from July 1985 until November 1987 — just after the 1987 sharemarket crash. In August 1987, I did a company review of Bell Group and interviewed [its chief executive] Robert Holmes à Court. I asked him how he was generating his profit.

I said it seemed to me that the book value of his BHP holdings should be rising and he said, 'Oh no, that's not the case'. The next day I got a call from his human resources manager asking whether I would work for them. Eventually I agreed to do so. That was just prior to the crash, but I actually left National Mutual immediately after the crash. By the time I joined Holmes à Court, his plans were already in disarray.

He was impressed with your analysis?

He basically wanted me on the inside of the tent rather than the outside.

Can you elaborate on this a bit more?

Holmes à Court had bought BHP shares at $5 and the shares were rising. If he sat there and did nothing and BHP went up to $8, his asset value would have gone up but there would be no impact on the profit line. So what he did was effectively start trading the shares around in circles on the way up, which made no difference to his asset value but meant every time he sold and repurchased, he realised a profit.

Every time he sold he realised profits and every time he bought again he replaced the stock he'd sold?

Even though he wasn't reducing the number of shares he was holding, he was still realising profits on the way through. He didn't want people to understand that one of the sources of his profit was just turning over his portfolio. If you think about it, the question is, how sustainable are these profits? And if you are just upping the book value all the time, the answer is they're not.

The relevant question is whether the book value of BHP holdings is rising. The true answer is yes, but the answer he gave was no. And from his point of view, did he want me sitting on the outside looking at this? He preferred to have me inside the camp — that was my interpretation.

But why would you agree to go and work with him if he was doing that kind of thing?

Because he was doing a lot of things that were very interesting. I had been at National Mutual at that stage for about fourteen years and, as I said, I enjoyed the corporate advisory work in London. To be involved with Holmes à Court's transactions would really have combined my market experience with my corporate finance advisory experience. It was really a way to bring those two things together. By the time I joined, Bell Resources was still in a reasonable financial position but, of course, Bell Group was geared on that position and Holmes à Court's personal company was further geared on that. He decided the risks were too high and moved into defence mode.

So you left the job at National Mutual to join Bell Group in November 1987. In the eighteen months or so in the lead up to the crash, which was the biggest bull market while you were at National Mutual, can you remember any of the stocks you held?

We had a fantastic run in that period. The sharemarket index between September 1986 and September 1987 was up 85 per cent and our portfolio was up 98 per cent. We were only a couple of points away from doubling the value of the portfolio within that twelve months.

> *October 1987 was probably the most exciting month of my career [because] we had so many defensive positions in place.*

It was, I guess, the flip side of 1974. In 1974, it didn't matter what you did, the market kept going down. In 1986–87 it was the opposite. It just continued to go up regardless of boundaries you set. We were using convertible bonds in that period to put defensive downside protection in place, while keeping the upside. We had such a good run. We were fully invested and the market was going up. It was one of those dream times that doesn't happen very often.

But when the market collapsed you had already moved on?

No, the best thing about it was that I was still there when the market collapsed. It fell 25 per cent in a single day, which was quite an event.

So what did that teach you about the market?

I don't want to make it sound like I was having fun while everyone was losing money, but October 1987 was probably the most exciting month of my career. We had so many defensive positions in place, so many put options in place and put options embedded in the convertibles we had been switching into that we outperformed by another 6 per cent in the month of the crash.

Can you give us an example of how you did it?

I'll talk about Elders as an example. [Elders boss John] Elliott had issued convertible bonds in five different currencies in 1986 and again in 1987, so there were ten sets of bonds on the market. We switched out of Elders ordinary shares into the bonds. Typically, they were structured so that the conversion price was set about 30 per cent above where the shares were initially trading. The market was going up very strongly, so it didn't take long for the share price to make up the 30 per cent. You were in a position at that point where you were getting 100 per cent of the share price upside, because the conversion value was pushing up the bonds, but if the share prices fell, the fixed-interest value of the bond held up much better.

And if the company went broke, like many later did?

If the company went broke, you lost 100 per cent of both.

So if they could pay their interest bill, the value of the convertible should hold up, within reason?

Within reason. We initially sold all our Elders shares and bought the bonds, but the value of the shares kept going higher and higher. So then we started using the option market to short shares to buy Elders bonds. We had run out of physical shares in the portfolio, so we were using options to synthetically short the shares. We were using short calls and long puts to have a synthetic position against the bonds. When the crash happened, Elders shares halved and the bonds went down 20 per cent, so there was a 30 per cent gain [the gain on shorting the shares minus the fall in the bonds] that we locked in on that. If the shares had gone up, we could have converted at parity — there was no risk — so we made a lot of money.

Can you just run through some of your other shareholdings and how they were positioned to handle the crash?

Part of it was that we didn't have things like [insurance and investment company] FAI in the portfolio — those sort of things.

Can you remember why?

Yes I can. The FAI share price was well above the value of the assets FAI held at the time. It was so high because of the idea that Larry Adler could continue to do deals into the indefinite future that would create more and more value and, of course, if he could do that, the shares were cheap. But we were looking at it from the point of view of the value the assets had at the time, not what the value of the assets would be if he continued to do great deals.

So back to your career path, what happened when you joined Bell Group?

While I was still at National Mutual, we bought a lot of put options over BHP shares [options to sell BHP shares]. We bought $9.66 put options over BHP shares, and National Mutual made a lot of money on them. In fact, we paid 2.5¢ each for these options, exercisable at $9.66. When BHP went to $7.00, which it did straight after the crash, those 2.5¢ options were worth over $2.50 — so we multiplied National Mutual's money a hundred times. National Mutual had options over 10 million BHP shares. They cost us $250 000, and were worth $25 million.

Why did you take that position?

Kim Slater [a stockbroker] rang up and asked me what I thought the $9.66 puts were worth. BHP was about $10.20 at the time. I said my model says they are worth 9¢, and he asked how many would I like. I told him that I wasn't a buyer at 9¢, because we already had enough. We had a lot of BHP puts in the portfolio, mainly because Holmes à Court had been selling put options left, right and centre.

Holmes à Court was selling BHP shares to improve his profits?

Holmes à Court's logic was that he would take over the company if it ever got that cheap, so therefore there wasn't a risk. If you are going to buy 100 per cent of the company, you don't mind putting yourself in a position where you can be forced to buy the shares and are generating income along the way.

So we already had a lot of BHP puts in the portfolio, and Kim rang up three days in a row, saying, 'Andrew, I have to sell these options'. It turned out that Holmes à Court had given his dealer instructions to sell a million dollars' worth of these options at 10¢ each. On the third day, Kim came back to me and said, 'There must be a price at which you will buy these things. I've just got to deal'. The price we settled on was 2.5¢. And the funny thing was, at that stage, the Bell Group dealer had to sell options over 40 million shares to get his $1 million premium. So we bought put options over 10 million BHP shares, and other institutions bought the other 30 million.

When I eventually turned up to work for Holmes à Court at Bell Group, I opened up the portfolio. There was the contract for the sale of options over 40 million shares! Book value cash received was $1 million but, with each option representing a liability of over $2.50, the market value was more than minus $100 million.

When you went to work for Holmes à Court, the sharemarket crash of 1987 had happened and his empire was very shaky. What was the feeling like in the office?

There was a degree of apprehension. I suppose they were asking themselves what they were going to do now. Holmes à Court was basically working out how he could stop the whole empire falling apart. And, of course, what he would do about those BHP put options. If you think about it, they had 40 million options exercisable at $9.66 — that is, they needed $380 million cash and they just didn't have that kind of money. I told him he needed to buy back the options for at least $2.50 a pop. He said that would be a loss of $100 million and he couldn't accept that. So he went to the Western Australian Government, and got the SGIO [State Government Insurance Office] to buy 40 million BHP shares off him at the market price of $7.00, which was about breakeven on his purchase price. That gave him the cash to buy the BHP shares at $9.66 as the put options were exercised against him. Effectively, he sold the stock at $7.00 a share and then bought it back at $9.66 a share rather than pay to extinguish the options at a loss.

How long were you at Bell Group?

Six months to the day, at which time he sold Bell Resources to Alan Bond. That occurred in May 1988. I left Bell that day, which was a mutual decision. The question then was, what would I do next? Should I go back to a large institution or should I look for alternatives? I guess by this stage I'd had a fair bit of experience and there were a couple of boutique fund managers starting to pop up. Robert Maple-Brown had set up in Sydney and that had set a precedent for setting up a boutique.

Were there many others?

Not really. Steven Sedgman had an interest in Security Pacific and Laurence Freedman had set up Equitilink, but that was about it.

John Nolan of asset consultants John A Nolan & Associates suggested it would be a good idea if I hung up my own shingle. So in July 1988 we opened the doors and we started managing money on 1 September 1988. Our first client was the State Electricity Commission of Victoria superannuation fund [now Equipsuper].

We had to go to the NCSC for a licence, and the solicitors told them we were going to manage money for State Electricity Commission of Victoria super fund, so we got our licence. Unfortunately, the licence specified that we could only manage money for the State Electricity Commission of Victoria super fund. We had to vary the licence so that we could grow the business beyond just one client. It would be pretty difficult setting up on your own without the prospect of any clients at all.

Can you give us some kind of idea of how much money you were managing when you started?

It was quite a small amount in today's terms. Even after two years it was still running at less than $100 million.

Was it a big financial risk to go out on your own after years of working for a big institution?

> *You buy value according to the assets of the company today, rather than assume that a company is going to be able to transform itself in the future.*

Basically, the income was enough to pay the rent and to pay the secretary, so unless I lost the client it was enough to do that. I couldn't pay myself.

It was pretty tough?

When you set up a new business like that, it's very much a scale business. If you don't get the scale, you are going to struggle, there's no doubt about that.

And what was your investment philosophy? Does it vary much from your philosophy some seventeen years later?

You buy value according to the assets of the company today, rather than assume that a company is going to be able to transform itself in the future.

How did you arrive at that basic principle of investing? Was it a conclusion you came to after your long stint at National Mutual?

I think it was just what we had worked out over the years at National Mutual. You so often see a leap of faith not working out. Holmes à Court was a case in point. The brokers who were supporting Holmes à Court were basically saying, 'He generated $200 million of profits last year and he can continue to do that this year'. Well, no, that's not the way I look at it. What you should do is look at the assets his company owns and decide what the value of those assets are and what earnings can be expected to come out of those assets — not what earnings you can expect to generate from trading, basically, playing the market and generating surplus income.

To put it another way, you have to look at each asset and decide what you think it can earn over the course of an economic cycle?

What we did then and what we still try to do is look at the earnings that are sustainable. The definition of sustainable earnings is what you can expect to achieve from the asset over a full cycle and not what it earns in the good times.

Why in 1988 did you decide to restrict yourself to investing only in the fifty largest companies on the Australian Stock Exchange?

The reason for that really was because we wanted a sustainable business. Obviously, you need a certain amount of income for a company to be viable. In this business you have two choices — either you charge high fees on low funds under management or low fees on high funds under management. I preferred to go the second route. From my training at National Mutual I suppose I was more comfortable managing a large amount of money on lower fees. And if you are going to achieve that, you have got to be in the large end of the market. It was hard enough to start a boutique in the 1980s and attract clients. It wouldn't have worked if we had decided to begin by managing small-capitalisation companies. In those days, it just wouldn't have attracted enough money to make the whole business viable.

Who worked with you? You mentioned John Nolan.

John gave me advice and our first two clients were clients of John's asset consultancy business. We spent the first two years just trying to prove our track record and establish a good reputation. It's all very well to say to a prospective client that I successfully managed one of the larger funds in Australia when I was at National Mutual and had a good track record. The question, particularly at the time, was whether that was done only because of all the research and support at National Mutual. Would it be possible to do it by myself? So it was necessary to start off fresh and generate a track record.

In those early days were you managing the money yourself?

Basically, it was just myself and a secretary for the first few years.

Was it tough?

It was interesting. The other reason I focused on the fifty largest companies was I didn't want to try to manage across the whole market. It is a mistake to spread yourself too thin. One of the big lessons from National Mutual was that you can't stretch a portfolio manager across too wide an area. There, a portfolio manager was responsible for managing money against an All Ordinaries benchmark. The All Ordinaries involved something like 500 stocks. Typically, the managers would be spending 80 per cent of their time looking at stocks outside the top fifty; yet those stocks represented only 20 per cent of the money. So they were spending 20 per cent of their time looking at 80 per cent of money, and 80 per cent of their time looking at 20 per cent of the money. It wasn't an effective way of doing things.

I took the view when I was at National Mutual that it would be better if we had people concentrate on different segments of the market rather than concentrate across the whole of the market. I guess that was part of the philosophy of setting up Balanced Equity — that it really would be better for me to concentrate on either small- or large-caps rather than try to do both. So it made more sense at the time to go for the large-caps segment.

And how did the first years go?

We outperformed quite nicely.

That set you up?

We then recruited Steven Fahey, who was an analyst from National Mutual, and Jon Bjarnason, who worked for National Mutual and County, as a dealer to help me, and our client numbers went from two to five. This all happened in our third year.

Are those two men still here working?

Jon is still a director, although he is not an employee anymore, and Steven is still here. He is the next largest shareholder and is responsible for our industrial research. And we still have our very first client from 1988, although it's changed its name along the way.

Do you remember the couple of stocks in those early years that helped deliver that outperformance?

To be honest, in the early years the stocks where we did really well were more ones where we were underweight. It's hard to credit now but companies like Bond Corporation, Orbital Engine and Hooker Corporation were in the top fifty at the time.[2]

What other companies did you try to avoid?

FAI was another one. We really outperformed because of the stuff we didn't have. And the other factor is that, in those early days we made a lot of money out of convertible arbitrage. Convertibles were issued in the heyday of the 1986–87 bull market and generally they had ten years to maturity. They didn't actually go away until 1996–97 and they were still there when we started Balanced Equity Management. We even made money on Elders again. As you know, Elliott made a takeover bid for Elders.

Can you recall the details of the bid?

Harlin, Elliot's private company, made the takeover bid for Elders. He didn't include the convertible bonds in the takeover and they traded at a discount to the shares. So we sold all of our ordinary shares in the takeover and bought the bonds at a discount to the shares. In the subsequent year and a half, Elders shares went from about $3.00 to $1.50 and eventually to about $1.10. The convertible bonds during the same period went down just 10 or 20 per cent. It was almost a replay of what happened to us at National Mutual at the time of the crash, but this time it was 1989.

So it was a big win for you in a relative sense?

Convertibles in general have been a big win for us. MIM had bonds that were 9.75 per cent Eurobonds convertible into ordinary shares at $3.16. They were trading at $100, around parity to the ordinary

---

2 Hooker Corporation was a property company run by George Herscu which ultimately failed.

shares despite the high yield. What happened there is that shares went down to not much over a $1, and the bonds were still trading at $80. So we've made quite a bit of money out of convertible bond arbitrage. Unfortunately, the opportunities in convertibles really died in that 1996–97 period when the ten-year issues expired.

Can you tell us how much money you manage today?

We are at $8.3 billion.

In the seventeen years you have run Balanced Equity, the size of the firm has increased significantly. Has your investment style changed?

The style hasn't changed at all. We've gone out to investing in the top 100 companies, though we only have about 1 per cent of our funds outside the top fifty stocks. We now have six analysts, a dealer and a compliance manager, so we can look at things in much greater depth. Besides that, nothing has changed much at all.

For many fund managers, size becomes an impediment to success. Do you think getting very big will hurt your performance?

We don't see capacity as a major impediment. We are only in large-cap, highly liquid stocks. We are very value-orientated in our approach. If a stock is cheap, we will be overweight; if it's very cheap, we will be more overweight. If we think it is correctly priced, we will not be too far away from the benchmark weight. So that really means that we typically move by ten, twenty basis points at a time. Some managers take the view that they just have the highest conviction stocks in the portfolio, and if they want to get out of one of them, they have to sell 5 per cent of their portfolio. For us, if something is getting more expensive or getting cheaper, we are typically moving ten to twenty basis points at a time, so even at $8 billion there is not a large number of transactions behind that, and all of our stocks are very liquid.

How long do you hold your positions for?

We hold most of our positions all the time. If we feel quite negative about a stock, we will go underweight compared to the index. If we feel really negative, we might not own the stock at all but this is fairly unusual. Of the top fifty stocks, we'd typically hold forty-five because there is only handful that we are that negative about that we want to be down at maximum underweight exposure.

From 1988 to 2005, what kind of performance have you delivered?

Over the period we have outperformed the relative benchmark by about 2.5 per cent per annum.

So the system works?

If you are patient and disciplined, it works. If you keep buying for long-term value, it does work. The only risk is if you get blown out of the water in the short term — a prudent investor structures the portfolio so any single position cannot cause too much pain. While some stocks might be causing some short-term pain, others should be coming good for you.

Generally, you keep buying stocks as they get cheaper and fall further below your valuation. There is only one risk to that theory — that is, if you are basically wrong, if it wasn't actually good value after all, and they keep going down and down. It comes back to your judgment. If your judgment is sound, there is nothing wrong in continuing to increase the position as it gets cheaper.

> *A prudent investor structures the portfolio so any single position cannot cause too much pain. While some stocks might be causing some short-term pain, others should be coming good for you.*

During the seventeen years you have run your own business, what has been the most difficult period?

We've only ever lost two clients because of performance, and they were both in 1996–97 when we underperformed, even though it was not by very much. Our underperformance was really because Coca-Cola Amatil was buying up franchises in Eastern Europe. They bought the franchise for Poland and it would have cost them $500 million, and the sharemarket capitalisation went up another $500 million. Basically, the market was saying that they had paid $500 million for something that was worth a $1 billion, so the market increased their market cap by $500 million. Steven Fahey thought the franchises they owned at the time could not get near the Coca-Cola share price, but the market was assuming that they were going to continue to be able to get franchises at less than what they were worth and therefore people should hop in early.

We went to a zero weighting in the stock at $12, and then the shares continued to rise, going up to $17. That decision caused us to underperform. Two clients terminated our services at that time. They are the only two clients we have lost because of performance. It was amusing to see the managing director of one of those clients in the press twelve months later complaining about the impact on companies of fund managers' short-term investment decisions!

Just getting back to Coca-Cola, you were eventually proved right.

They went down to $5.

For you, is that what investing is all about — you have got to take that medium- to long-term view and have that patience?

You first have to make sure you have done your arithmetic properly. If you are convinced you have, you just have to have the courage of your convictions and stick with it.

The only other time we underperformed was in the dotcom bubble, were we didn't have the TMT [telecom, media and technology] type stocks in the portfolio, but at that stage I think we were compatible with our client base and we didn't lose any clients.

How did you perform during that boom of 1999–2000?

We underperformed by about 4 per cent in the six months leading up to the eventual bust in March to April 2000.

Of the media and technology companies, News Corp, PBL, Fairfax, Optus, Hutchison and Telstra were in the top fifty at the time. There was still enough there to get yourself into trouble if you were not in them. But, obviously, that all came to an end.

In our research we found it very difficult to find any interviews you have given over the last thirty years. Given the amount of money you manage, this is amazing. However, at the height of the tech boom on 29 February 2000, you gave an interview to Alan Kohler on the ABC's 7.30 Report. In the interview you effectively said that when sentiment does turn on technology stocks, it will turn very sharply. The panel included a stockbroker who commented that the tech boom was not a South Sea Bubble situation where the mania was based on nothing at all. He went on to say that information technology would provide some huge opportunities to save money and generate profits, and that people couldn't afford to stand out of that. You responded by commenting that, although March hadn't started, it was hard to imagine there would be a further increase in the market this year. A month later, the technology crash came.

Let's look at the market now. The Australian sharemarket has experienced its best two and a half years since the lead up to the 1987 crash. Do you see a lot of value in the market or are you more concerned about individual stocks?

We have a philosophy of being fully invested all the time, so that means that we are 100 per cent invested and our performance over the last twelve months has been almost the same as the index.

It is not easy to find bargains in the market. We are actually quite pleased that our performance in the last twelve months has been the same as the index, because we have a conservative portfolio and we should outperform the index if the market heads down.

We try to avoid paying anything for the blue sky. That's really the key to it. We don't pay for blue sky and, of course, in a bear market, the market doesn't pay for blue sky. In a bull market, it does. In a bull market, people start to give credence to future growth prospects and the earnings multiples expand and a lot of blue sky is built into the price of many stocks. In a bear market, the blue sky deflates quicker than the overall market deflates, meaning if you did not pay for the blue sky in the first place, you should outperform.

The market over the last twelve months has built in some blue sky and indeterminate earnings are being factored in. That sort of environment is not very supportive of our process, so we are not unhappy that we have managed to maintain parity with the market in the last twelve months.

> *We don't pay for blue sky and, of course, in a bear market, the market doesn't pay for blue sky. In a bull market, it does.*

Do you look at the overall market and the direction it is taking?

As I said, we are always fully invested. Part of the reason for this approach is basically because we are trying to concentrate on a small number of things, because you can't concentrate on a large number of things and get them all right. So one of the things we don't concentrate on is which way the market is going.

So you take market direction out of the equation?

We try to focus as much as we can on the relative value of companies within the stock market; choose which is the best value stock today and don't try to do the macro call.

You've talked openly about your stock selection in the early years, but could you tell us best and worst calls in more recent years?

There haven't really been a lot that have gone markedly wrong. I've got bad calls in my personal portfolio — like buying Pasminco[3] because it got so cheap, and then it went bust. But on the Balanced Equity side of things, I really can't think of too much.

Your best calls would have probably been three years ago when the market was at a low point.

Buying Boral at $2 was an absolute classic for our stock selection process. It was back in 2000 and the goods and services tax (GST) was being introduced. Everybody could see that there had been a huge pull forward in home building, as people tried to beat the introduction of GST. There was a shortage of bricklayers and bricks, plasterers and plasterboard. Everybody knew that once we got past 1 July, building activity was going to fall dramatically. People were basing their views about stocks like Boral on that big drop-off in activity that would happen in July and the following months. As a result, most people were unloading stocks like Boral, because their earnings were going to drop off a cliff and they couldn't see the other side of that valley because the fall was so far down.

The way we look at things, though, is not to worry about that but to work out the earnings over a full economic cycle, ignoring the fact that there had been a pull forward effect. While we knew there was going to be a real fall in building starts, we tried to concentrate on the five-year average. Based on that analysis, we thought we could justify Boral's share price because it had been sold down to the point where it was trading with very low risk.

Put more simply, if you look to the other side of the valley, you can see that people will at some time start building houses again.

How overweight did you go on Boral?

Heavily overweight. One of the brokers had a valuation of $3.63 but a sell recommendation at $1.90 because he could see no catalyst to drive the stock higher to its true valuation and cause the underlying value to emerge. You don't have to see the catalyst if you

---

3   Pasminco, a base metals miner, went under in 2001 but resurfaced in 2004 under the new guise of Zinifex.

are confident that the earnings will emerge. Why do you need to know what event will cause it to emerge? It will emerge.

Do you have any mentors?

John Nolan was there on day one when I walked into the National Mutual office on 2 January 1974. He'd be the person who has had the greatest influence on me. He was always looking for the commonsense approach. He made sure you were always checking back to see if things made sense. He was a country boy and always applied the sanity test of whether a situation is sustainable in the long term or whether it is just the fad of the day.

You are in the business for the long term?

The market is more sophisticated than it is given credit for. There is a very simplistic view that if a company's earnings are down, the share price is going down. Actually, if the reason that earnings are down is because the company is investing to deliver in the long term, the share price may not fall at all, particularly if the management has credibility.

It is not easy to outperform the market. If the market had a simplistic short-term view, it would be easy to outperform it, wouldn't it? I really don't believe the theory that the market is so unsophisticated and short-term in its outlook.

Sisson, like other investors in this book, is fundamentally a value investor. He is, however, more comfortable than others with investing within the boundaries set by using the major sharemarket indices as a guide to which stocks he should choose from. This means that his funds hold most of the stocks that comprise those indices (in his case, mainly the top fifty stocks on the Australian Stock Exchange).

Despite this, like our other Masters, Sisson is still very much a stockpicker. He constructs the portfolio such that the fund holds a greater than index-weight exposure to those stocks he likes, and a smaller than index-weight exposure to stocks he doesn't like.

By picking from the top fifty stocks, Sisson isn't exposed to the small-capitalisation stocks that, although less liquid, arguably offer a greater opportunity for factor gains. He can also focus only on stocks that determine in the most part the performance of the overall sharemarket and the indices that most investors refer to each day as a bellwether of market conditions.

Sisson also illustrates how the use of options and convertible securities can be handy tools to manage risks while maximising returns. In the same way that he uses the indices as a tool for successful long-term investing but refuses to pay a premium for stocks making big promises, he also takes calculated risks and this has proved a good formula for long-term investing success.

I think you still need to be well diversified and keep some cash in times like this, but I'm not saying I'm terribly pessimistic. I just think you should be a bit cautious.

4

Retiring is hard to do
Robert Maple-Brown

Many readers of the first edition of *Masters of the Market* remarked that of all the Masters, Robert Maple-Brown was their favourite, or at least the fund manager to whom they could most relate. The response from readers vindicated the authors' decision to devote the first chapter of the first edition to Maple-Brown, one of the founding fathers of the Australian funds management industry. Maple-Brown's conservative philosophy of value investing with an eye for the long-term undoubtedly has broad appeal.

The potential disappointment for readers this time around is that Maple-Brown has since retired from day-to-day stockpicking. Even so, Maple-Brown is not that hard to find. He still owns about half of the firm that bears his name, Maple-Brown Abbott. And he still spends half his week in Maple-Brown Abbott's Sydney offices, as well as chairing the firm's monthly investment strategy meeting.

Even from the sidelines, Maple-Brown has plenty of insights to offer. His firm retains an enormously high standing in the industry, even though the industry itself has become more competitive as a result of some of the stars at large institutions deciding to start their own firms. Maple-Brown Abbott still commands the awe of its peers and it is difficult to fault the firm's long-term performance, even if it does not top the performance tables in some years.

With its main balanced fund (investing in all the asset classes), Maple-Brown Abbott hasn't done quite as well as the average of its peers in recent times. Then again, the bull market conditions since March 2003 haven't been ideal for Maple-Brown Abbott to be a sizeable outperformer. Maple-Brown Abbott tends to show its true colours when other funds are underperforming during bearish market periods.

Still, the firm's funds under management have grown strongly in the past two years because its performance has remained consistent. Those funds, managed primarily on behalf of wholesale clients, now total more than $18 billion, up from $16 billion since we last spoke to Maple-Brown in 2003. Since inception in 1986, the main Maple-Brown balanced fund has returned 11.8 per cent a year. In the ten years to 31 May 2005, it returned 9.8 per cent a year — against 8.5 per cent for the mean in the Mercer survey of pooled funds.

In recent years, the firm has also diversified its offering to include Asian and Asia Pacific funds. Those funds have clearly outperformed their benchmark since inception.

Maple-Brown had his first taste of the sharemarket as a broker at establishment firm McNall & Hordern in the 1960s. There he met Tristan Hearst, a client of the firm and arguably Australia's first fund manager. Hearst was also an avid exponent of fundamental analysis, inspired by the teachings of legendary American investor Benjamin Graham. Hearst found a receptive audience in a young Maple-Brown. Among the lessons he taught Maple-Brown was the need to do extensive research and careful analysis before buying stocks.

Maple-Brown then honed his accounting skills at Deloittes, before entering the funds management industry in the 1970s as a portfolio manager for Rothschild. There he identified a number of stocks that remain a successful part of the Maple-Brown portfolio to this day, including Frank Lowy's shopping centre empire Westfield and plumbing supplier Reece.

Maple-Brown also did much to improve the transparency of the funds management industry to its end investors. Rothschild became the first fund manager to advertise its investment returns, at a time when some institutions didn't even know how to calculate them.

A desire to focus solely on his love of investment management saw Maple-Brown join forces with Rothschild corporate finance executive Chris Abbott to start Maple-Brown Abbott in 1984. Maple-Brown Abbott's first client was the Myer family. Their close relationship continues with the recent purchase of a 25 per cent interest in financial services company The Myer Family Office. The company provides accounting, taxation and investment advice to high-net-worth individuals.

Maple-Brown Abbott has been a resilient and successful investor through all types of markets. The firm's longevity is testament enough to its success. Maple-Brown's investment style involves maintaining a long-term investment horizon while using conservative assumptions to value stocks. Often this means employing a contrarian approach by buying stocks that have fallen hard.

We caught up with Maple-Brown at his Sydney offices at 20 Bond Street, the old Australian Stock Exchange building, on Wednesday 13 July 2005. The Australian sharemarket had just registered another 20 per cent plus return for the financial year. The interview was carried out just a few weeks out from the start of a corporate profit reporting season some feared would be the source of disappointment.

———————•———————

You seem to be in the office a lot for someone who has officially retired. Can you explain?

I guess I have a lot of interest still in Maple-Brown Abbott. It's a substantial investment for me and I am keen to keep up to date with what's happening in the firm. I also got a bit bored with sitting at home. I promised myself I would play golf but I haven't got around to doing that yet. I guess I am still too interested in what's going on in the city to spend too long playing golf.

I also have a friendship with the Myer family and have recently bought into a subsidiary of the Myer family company called The

Myer Family Office. We are opening a Sydney branch and that's going to take a little bit of my time in terms of helping set up that business. I guess I am still keen to start up new businesses in the financial services sector.

So does that mean that you are effectively creating a new funds management business via the Myer Family Office venture?

Yes. It is. It's a completely different business. Basically it gives Maple-Brown Abbott a bit of an intro into the top end of that private client market. We have never been in that retail space and don't really want to be, but we want to make sure we don't lose touch with the top end of that retail market.

Are you pleased with how Maple-Brown Abbott has been travelling since we last spoke?

Yes, but it's pretty competitive out there. There are more boutiques starting all the time. Boutiques seem to be pretty popular with the institutional advisers so I suppose it's just become more competitive. The business is still going pretty well. Our entry into managing Asian equities is developing well.

Maple-Brown Abbott, of course, was possibly the original boutique.

I am not sure what the definition of a boutique is these days. If it's being owned by the people who work there, we are still a boutique I suppose. If it's got something to do with the amount of funds under management, we are probably not a boutique.

I think it's still all about picking stocks and you have some successes and you can go through some flat periods.

You are sizeable in terms of funds under management ($18 billion as at 31 March 2005) — is it getting harder to outperform the market?

I have never thought the size of funds were a constraint on performance. We have always invested heavily in the top 100 companies and we are still not a substantial shareholder in many companies. Our competitors say that size of funds under management is a problem for us. I think it's still all about picking stocks and you have some successes and you can go through some flat periods. But I don't think it has much to do with funds under management.

Have you stuck to your value investing philosophy through this period?

I am sure they [Maple-Brown's fund managers] are very focused on value and I don't think anything has changed in that regard. But picking good investments is an art as well as a science and it doesn't always work in the short term.

Some of your competitors might have looked at your retirement as an opportunity to buy the business, but you have a son working in the business and don't appear willing to sell.

I have an ongoing commitment. The business has my name on it and I think it would change if it were transferred to anyone else. I have a long-term interest in being part of the business, so nothing much has changed there.

You still own about half the business, don't you?

About half the business. It comes and goes a bit. Chris Abbott owns 20 per cent and the staff own the balance.

Have you had a lot of offers to buy the business?

We have had plenty of offers over the years.

In more recent times?

We have had but I wouldn't want to talk about them. The offers go away very quickly because I just say no. I am not interested in making a pile of money out of it. I am interested in having a good business going forward. I think my commitment to The Myer Family Office shows that I am committed to the longer term business of Maple-Brown Abbott. I wouldn't bother to do that if I wasn't.

Will The Myer Family Office also invest in shares?

It does have some products that it will manage itself. It won't compete with Maple-Brown Abbott, but some products will be managed by Maple-Brown Abbott — as long as Maple-Brown Abbott performs. There's a relationship there. For any Australian equities product, they will certainly look to use Maple-Brown Abbott as long as Maple-Brown Abbott is a good Australian equities manager.

How did the association with the Myer family form?

The Myer family were effectively my first clients at Maple-Brown Abbott, so it goes back a long while. And I am on good terms with the family — this is another example of a bit of cooperation, if you like.

Even in the past two years the market seems to have changed a lot with the rise and rise of hedge funds and the boutiques as you mentioned earlier. Has that changed the way Maple-Brown Abbott does business?

I am sure boutiques will come and go. I will not be surprised if some of the boutiques don't survive — I think it's much harder to get the economies that we have, because you need so much more investment than we ever had when we started. The compliance and staff requirements are much higher than when we started. There's quite a big commitment required to start a boutique.

Hedge funds are popular perhaps, but I think it will depend on how good the people are who run them. A successful hedge fund will do very well. An unsuccessful one won't last very long. I think it's as simple as that. A hedge fund needs very good management in my view.

Do you see Maple-Brown Abbott ever offering funds like absolute return funds (a type of hedge fund), which appear to be more popular?

I don't think you will see us go along that track in the immediate future, but they are products we have looked at. We are not into active share trading. We are into active management of portfolios. We have never been share traders. I can't believe we will ever be share traders. I think share trading is one of the hardest businesses in town. Everyone wants to do it and everyone thinks it's easy. But my experience tells me it's pretty difficult.

So, philosophically, it's not what you would want to do?

Philosophically it's against what I would want people to do but I don't have total say in what goes on here anymore. They may decide to do some of these sorts of products, but I think for the moment they are pretty happy to run with Asian products, Asia-Pacific products and Australian equity products.

You are a little reluctant to talk about Maple-Brown's stock holdings, but maybe we can ask you in broad terms about the last few years in the market. Did the market doing so well surprise you?

Yes. I think the market, the Australian equity market, has done better than I would have thought. That's probably due to a couple of factors. Long-term interest rates are still quite low and I think corporate profit growth has been quite good, probably helped a bit by resources stocks and commodities generally. We have been through a pretty good period. Will it continue at this sort of rate of growth? I would say not. I mean the sort of rates of growth we have seen in Australian equities in the past two years are very good. But you would not be forecasting 26 per cent per annum total return as we had for the year to June.

The average for the last couple of years is over 20 per cent, and that's a rate of growth that is unsustainable.

But I'm not as pessimistic as some people. The market's a little bit expensive but the earnings outlook is not too bad — there's a pretty reasonable dividend yield there and the economy still seems to be going okay. I am reasonably happy with Australian equities.

There's a bit better value in Asia but apart from that I don't think I have too much of a problem.

Generally, if we saw two 20-per-cent-plus years, most people would say there's a bubble forming in the market; however, not too many people have been saying that.

There is a bubble there, but it's not a huge bubble. That's what I'm trying to say. The PEs are okay as long as the earnings growth comes through, but the earnings growth expectations are quite high and there will be some disappointment.

Are there particular areas you think look expensive — resources or industrials?

I think it's everywhere and I think the market is generally expensive on current earnings, but it is probably reasonable value if the forecast earnings are achieved. A lot depends on earnings.

In the last few years, we have seen the resources sector firing, which has probably been long awaited.

There are a couple of things there. If the [Australian] currency was to firm up, that might hurt that a bit, and if China slowed down a bit more, that might hurt as well. The oil price is very high. Will it stay at $US60 a barrel? It's been a long time below that and plenty of people are saying it will go to $US100 a barrel, but it is anyone's guess. BHP Billiton and Woodside have had a big run on the back of the huge increase in the oil price. Is it sustainable? I don't know. But it may not be.

In what stocks has Maple-Brown fared particularly well?

We have done okay in some stocks and we have missed some stocks too. I don't think there's too much to talk about and I don't really want to talk about individual stocks. One, I'm not too familiar with it and, two, we don't talk about individual stocks.

What role do you have in investment decisions now?

My only role is to chair the monthly investment strategy meeting, so I'm interested in the broad asset allocation of our balanced funds. I am not involved at all in deciding whether to buy Woodside or BHP. That's someone else's decision. I have some input into the asset allocation in the balanced fund but I don't have any impact on individual stock decisions. I attend all of those meetings and put in my three pennies' worth. It's a consensus and I am really there just to keep an eye on the process and make sure everything's reasonably sensible.

Do you have strong views on asset allocation?

No. I think the consensus generally applies. I probably have stronger views on individual stocks that don't go anywhere or I have no influence on.

So I am still pretty interested in what goes on and keep an eye on what's happening. And I am keen for it to continue to do well. That's all I am interested in really — for the purpose of our clients. I'm a client and a lot of my family are clients. I just want to make sure the clients do well, basically.

Are there any other interests you are pursuing as well?

That's about it. I have a couple of non-profits I think you know about — the University of NSW and the Sir David Martin Foundation. I am also the director of the Institute of Chartered Accountants in Australia. I'm not doing too much but as you point out I spend a fair bit of time here.

Exactly how long do you spend here?

I spend maybe half a week here. I spend a bit of time at my property [a sheep and cattle property near Cootamundra] and a bit of time on non-profit activities and a bit of time in Melbourne with the Myer family. I am probably down in Melbourne one day a month.

Is it fair to say the Maple-Brown name is going to be around for some time to come?

I don't think there is going to be any change and the business is likely to be around for a while. I wouldn't expect any change there.

Are there any other issues currently in the market that concern you?

Not really, but I have been a little bit intrigued that bond markets have gone down. Yields have gone down and prices have gone up; equities have gone up but inflation also seems to have gone up a bit. They don't seem to be in sync like they used to be. Maybe that's a warning that something funny is going on. There's a lot of money around still, I guess, and maybe that's helping buoy both of those markets [bonds and equities]. I think you need to be a little bit cautious about the outlook. We have had a good run and it would be a good time to have some cash around.

There's a lot of talk about the 'weight of money' (from takeovers and so on) but, on the other hand, some investors believe those types of theories are a load of baloney.

The theory's a bit baloney but there's no doubt in the short run it does have some impact on the market. It affects market liquidity and you see that. The housing market is of concern. A lot of people's expectations there are too high. People still think houses go up in price by 20 per cent per annum. It's more likely to go sideways or down. Someone did a survey in America recently and the expectation is that the housing market will go up 20 per cent per annum for the next ten years. Well, houses are going to be worth a lot of money if that happens. There's certainly a cycle there and there's a cycle in everything.

But on the economy overall, you seem quite sanguine.

I'm okay but not very optimistic. The economy's okay and the government has done a great job in terms of managing the economy. I give them credit for that. But we

> *We have been through fourteen years of strong growth and the party won't go on forever ... The business cycle is still around.*

have been through fourteen years of strong growth and the party won't go on forever. You just need to be aware of that. The business cycle is still around.

And sharemarket investors might want to maintain a diversified portfolio in that event?

I think you still need to be well diversified and keep some cash in times like this, but I'm not saying I'm terribly pessimistic. I just think you should be a bit cautious.

———————●———————

For the first time most of us in the investment community can remember, Robert Maple-Brown is feeling a little bit edgy. Retirement, after thirty-five years of managing money, is easier said that done. To cure his itch to hang around the city and talk about the stock market, Maple-Brown has convinced his former colleagues at Maple-Brown Abbott to allow him to come into the office two or three days a week. And it doesn't seem his colleagues will be getting rid of him in a hurry.

Maple-Brown's reaction to retirement is in complete contrast to the way he invests. He is always calm and seemingly not overly worried about the day-to-day machinations of the market. As an analogy, if you were riding on a bus and about to take on a windy, narrow road, you would want Maple-Brown in the driver's seat.

The last two years have seen the Australian sharemarket go from the early stages of a bull market to a stampede. Not only have company profits ballooned but price/earnings multiples have expanded. Not a great environment for people looking for value. For Maple-Brown, though, this is of little consequence. Sure, many pundits may claim he has become a dinosaur and that value investing is yesterday's story, but Maple-Brown has heard it all before. Only five years ago the technology boom produced a similar reaction from the investment community. Maple-Brown is more interested in sticking to his time-honoured process of value investing and reaping the rewards for himself and his investors over a long period of time. He might underperform the market on any given year or even eighteen months, but over the long term, Maple-Brown Abbott has outperformed the market despite growing from a minnow to a monster. And like you would expect from a champion like Maple-Brown, he does not use size as an excuse to underperform.

We look for monopolistic-type assets. If you go back, there were times in the 1980s (and in the case of Ron, even earlier than that) when we were looking for things like gas companies or whatever where the pricing power was there because of semi-monopolistic traits. For us, it is an important factor in trying to understand the franchise value of a company we are buying. If you are a 'me-too' manufacturer with no particular strategic position, our assessment of value will be materially less than for a competitor that has significant market share and some element of pricing power.

Sticking to their knitting
Sir Ron Brierley and Gary Weiss

Sir Ron Brierley and Gary Weiss seem more at home in the 1980s. Back then, the corporate raid was in its heyday and the pair initiated some of the most audacious takeover bids the Australian sharemarket had ever seen.

Like many of the corporate raiders of that period (most of whom fell by the wayside), controversy has usually surrounded the antics of Sir Ron and Weiss. This is probably not surprising given their activities at GPG's predecessor, Industrial Equity, often involved taking on establishment targets and confronting an underperforming company's board and management.

It is testament to Sir Ron and Weiss's skill and determination that their investment company, Guinness Peat Group (GPG), is one of the few corporate raiders to have stood the test of time, despite the term 'corporate raider' being associated with the unhealthy excesses of that decade.

Even in these more measured times, controversy is still not far away from GPG — but it is clear from our interviews that it is something that Sir Ron and Weiss revel in.

Born in New Zealand, Sir Ron first embraced the sharemarket as an eighteen year old in the 1950s. His first investment generated a quick return of 30 per cent and from that moment on he didn't really contemplate a career other than investing.

His fifty years in the sharemarket game have been littered with bold, sometimes outrageous investments, and decisions that could only be carried off by someone with an extreme intelligence and an abundance of gall.

As a man in his early twenties, Sir Ron decided that he would raise funds from the public and establish his own investment company, despite having virtually no track record in this area. Somehow he convinced the public to give him £20 000. Not happy with just playing the NZ sharemarket, he set sail in the early 1960s across the Tasman, determined to make his mark on the potentially more fertile playing fields of Australia. He quickly established an investment vehicle in the form of Industrial Equity, which in the 1980s would become the third biggest company listed on the Australian Stock Exchange.

Sir Ron's cunning was well complemented during that period by Gary Weiss, a lawyer by training. Weiss came to IEL in 1984 and quickly established himself as a brilliant tactician.

The fall-out from the crash of 1987 saw IEL taken over by John Spalvins's Adelaide Steamship in 1989. Sir Ron was 'frozen out' by new management of his other vehicle, the NZ-based Brierley Investments (BIL), even though he nominally remained 'founder president'.

In the early 1990s, Sir Ron founded a new vehicle listed in the UK, Guiness Peat Group Plc (GPG), to recreate the philosophy behind IEL and BIL. A controlling stake in financial services group Tyndall formed the cornerstone of GPG's initial investment portfolio. GPG runs a small investment team and employs around 25 people to identify investments primarily in the UK, Australia and New Zealand.

Like its predecessors IEL and BIL, GPG is still feared, often seeking out weakened companies through a raid on their share registers followed by a demand for board seats or wholesale change.

In our 2003 interview, it became clear that both Sir Ron and Weiss love doing deals as much as making money, and truly enjoy the intellectual challenge of outwitting others in the process of making an investment or undertaking a takeover bid.

The choice of bombed-out targets is very much in keeping with GPG's strict adherence to a value style of investing, but very much augmented by GPG's 'catalytic' role in encouraging the target to change its management or corporate strategy. This willingness to be closely involved in the target company's management has often enhanced the potential return on an investment. GPG's investment process often involves incredibly detailed research to exploit loopholes in corporate law or companies' articles of association, unlocking value from investments in a way that most others — even professional investors — would not be brave enough to attempt.

Sir Ron's cheeky style is perhaps best understood by examining tilts at the likes of AGL and Woolworths back in the 1980s as part of the rise and fall of IEL (passages from the first edition of *Masters of the Market* covering these two episodes are reprinted here).

GPG hasn't been involved in quite as many hostile situations of late. But for chief executives and boards, the emergence of GPG on their share registers is still a reason for incredible discomfort and often a signal to start thinking about an alternative career.

From a shareholder's perspective, GPG's role is often the part of saviour. It is a role GPG played in 2002–2003 by buying a stake in troubled trans-Tasman insurer Tower, assuming several board seats, underwriting a life-saving capital raising and helping to devise a new business strategy for the company.

At the time of writing, GPG was up around $100 million on paper on its investment in Tower, which subsequently spun off its Australian financial planning and trustee arm to create Australian Wealth Management (now 34 per cent owned by GPG).

Sir Ron and Weiss have a natural preference for investing in old-style manufacturing businesses and, like some other Masters, only invest in companies they can truly understand (as Peter Lynch says, 'Never invest in any idea you can't illustrate with a crayon').

In GPG's case, this preference reflects a liking for companies that are asset rich but might have depressed share prices because of mismanagement. In Sir Ron's own words, GPG looks for companies that are 'better dead than alive' or are potentially worth more than what they are trading at if their assets were sold.

The investment motto 'sticking to your knitting' has more than the usual connotations for GPG these days. The fortunes of GPG are now closely tied to that of Coats plc, GPG's biggest investment and the world's biggest maker of threads. The business has a book value of $500 million but GPG is hoping to significantly profit from the turnaround in the business, in part through developing Coats's strong global position in the crafts market, including handknittings.

Investments like Coats potentially take years to realise their potential, but GPG has an impressive track record. GPG's shareholders' funds have grown from £49 million in 1992 to £514.4 million as at 31 December 2004. During this period, GPG's reported net asset value per share has increased at a compound growth rate of 17.4 per cent a year, more than 5 percentage points above the S&P/ASX 200 and double the FTSE 100.

GPG has moved onto lower profile, but potentially lucrative, corporate targets in the two years since our 2003 interview, a period when the market rose strongly. We spoke to one half of the duo, Gary Weiss, on 18 July 2005 at GPG's Circular Quay offices overlooking Sydney Harbour.

———————●———————

How have you fared in the bull market of the past two years, given this time did not represent ideal conditions for a value investor like GPG to shine?

That's true. Whether it is fortuitous or whatever, we have been fairly preoccupied during this period with the prosecution of our existing major investments, some of which are significant turnaround stories. So we really have not been in a good position to undertake major activity in a significant way anyway.

Markets have clearly been on the rise — hardly a situation that's conducive to the type of value investing that we employ but, as I said, we have been preoccupied with dealing with our current investment portfolio.

Are you saying you haven't used this period to realise many investments or make new ones?

We have made some reasonably modest investments but there have been no major transactions in the past twelve months. The focus has been on getting those areas in which we are already invested right, and to continue to develop those assets that are more mature with a view to disposal.

By the time you come to publish, there will probably be a few things that will have evolved where we would have realised some of our investments.

That having been said, there's been some very good improvements in value in some of our significant investments, which all augurs very well for the future.

Was your lack of activity due to the market being overvalued or other factors?

It's probably a combination of things, some of which I have already indicated. Take Coats, for example. We have somewhere in the region of 37 per cent of our assets tied up in this one investment. Coats has been quite consuming in terms of GPG's involvement. It is the most geographically widespread investment we have ever undertaken. It's not the biggest — in days of old we have owned companies much bigger and, indeed, with more employees. For example, Woolworths [Industrial Equity took control of the grocer in 1987] had about 65 000 employees but they were, for the most part, all based in Australia. Coats has about 28 000 people in sixty-eight countries around the world.

What has been your best investment since we last interviewed you for Masters of the Market *in 2003?*

This is probably very much leading with my chin. But I would like to think that Coats will be the best investment that GPG's ever made. I hope that does not prove to be false or excessive optimism, but Coats certainly possesses the fundamentals of being a very, very good investment for GPG.

Can you explain why you believe Coats will be a good investment for GPG?

I suppose when you go back to look at some of the basics, Coats is a company that has been in the threads industry for 250 years. It has a superb pedigree in terms of brands, its intellectual property and its franchise value. It is undoubtedly the world leader in threads and, of course, a significant part of its production is directed towards areas that are reasonably fundamental — unless nudity is embraced in a very large way globally. The clothing industry — or the textile industry more generally — will continue to grow. Coats will clearly be a participant in that, being as it is the number one player in the thread industry globally.

And what has your worst investment been?

Well, I think if one undertook a review of GPG's investment performance or took a snapshot of its investee companies over the past twelve to fifteen months, undoubtedly the worst performing part of our portfolio has been our investment in Capral.[1] Without going into excessive detail, Capral is a significant restructuring story that has taken a lot longer and been a lot more painful than anyone had anticipated. That was reflected in the results to 31 December 2004, where the company not only reported a material trading loss but also took the opportunity to write off a future income tax benefit that had been an asset on the balance sheet. This resulted in a loss for the period of $70-odd million. It impacted on the results of GPG, a significant holder with two representatives on the board, because of the application of equity accounting. So, as I said, on any objective basis Capral has been a significant underperformer. However, it has now completed the construction of a major new facility in Queensland. We have now appointed a new chief executive [former Onesteel head of distribution, Robin Freeman] and I would like to think that the worst days of Capral are behind us. But one shouldn't underestimate the challenges that exist today.

What lessons did you learn from that experience?

Restructurings are easy to do from an academic standpoint — that's probably an absolutely trite observation — but far less easy to implement in a practical way. Some go easier than others. Certainly, closing [manufacturing] capacity without constructing new capacity is a lot easier than trying to achieve both at the same time while also seeking to meet customer requirements. Of course, we have a much larger restructuring than Capral underway at Coats, where we are closing capacity and constructing new capacity in a

---

1   Capral is an aluminium fabricated product supplier.

global sense. That's not without its issues but in both cases, the reconstruction that has occurred is absolutely necessary if these companies are to continue to be viable forces in their respective industries.

In the case of GPG, to reiterate what we have always said, we are financial investors. We don't manage the companies we invest in. We have management teams to do that. Our job is to provide the financial and strategic support to enable the management team to implement a course that the board has agreed upon. Probably at Capral, it has been far more challenging in practice than management had contemplated, but GPG has been a stalwart supporter of Capral. We believe in the end vision of the company. We believe the company has the potential to be a very serious force in the aluminium industry in this country.

> *Our job is to provide the financial and strategic support to enable the management team to implement a course that the board has agreed upon.*

Again, with our disclosures on all these companies, we don't pretend something to be that which it isn't. If it is hard and difficult, we are the first to acknowledge that to our investors, and these complex and major restructuring exercises are very rarely seamless and very rarely proceed without any hiccups along the way.

How confident are you that Capral will turn out to be a good investment?

We are reasonably confident. We would like to believe that its worst days are already behind it.

There are a lot more cashed up private equity funds looking at the types of assets that have traditionally been GPG's bread and butter. Has that noticeably changed the way you invest?

Clearly, asset prices have gone up significantly. There is such competition for quality assets that prices are far from cheap. But probably with only a handful of exceptions, the private equity firms do not undertake the sort of initial activity in an investment that we do. Very rarely do they start buying shares in a target company on-market. Very rarely do they agitate for change. Very rarely do they themselves initiate a hostile takeover of a company. To that extent we continue to enjoy an area of activity that is underexploited by the private equity people. But, clearly, when any asset is up for sale in a retail environment, it is difficult for GPG to compete based on the value equation.

Do you think that some of the private equity funds, which have made great returns in recent times, will fall on hard times?

If there aren't some duds in the investments private equity funds have selected, it would come as a huge surprise. No matter how clever or talented you are from an investment point of view, you inevitably are going to have some failures or significant underperformers. It goes with the territory.

You have never invested significantly in the resources sector, which has been resurgent in the past year. Why is that?

We invest only to a very modest extent [in resources]. That's an area, quite frankly, where we have considerable difficulty in relation to determining value. As someone famously said, 'A goldmine is a hole in the ground with a liar at the top'.[2]

The companies you mainly target are down and out …

Or have a role for us to play. I guess a small example of what we have done in the last twelve months that would illustrate the 'catalytic' role we like to carve out would be our involvement in Rattoon Holdings and the bid for beneficiaries' stock in Tattersall's.[3] I would like to think that the activities that Rattoon undertook initially in buying beneficiaries' stakes was, in itself, a catalyst for Tattersall's to come out with a full sharemarket listing.

When did Rattoon first make offers to beneficiaries?

Quite a long time ago. Probably eighteen months ago.

---

2   The quote is often attributed to Mark Twain but there is no record in his writings of him saying it. It is said that the saying is usually attributed to Twain because he was such a prolific quipster.

3   Tattersall's, which holds lottery and gaming machine licences in Victoria, listed in July 2005 with a $2 billion-plus market capitalisation after raising $310 million from investors. The float followed a decision by so-called 'beneficiaries' — descendents of founder George Adams and his associates — to convert their interests into shares. Rattoon — in which GPG is a major shareholder — made offers to buy the beneficiaries' holdings prior to the float but held only around 1 per cent of Tattersall's shares at the time of writing.

Tattersall's was an interesting float.

We were quite disappointed that Rattoon didn't achieve a greater level of take-up among beneficiaries, but this is a modest illustration of GPG's catalytic role.

Rattoon was actually offering a higher price than the float implied, which seems a little contrary to your natural philosophy. Can you explain that?

Well, I guess we were looking for significant stock and had we achieved that it would have given us a strategic position, which is always more valuable than the handful of shares that trade on the market each day.

How much does GPG hold in Rattoon?

It was about 15 per cent of Rattoon but we had agreed with others to underwrite a significant capital raising to finance the offer that Rattoon had made to beneficiaries.

You have had some experience investing in the gaming sector, but Tattersall's is a company with some risks associated with the renewal of its licences in the coming years. What did GPG and Rattoon like about Tattersall's?

We have had some experience in the sector but I wouldn't overstate that. Tatts is clearly a very well established name and a well-established franchise. There are risks in any form of business activity but arguably the doomsayers, with respect to Tattersall's, are going to be proven somewhat wrong. The other point is that I don't think the consolidation of the gaming industry in Australia is complete.

They have a big wad of cash and no debt so that puts them in an interesting position.

As to what they are going to do, we are not in a position to comment — not as yet.

Australian interest rates haven't moved up as fast as some people might have thought. How does that affect the way you invest?

Not to any significant extent. GPG itself, apart from capital notes on issue in the New Zealand market, has no bank debt and that's how we choose to operate. Our investee companies themselves have debt; and in some cases quite significant debt. But the current rates of financing, compared with some of the rates of interest that

Ron and I have seen over the years, look reasonably benign. So it's not huge in terms of our decision making, unlike a leveraged private equity-type investor, where interest rates are critical and sensitivities to movements in interest rates can have a significant impact on valuation.

Do you have a view on the impact of China's growth on the Australian sharemarket and the stocks you invest in?

Beyond stating the bleeding obvious that the manufacturing sector in China is going to continue to grow and grow, I can't really take it much further. GPG has an increasingly significantly exposure to the Chinese economy through our investment in Coats. We [Coats] also have a very significant business in India that dates back to the days of the British Raj. We have, in fact, a much more significant share in the Indian textiles industry than we do in China. We have major exposure to South America too and it is on the cusp of being a significant force in terms of low-cost manufacturing. As to China, there's just no getting away from the fact that it is clearly going to be the industrial powerhouse of the world over the next little while, with India rapidly coming up behind. From a GPG point of view, we have — as I have indicated — a material exposure [through Coats] to those two countries in particular.

But you have invested in a lot of Australian-based manufacturing companies. Can you still confidently do that, given the lower costs of manufacturing in some of these other places?

Capral is an example that belies the proposition that everything in the world will be ultimately manufactured in China. There are reasons why a number of industries involved in domestic manufacturing still have a role to play — large bulky items, long lead times and things like that are matters that clearly have an impact on the viability of a domestic manufacturing base. Take Capral, for example; if one looks at the modelling that's gone into our new plant, we should be cost-competitive with imports from China in particular, but with the added advantage of having significantly shorter manufacturing lead times and a customer service profile that is domestic and can more readily deal with things such as damaged goods or goods that are not in compliance with what's been ordered, or whatever.

So clearly Capral is an example — so far not a very successful one — but an example nonetheless of the belief that domestic manufacturing still has a role to play.

What single issue do you think will drive the Australian sharemarket higher or lower in the next few years?

The Australian market will continue to be heavily influenced by the direction of major global markets. The two things that will have an impact on global markets are economic and political risk.

If one has to take Australia as a subset of that, I think the proximity to the fastest growing region of the world should provide some underpinning to the Australian sharemarket, together with the sheer volume of funds generated from Australia's superannuation regime, which clearly need to be invested. Domestic equities are still going to be a significant asset class for the investment of these funds.

> *The proximity to the fastest growing region of the world should provide some underpinning to the Australian sharemarket.*

But, nonetheless, confidence is clearly a very important factor. There exists the potential for something to emerge from left field that could shake confidence with a consequential impact on markets.

The Australian sharemarket has had a great run. Do you foresee leaner times ahead?

I am going to probably incorrectly parrot the views that my close colleague Maurice Loomes said to me in the recent past, but when you look at corporate Australia's share of Australia's GDP, it has been at a very high proportion. The question that arises is whether that is sustainable. We have seen periods of pressure in terms of wages and so on, which is clearly going to affect margins. Then there's fuel prices. The real issue is, how many companies are there in Australia that truthfully have genuine pricing power? If you don't have pricing power and there is a continued upsurge in costs of doing business (whether it's fuel, labour or construction costs or whatever), that will have an impact on margins. To my mind, the Australian market is priced on the expectation of continued growth in profits.

To what extent do you look for companies with pricing power in their industries?

We look for monopolistic-type assets. If you go back, there were times in the 1980s (and in the case of Ron, even earlier than that) when we were looking for things like gas companies or whatever where the pricing power was there because of semi-monopolistic traits. For us, it is an important factor in trying to understand the franchise value of a company we are buying. If you are a 'me-too' manufacturer with no particular strategic position, our assessment of value will be materially less than for a competitor that has significant market share and some element of pricing power. Coats, for example, has been the global leader in its field, and with the technical skills that have been built up over 250 years it is the sort of company where we perceive the value is underpinned by a franchise that comes from having those sorts of qualities.

You are famous for getting involved in a corporate stoush at GPG. Have there been any notable ones of late?

No. It's been quiet in terms of hostile activity. In truth, we have been heads down and looking to maximise the value of what we have. But even in situations like [life insurance company] Tower, where we were instrumental in putting forward the proposal to spin off Australian Wealth Management, the position was so compelling that there was no disagreement at all around the board table. Probably the only recent example of corporate activism in the past twelve months has been the Farm Pride Foods situation, where we did requisition a meeting to put one of our people on the board. Reasonably predictably, the company caved in at the eleventh hour.[4]

To reiterate, between Capral and Coats we are talking of investments that comprise the best part of 40 per cent of GPG's portfolio. Those companies have been undertaking major restructurings and that's where the clear focus has been. And in a similar vein, the work we put into Tower has now been vindicated in terms of both the sharemarket rating Tower is enjoying and its performance in Australia.

We've got 31.5 per cent and another 3 per cent under a swap arrangement of AWM [the Tower spin-off] and that swap will go to a shareholder vote in September for approval for us to acquire those shares. It has been a very pleasing development over the past twelve months to see the emergence of Tower from the critical care ward.

Tower is an interesting example because life insurance is a complex business. Was it hard to work out when that stock had bottomed at the time you decided to invest?

Unfortunately, we didn't quite pick the bottom. Our timing there wasn't entirely spot on. We probably purchased our initial strategic

---

4   Farm Pride is a grader, packer, supplier and marketer of eggs and egg
    products.

stake a few months too early but, nonetheless, we have worked very hard in the rehabilitation of Tower. You're perfectly right that it is a complex business and it needed in the first instance the restoration of capital, not only for regulatory requirements but indeed to rebuild stakeholders' confidence in the company. GPG underwrote that exercise and we have been closely involved in the fundamental exercise of rehabilitating the company on both sides of the Tasman. We still think there's a lot of work to be done at Tower to improve the performance, but we are quite pleased with the progress the company has made.

Now the market is saying Tower has excess capital and is looking at ways to spend it.

They are but one needs to await the full impact of the application of IFRS [International Financial Reporting Standards], not only on Tower but indeed on financial services companies generally, to see how the new rules affect stated balance sheets and we will see how it goes from there.

In terms of the GPG investment team, has it changed much since we last spoke?

It's been very stable. All up, including secretaries and librarians, we have twenty-five people around the world.

Sir Ron is overseas for the cricket, but has he had any thought about retirement?

I doubt that, but it's a question that should be directed to Ron.

Are you looking to invest your spare cash at the moment?

We are currently holding significant cash on deposit. In Australian dollar terms, it's about $500 million and with some more likely to flow depending on the outcome of some asset sales in the course of negotiation. We are investing in a reasonably modest way at the moment in a number of interesting industries that could have some potential, depending on how these things go.

We are in a very good position and Coats is demonstrably a better company than it was twelve or eighteen months ago. We have already canvassed Capral, and when you look at the public scorecard for our

Tower involvement, there has been some material value creation for GPG shareholders.[5]

How long do you hope to hold your individual investments? You have held some for a very long time in the past.

We have. For example, Tyndall we held for something like nine years. Tasmanian Perpetual Trustees, which we just sold, had been a core component of our portfolio for something like thirteen years in various forms. So there's no hard and fast rule on how long we like to keep investments. We sell when we have achieved the sorts of returns we have been looking for. Often this will coincide with a company going into a new phase of its development. Take our investment in Reinsurance Australia [now Calliden], for example. When ReAC nearly collapsed, we averaged down our investment and took a position to help with the workout of ReAC. That has being largely completed and it has gone on a new tack of being a general insurer. While there is still a tail of claims on the workout reinsurance side, the restoration of value has to a large extent been completed. It gives you some idea of our modus operandi of buying when all looks bleak and working to restore value.

How much did you make on ReAC?

Relative to GPG today, a useful if somewhat modest contributor would probably be the best description of it.[6]

> *A good example of Sir Ron and Weiss's approach is IEL's controversial raids in the 1980s on AGL and Woolworths, illustrating the pair's typically unorthodox, often controversial and usually mischievous and amusing approach to investing. The following edited passage from the first edition of* Masters of the Market *is an entertaining classic discussion on how the raids unfolded. We began by asking Sir Ron from where he sourced his investing ideas.*

Sir Ron: Well, some of them came from disciplined research. Others came from opportunism. You can pick up today's newspaper and

---

5   At the time of writing and including its investment in the lower spin-off, AWM, GPG was up close to $100 million on its initial investment.

6   ReAC reported a loss of $467 million in 1999 before putting its businesses in 'run-off' in order to extinguish its insurance liabilities. The protracted run-off process left ReAC with a small pool of capital to restart its general insurance activities in 2004.

> *You can pick up today's newspaper and see a company that's come out with a bad result, so there's a distinct element of opportunism based not only on perceived value but also on strategy.*

see a company that's come out with a bad result, so there's a distinct element of opportunism based not only on perceived value but also on strategy. GPG became very skilled and IEL became very skilled, somewhat controversially, in exploiting what you might call loopholes and inconsistencies and anomalies in various regulations, laws and conventions in order to gain a superior strategic position. Things came just instinctively, because after you were working for years and decades in an IEL-type atmosphere, it just attracted ideas and opportunities.

I can remember one morning when I said, 'Have we ever looked at Woolworths?' Woolworths was getting into lots of strife — it had a liquidity run at one stage. One of our colleagues, who was reading the paper, put it down and said, 'Too good for us, Ron' and resumed reading his paper.

When was that?

Gary: I can tell you. It would have been 1985. We raided it in 1986.

Sir Ron: From being 'Too good for you, Ron' about six or twelve months later we were actively raiding Woolworths. It could be said that Woolworths was probably the greatest deal that IEL ever did.

What were you trying to achieve?

Gary: I was just wondering, before we discuss Woolworths, whether we could talk about an earlier transforming deal — not only, I suppose, from a corporate standpoint for IEL, but also in a personal sense.

I can well recall three or four days after having joined IEL — and I'd only met Ron once before — he sort of shuffled into my office with a few folders and said, 'I'd like you to look at these folders, there must be a way into this company'. He then deposited on my desk a heap of folders on the Australian Gas Light Company, which at that time was a real bastion of the New South Wales establishment.

Ron had always liked AGL. Previously, he'd had a bit of a foray into the shares in the early 1970s and been warned off by the company. I think that's a fair way of putting it. So this was for me a wonderful exercise because it harnessed all my strengths. I was, from a legal standpoint, going back and looking at the origins of AGL. What I identified were some very obvious loopholes in AGL's structure and the ability then to take advantage of them in the practical sense.

We started buying shares in AGL. I was responsible for this and worked very closely with Graeme Cureton, who was IEL's investment manager [Cureton now works at GPG]. I was responsible for setting up the structures and so on.

What were the loopholes?

Gary: AGL, contrary to what they'd told everyone, wasn't a company. It was a statutory partnership established by its own Act of Parliament. It had proprietors (rather than shareholders) and so on. But it purported to everyone that it was effectively a company. It had its own rules so it never produced consolidated accounts. When the stock exchange used to grizzle, they'd say, 'Well, we're not a company so we don't need to comply'. They had the best of all worlds. And they had a purported shareholding restriction that limited the interests of a single proprietor, or associates, to 2 per cent.

I went back to the company's founding statute and traced every amendment and every regulation that had ever been made relating to AGL. As Ron told me after all of that, he reckoned I knew more about the company than they did.

Not being a company, it wasn't subject to the usual rules and regulations that applied to companies, but similarly, therefore, some of the protections that were afforded to other companies, like substantial shareholding notices, did not apply to AGL. The need to lodge substantial shareholding notices only applied to listed public companies. 'Company' was the defining term and AGL wasn't one. It also wasn't subject to the takeover code, because it wasn't a company.

I went through all this with Ron and then Ron asked, 'How do we deal with the shareholding restriction?' I came up with a very strong argument that usually articles of association of conventional companies have contractual effect. They're publicly available and bind members of the company, both existing and prospective. But what about by-laws in this entity? I took the view that they didn't have the impact at all of articles and if they were binding, they were only binding on the proprietors at the time when this by-law was enacted in 1936. To deal with all of this, we set up nominee companies so that once we got to 2 per cent, we switched to another nominee and so on.

AGL tried to find out who was behind the trading by issuing the old section 261 notices but again they only applied to companies. Whenever they were issued, the broker would go back and say to the company, 'Are you allowed to issue these sorts of things?' The inquiries would sort of disappear.

I'm sure you were helping the brokers answer that question.

Gary: Absolutely.

AGL was a wonder. It was absolutely one of the great stores of value. When we bought into AGL, it had a market capitalisation of about $150 million. That was only equal to the value of its shareholding in Santos. The rest of the gas company you got for free. AGL had about 12 per cent of Santos and the market was attributing absolutely no value to its New South Wales reticulation system nor its vast land holdings and so on, of which we knew there were plenty.

Anyway, we started buying. We had nominees all over the place with some bizarre names — The Countess of Naples, Cessnock Flying School, Gary Sobers Indoor Cricket Centres from Gibraltar. We went through 10 per cent and I asked Ron, 'Shall we keep buying?' He said, 'Oh yeah'. We went through 15 per cent. I asked, 'Ron, what will we do?' He replied, 'Got to keep buying'. We got to 20 per cent and Ron said, 'Keep buying'. We got to 41.5 per cent. By this stage, we were aware that the government was going to review the status of AGL and, indeed, a report was commissioned that called for AGL to be brought into the new world.

Ron was convinced that AGL knew we were there and was somehow secretly loving all of this. I assured him that they had no idea whatsoever. He then went to lunch one day to a Liberal Party function and sat next to Maurie Williams, who was the general manager of AGL at the time. Ron came back just after that lunch and said, 'Maurie hasn't the faintest idea we're there'.

Then the government announced that they were going to effectively incorporate AGL. Under the legislation that was being announced, they were going to 'grandfather' shareholdings that were in place. Even though there was a limitation of 2 per cent for everyone else, some feted organisations had more — MLC, in particular, and AMP had I think 8 per cent and 5 per cent. To protect their position [so they didn't have to sell], they were allowed to grandfather their holdings. The way in which it was done was to make exempt those holdings in place when the legislation was to be enacted. So then, virtually on Christmas Eve 1985, we announced that we had 41.5 per cent of AGL. On Christmas Eve, we delivered a requisition to AGL that a meeting be convened to appoint us to the board.

Then all hell broke loose, putting it mildly. The Premier of NSW got involved. We were summoned to meetings by the Minister of Energy. Ron had already departed on holiday so I had the task of attending this meeting with Bill Loewenthal. The minister was furious, complaining we'd made the government look like mud.

Then the threat came out, 'We're not going to register any of your stock'. I said, 'Well, with great respect, Minister, it's already registered'.

He said, 'Get me the top twenty list'. He came back and said, 'Right, now, Cessnock Flying School'. I said, 'Yes, Minister, that's us'. 'Countess of Naples.' 'Yes, Minister, that's us', et cetera. He then worked out that AGL had been so stupid and had made the government look like mugs. In the end, we brokered a deal with the NSW Government that allowed us effectively to keep our shareholding.

Sir Ron: It took me a year to do it — travelling between the chairman's office and the minister's office and sometimes the Premier's office. Not a year I'd like to repeat, Gary.

Gary: But the upshot of it all was that we became by far the largest shareholder in AGL. Ron was appointed to the board and still sits on the board of AGL today. He's the longest serving board member. I'd say probably, Ron, that was the one transaction that really brought us together from an intellectual point of view.

Sir Ron: We didn't actually finish up making a lot of money out of it because it coincided eventually with the takeover of IEL itself. But as a legal, intellectual and mischievous exercise, it had a lot of intangible value for IEL.

Why were you requisitioning the AGL shareholders meeting on Christmas Eve?

Sir Ron: Well, that wasn't quite as bad as it sounds because legislation was due to take effect on 31 December. I wanted to sort of tell the company anyway. There were some very good reasons why I was anxious to reveal ourselves on Christmas Eve, so that we had contact with the chairman before all this came about a few days later. But, yes, the fact that it was Christmas Eve added a sort of further mischievous aspect to it.[7]

It was one of my specialities — to make takeover bids or raids at Easter or Christmas. We made one bid on Christmas Eve and all it succeeded in doing was stuffing up our Christmas. That taught me a lesson — no more raids on Christmas Eve.

Gary: When Ron says IEL didn't make a huge amount of money out of AGL, that's true in the sense that, ultimately, IEL was taken over by Adelaide Steamship. Adsteam was under a lot of pressure at that time to dispose of its AGL holding, which it did at prices that were a fraction of today's prices.

AGL would be worth several billion dollars today.[8]

Gary: AGL was in all the papers and, really, on the back of CUB, Cascade and a host of other takeovers that we were making, that put IEL on the map. I think just the subtleties of getting to 41.5 per cent of a major listed entity without anyone knowing was fairly well regarded in the marketplace. That then brought us to Woolies, which was absolutely in disarray and we started buying stock. The market capitalisation of Woolworths was about $500 million or $600 million at the time.[9] We pounced right when it was on its knees.

You said earlier Woolworths was initially thought to be 'too good' for you. What made you actually commit to start buying shares?

Sir Ron: As I recall, I'd been on a trip to New Zealand and came back and discovered we'd bought 20 per cent of Woolworths, which I was quite pleased and surprised about. I said, 'Oh, I thought you said it was too good for us' and someone said, 'Oh well, that was yesterday'.

Gary: The person who made that statement was our chief investment analyst at the time, Peter Pedley, who is still a legendary character.

---

7   Sir Ron was finally appointed to the board of directors after his lengthy battle with AGL early in 1986. The stake was diluted back to around 30 per cent before being on-sold to investors in 1991.

8   AGL had a market capitalisation of $6.6 billion at the time of writing.

9   Woolworths's market capitalisation was more than $17 billion at the time of writing.

Peter had a firm view that companies that have gone about their business and done reasonably well, even if they were cheap, weren't appropriate targets for IEL. So when he made the comment he wasn't all that conscious, I think, that Woolworths had started on the slippery slope of really destroying value. But then I think he looked into it when it got down to quite reasonably attractive levels and was convinced that it was for us. They'd stuffed up in such a bad way that he regarded it as almost a public duty for us to get involved and restore Woolworths to its former glory.

What made you think it was worth a lot more than it was trading at? Is it purely that a good manager could run it better or were there assets there that weren't getting a good return?

Sir Ron: Woolworths was a very big property owner and had huge cash flow. Money just comes in over the counter, so that's a good start. The name Woolworths is not just famous in Australia, it's famous worldwide. [Our investment] was based on the most conventional analysis. It still didn't look all that cheap relative to the balance sheet but once you interpreted the balance sheet and costed in potential, it looked rather different. It was that instinct that proved to be absolutely right because it was worth $900 million [the share price went up as IEL accrued a stake], which, given Woolworths was essentially the same organisation although larger today, was a ridiculously low capitalisation.

Gary: Anyway, we started buying. The market got wind of our activity. By the time we'd bought about 2 or 3 per cent, we were reading in the newspapers that we were rumoured to be buying. The share price kicked up and no stock was flowing to us. Fairly soon thereafter, we had a call from someone, who shall remain nameless for the purposes of this publication, who said, 'Look, I've been offered some Woolworths shares. They're not of particular interest to us but would you like to buy them?' And it was someone, it would be fair to say, who was from a sort of establishment institution but with whom we had a very good relationship. I said, 'I would love to do that, thanks. Why don't you just book them in your nominee name, send us the contract note and we'll send you the cheque?' And they said, 'That sounds fine'.

The broker involved, again who shall remain nameless, but a household name, thought, 'I've got a buyer here, you know, an establishment sort of buyer, I'll see what else I can do'. So he rang around a number of the major holders of Woolies and said, 'Look, I've got this establishment institution ready to buy'. All these sellers wanted assurance that they weren't selling to IEL, which the broker faithfully gave. He knew nothing of our arrangement and within two days we'd bought 19.9 per cent of Woolworths. The institution kept ringing and saying, 'I've been offered another $5 million, another $10 million'. I'd say, 'Yeah, take them, take them.'

Why didn't the sellers want their shares to fall into IEL's hands?

Gary: AMP and other institutions didn't want to deliver Woolworths to us. Selling to a sort of quasi-establishment institution got them off the hook. After the second day, when we were about to notify our 19.9 per cent shareholding, I rang the broker and said, 'Look, I was just wondering whether you had five minutes to come up for a cup of coffee'. He replied, 'What's it about?' I said, 'Just come up. It could be very interesting'.

I took him into a room and I said, 'Now, I want to talk to you about the Woolworths shares you've been buying for us for the last two days'. And he said, 'I beg your pardon?' I said, 'Well, the shares that you thought you were buying for X are actually being bought for us'. This bloke went absolutely white. I said, 'Look, I'm going to leave you alone for five minutes. There's the phone if you want to ring your client; I'm sure they'll confirm it'. When I came back this bloke was absolutely shaken. We bid him farewell. Later that day we announced that we had 19.9 per cent of Woolworths.

That was the start and then there was another 20 per cent we ultimately bought through a fairly tortuous way but using our legal and technical skill base. Woolworths had another 20 per cent in Safeway. They sold their 20 per cent parcel to a company called Rainbow Corporation in New Zealand, which was a casualty of the 1987 crash. Then, in due course, BIL bid for Rainbow Corporation. In between, we bought control of a company in Queensland that had a few Woolworths shares. Within the loopholes, if you made a takeover bid for a company that effectively took you through 20 per cent because it owned shares in another company, somehow that cleansed it.

Sir Ron: We bought the company in New Zealand, which was purely a New Zealand deal so, after that, IEL had 20, BIL had 20. They were quite separate holdings but in reality we had over 40 per cent of Woolworths.[10]

I said, 'Well, look, that was a New Zealand deal, it's nothing to do with IEL', and that would have been legal. Bryan Frith, a financial commentator, went on and on about this — that we now had 40 per cent and therefore we'd effectively breached the 20 per cent shareholding limit and it shouldn't be allowed. We got into a huge wrangle, the sort of wrangle that only IEL could get into — and which I've been accused of actually provoking. But that's not true, is it Gary?

So, finally the NCSC [National Companies and Securities Commission] took legal action against IEL or against BIL, or against the two — against everyone. The judgement eventually was, yes, there had been a breach of the Act, which in my view was a poor judgement. That then set the situation for another stalemate — because the Act had been breached, but by no single party. But all together there had been a breach of the Act — a classic situation. It was a complete stalemate.

One day Rodney Price [IEL's chief executive] came into my office and said, 'If there was a proposal that we pay the corporate watchdog $1 million and made a takeover offer for the rest of Woolworths, you know, what would you think about that?' Of course, Rodney was half expecting me to say, 'No, I'm going to fight to the end, the judgement's wrong, you know, there's a point to be proved here'. But I said, 'Oh, that sounds great, let's do it'. $1 million in the Woolworths context was nothing really, a fraction of a cent a share. But this was a fantastic precedent — you've allegedly breached the Act, you just pay a franchise fee to the NCSC and away you go. I liked the principle. Rodney and I weren't having any arguments.

Gary: It's the exception to the rule, I can assure you.

Sir Ron: So there was a bit of argy bargy on that. Rodney paid them $1.1 million and we were cleansed on the basis that we bid for the rest of the company. Actually, this was close to Christmas as well and the so-called minority shareholders couldn't get in quick enough. There'd been all this wrangle about IEL getting control but when there was a bid for their shares, they couldn't accept quickly enough.

---

10 The takeover threshold is 20 per cent; therefore, if a company or individual buys more than 20 per cent of a company, they are required to launch a full takeover for all of the shares.

No consideration of the merits of staying in. Next thing we owned 100 per cent of Woolworths at an overall cost of $925 million.

And earlier, of course, we'd been caught in the middle of the crash. We actually wanted to bid for Woolworths but didn't really have the wherewithal to do it. I've been unfairly maligned in this respect because one of our people came up with innovative schemes to offer paper and options but really it didn't hit the spot. What it amounted to was people handing over their Woolworths scrip to IEL and getting back some lesser paper in return. It wasn't a goer and we had to bid cash. It was — apart from the Adsteam structure, apart from corporate governance, apart from ratings agencies, and one or two others — the greatest corporate hoax of the century, the IEL bid for Woolworths. Thanks very much — a, to Bryan Frith and, b, to the NCSC, as it then was.[11]

———————●———————

Sir Ron Brierley has spent much of the Southern Hemisphere winter watching the Ashes cricket series in the UK. Sir Ron rarely misses an opportunity to watch international cricket, even when his beloved New Zealand black caps are not involved. You get the feeling, though, that Sir Ron would love test matches more than one-day cricket. In fact, he would probably have a persuasion towards a whole test match series, if his cricket viewing replicates his investment style.

Unlike many of the professional investors in the Australian market, Guiness Peat Group has managed to escape the rigours of monthly performance reporting. Instead, the group invests for the very long term, taking each project on its merits, hoping, with a great degree

---

11　BIL/IEL won effective control of Woolworths in April 1987 after buying 32 per cent of New Zealand's Rainbow Corporation, which had earlier bought Safeway of the US's 19.9 per cent stake in Woolworths. This sparked an 18-month battle with the then National Companies and Securities Commission. In November 1988, IEL unveiled a full takeover bid for Woolworths, then Australia's second biggest retailer.

of research behind them, to turn underperforming companies into much better operations. The group's big investment in the UK-based textile business Coats is a work in progress. It has taken, and will continue to take, years to generate returns acceptable to the group, but they will persist and be rewarded if the end goal is achieved.

The same can be said for some of the group's other investments, such as Tower in New Zealand and Capral in Australia. However, Sir Ron and Gary Weiss like to play the game and, like a great cricket test match series, each session and each day has a new twist. In the end, however, it is the series result that matters and not every individual umpiring decision.

The one aspect investors can be sure of is that this approach will not change for as long as Sir Ron and Weiss remain captains of the team at Guiness Peat Group.

I have always been a great believer — and we were brought up in the old school — that if anything had a PE of twenty or above, it was getting pretty expensive.

6

Tried and tested
Jim and Robert Millner

As one of Australia's most established corporate empires, Washington H. Soul Pattinson has seen plenty of booms and survived plenty of busts, including the Great Depression. For those investors lucky enough to have held on for the ride, the empire has just got bigger and bigger. This continued growth from humble pharmacy origins has generated a fortune for both those investors and the family who controls its investment decisions, the Millners.

It has often been said that the Millner empire seems to be run like it is another era, but that probably reflects the fact that the family has always followed tried and tested investment principles — backing good management, not overpaying for assets and buying real businesses. The family's success has snowballed in recent years. When the first edition of *Masters of the Market* was published in 2003, the Millner fortune was estimated at $170 million. According to *Business Review Weekly*, in the period since the family's wealth has exploded to $539 million.

The Millner family's history is now reasonably well known, but is worth recounting. Jim Millner joined the family pharmacy business — founded in the 1800s by Caleb Soul and Lewy Pattinson — as a trainee in 1938. Any thoughts of an immediate business career were interrupted by World War II and his subsequent capture by the Japanese after the Fall of Singapore. Rather than emerge forlorn after the hardships of a prisoner of war camp, Millner was energised and set about reinvigorating the group's core pharmacy business on his return.

Seeing the trends offshore, Jim led the evolution of the pharmacy chain into a broader retail offering, despite the long-standing laws and restrictions around pharmacy ownership (lasting to this day) that made the task difficult. Success breeds success for the Millners, and Jim wisely began to invest the proceeds on building a diversified investment empire. One of Jim's greatest investments was undoubtedly Brickworks, still held to this day — despite the occasional attempts by corporate raiders (most recently Sir Ron Brierley) to seize control of the business.

Jim, a man of few words but great determination, also made a lot of money by buying mining shares during the 1960s resources boom. Over the decades, the group's interests expanded to coal, including the Adaro mine in Indonesia, and television, with Newcastle-based television station NBN purchased cheaply from a distressed 1980s entrepreneur. In all cases, Millner saw value and bought cheaply, using the cash flow from one investment to buy another. At the same time, he gradually accumulated a broader investment portfolio through investing in stocks across the market, never assuming he could make a fortune overnight.

The odd corporate controversy just made the group stronger. For years, the Millners defied calls to unlock the cross-shareholding relationship between Brickworks and Soul Pattinson, and that structure still stands and continues to insulate it from takeover.

Given Jim didn't have children, the challenge for the next generation of Millners fell on the shoulders of Robert Millner, Jim's nephew. Robert took over the chairmanship of Soul Pattinson in 1998 (another nephew of Jim's, Michael, is also on the group's boards) and has since managed to take the empire to new heights.

Still, Soul Pattinson hasn't lost the sense of tradition that can sometimes give the casual observer the impression that the group is operating in a timewarp. As such, the group can be easily underestimated. The group's investment strategy looks disarmingly simple, perhaps explaining why it hasn't attracted the kind of following from institutional investors that other companies of a similar size have.

The group's approach to investing still looks incredibly simple, but the group's structure is such that its tentacles now spread throughout the Australian business scene. Like his uncle, Robert has clearly put his stamp on the group. Robert has released hidden value in a number of assets, taking advantage of times when certain types of assets were popular with investors.

Spin-offs from the Soul Pattinson empire in recent years have included the health products group Clover, telecommunications and media company SP Telemedia, coalminer New Hope Corporation and listed investment company Brickworks Investment Company. One of the biggest changes in the portfolio came under Robert when the old pharmacy business was vended into drug wholesaler Australian Pharmaceutical Industries in return for a 25 per cent stake. While this investment has had some difficulties, Soul Pattinson is again instrumental in the evolution of the pharmacy trade as API creates a new retail format in preparation for another assault on the industry from the likes of retail giant Woolworths. The Millners have truly earned their place among Australia's great industrialists and investors.

Soul Pattinson is now more than ever a pure investment company and, as well as setting up a separately listed investment company, it also has a specialist funds management company seeking funds from outside the Soul Pattinson empire.

We spoke to Robert in Soul Pattinson's newly refurbished offices above the original Soul Pattinson pharmacy in Sydney's Pitt Street Mall.

———————●———————

How have Soul Pattinson and your related companies fared in the two years since we interviewed you for the first edition of Masters of the Market*?*

Obviously, with our family companies we don't benchmark anything. With a lot of the companies [controlled by Souls], when we have surplus cash we reinvest that in the —————— businesses. That's particularly so in the various Souls operations but also with Brickworks, SP Telecommunications and New Hope Corporation — we reinvest the dividends.

When we have surplus cash we reinvest that in the businesses.

In Soul Pattinson, for the twelve months ended 31 December 2004, if you include Brickworks, we made a return of 60.14 per cent and, if you take Brickworks out of that, you get 67.63 per cent.

So that's the share portfolio within Souls?

That includes all of our equities within the Souls portfolio. As at the end of April, Souls had about $370 million invested outside of our operating businesses such as API and Brickworks. But if you take the whole lot, including Brickworks, Clover and so on, it's about $2.2 billion. We have had a very, very good twelve months. Mind you, everyone did, didn't they?

But you still outperformed the index quite comfortably.

New Hope had a wonderful year and, obviously, we had a lot of shares in BHP Billiton and WMC Resources [since taken over by BHP]. The banks all went up.

With Brickworks in or Brickworks out of it — either way, we have more than doubled what the market's done.

So what was the best call you made?

For the past twelve months in Souls, Macquarie Airports was our best returning stock. For two years, it's up about 273 per cent and for one year, it's 92 per cent. Next best was WMC Resources.

Were they stocks you always held?

We haven't had Macquarie Airports for that long, obviously. We took those up in the initial float and bought some more when they were unpopular shortly after listing. Another good stock for us was

Hills Motorway — obviously, thanks to the takeover [by Transurban in early 2005]. Over two years it is up 111 per cent and 70 per cent over one year. New Hope, of course, has done well.

Why did you see them as good investments at the time?

We have done very well out of all of our investments in the Macquarie Group over the years. We have had Macquarie Bank shares virtually from day one. Our initial cost was $1.7 million and now at the end of April they were worth $9 million. We have had Macquarie Infrastructure Group, which we have more than doubled our money on since we bought, mostly at the initial float. When Macquarie Airports came up, we thought they were great assets [Sydney Airport].

With WMC Resources (formerly Western Mining Corporation), we have held it for many years, as we mentioned in the first book.

It must have been a little sad to see it taken over this year by BHP Billiton.

I was happier that BHP got it than Xstrata. Olympic Dam is a great asset and you don't want to see those assets sold off overseas. We haven't got much left in the resources sector. Everybody's in agreement that it [WMC] hasn't been terribly well managed over the years. They have made a lot of boo-boos but to get in with the low base that we did, it has still been a very good investment for us.

Can you run through your worst investments?

Everyone has investments that don't perform too well. Our worst investment, unfortunately, is one of ours [in the family of Souls-related companies] and that's Clover. It's come back. It was floated at 30¢ and got to highs of 66¢ to 67¢. It's a biotech and a lot of biotechs have fallen out of favour. However, in the past six months it has increased its profit from its previous six months and paid a final dividend the year before. Unfortunately, with biotechs investors want to see announcements every week to keep it front of mind.

Our second worst one was Lindsay Brothers. We took a stake in Lindsay Brothers when they floated. We have a relationship via Brickworks. They are our agents in Port Macquarie and Coffs Harbour and we have a very close relationship with them that goes back a long way. Both Brickworks and Souls took stakes in that float when it came on. Obviously, the higher price of fuel has knocked them around and some of their business in the south of the state was hurt by the drought.

The other poor one has been Wattyl, which we have been a long-time investor in. We did take a bit off the top a few years ago but they seem to have gone from one disaster to another over the years. I don't think they have ever recovered from the ACCC telling them they couldn't do the Taubmans merger deal. They raced over to America and tore up their money there.

So they are our three worst — unfortunately, when you have a large investment portfolio you always have a couple.

What do you think the future holds for a company like Wattyl?

I don't think it's been managed particularly well for a long time. They probably haven't cut their costs as much as they should have done. Again depending on what the ACCC allows people to do, I would think that someone would probably take them over because there will be a certain price where it will be a bargain for somebody. It comes back to management. They have had quite a bit of management change.

Even as we speak the managing director Ian Jackson has resigned and there have been nearly a handful of people in the job in the past five years.

> *We have always maintained we are long-term but, if you have cash around, you can move in those times where the market dips.*

Do you think the recent weakness in the market throws up a lot of opportunities?[1]

Yes. Stocks like Coca-Cola have certainly been knocked around in the past week. Tabcorp's another one. We have always maintained we are long-term but, if you have cash around, you can move in those times where the market dips.

How much cash would you be holding?

Souls always has a lot of cash. The family companies are always well cashed up so we can always move quickly if we want to do something. It is always important to have cash. I can remember in 1987 when the stockmarket crashed, we went to the Union Club to have lunch. Everyone had their head in their hands and some

---

1   The Australian sharemarket dipped in April and May before a share recovery.

were almost crying. We had a wonderful morning because we were buying. We had cash. We could move quickly.

What do you think the best performing sectors or asset classes will be?

The results for the banks have come out recently and again their results have been excellent and they have put their dividends up more than the market was expecting. You look at the yields and they are 5 per cent or better.

I think the resources sector will run on a bit longer. I know from our experience in the coal mining business our prices are locked in at least until April next year [2006]. The iron ore prices have been settled so people have twelve months' profits coming out of the resources stocks. I think they look good at least for the next twelve months or so. And oil does not want to go down.

If you go back and have a look, there's probably five or six points as to why we have had this resources boom. We have not had one of these since the late 1960s or early 1970s. We have had a lack of investment. Most of the mining companies have been run like industrial companies, where you are being paid 40 to 50 per cent out as dividends, whereas years ago — thirty or forty years ago — if you bought a mining stock, you never received a dividend. All of their money went back into exploration. There's been a huge shortage of money spent on exploration. The shipping industry three or four years ago was at rock bottom. No-one spent any money on ships for a long, long time, so you have had this sudden turnaround with not enough ships to cart the commodities around. Shipping rates have gone through the roof. And there's been low stocks. Inventory around the world of nearly everything has dwindled. There's been port restraints, particularly for coal exports, which I probably know a bit more about than some of the other commodities. Both here and in South Africa there's been constraints on ports — Richards Bay in South Africa; Newcastle and Darymple Bay in Australia.

But I know what's going to happen. As soon as everyone spends money on infrastructure over the next three to four years, it will increase the capacity by another five to ten million tonnes and those are the times you get oversupply. That will put pressure on prices.

The cycle is well and truly alive.

Of course it is. Again you have China coming on and Asia, which has seemed to lurch from one disaster to another — whether it be tsunamis or meltdowns or Bali bombings — it hasn't had much going for it for a long time. And then you have India coming through.

Obviously, in the Soul Patts group with our interests in New Hope we have done extremely well there. Again, we have large exposures to BHP and WMC; we have never been a big Rio Tinto holder but we have shares like Iluka that have done well and we are quite large shareholders in Woodside.

In relation to movements in interest rates, how will they affect your investment approach?

I don't think it will be affected because if you are a long-term investor, you are going to have periods of high interest rates. High interest rates are good for us in a lot of ways because we have always had cash. If you can get 7 or 8 per cent for your money rather than 4 per cent, it's going to add a lot of value to your wealth as well.

Unfortunately, we go through these cycles. When interest rates are high, you are a lender; when interest rates are low, you are a borrower. Anyone who can lock some money in for five or seven years is going to be in good stead when interest rates rise. Unfortunately, it's just going to be one of those cycles we go through. We seem to get it every five to ten years. If you have a lot of holdings in banks, that is good because they tend to make more money in a higher interest rate environment.

I have been fortunate to go to China in the past twelve months. The first time I went there I was absolutely staggered. I thought I was in Singapore. This was in a place called Xiamen City, which is in the Fujian Province. We are looking at a joint venture there with our pharmaceutical operations in Malaysia. The interesting thing about China relates to some interesting figures that came out of the US after the Second World War. In the US, people built houses and in the house they had electricity and as they became more affluent they had airconditioning and heaters, TV sets, fridges and freezers, with an increase in demand for power. China is going through this now as they are getting out of where they used to live and into apartments or houses, and that's one of the reasons for the demand for steel and iron ore and things like that. China used to be a net exporter of coal. That's one of the reasons the price of coal has jumped because now they are needing to import.

So what else impressed you about China while you were there?

The sheer development of the infrastructure was frightening. When they are building new areas they design four or five lane highways to start with. There are magnificent bridges and huge shopping centres that have popped up and huge department developments.

I may have been a bit naive — I didn't know what to expect because over the years I had heard a lot of sad stories about China where people haven't made a lot of money. They have gone in there and not been able to be paid in hard currency. People have wanted to pay them in cut glass and this sort of thing. But going around and actually seeing things, it is quite frightening. In places like Shanghai and Beijing, which are bigger, all of the big multinationals like Kodak and so on are there.

Do you think Australian companies will make money in China?

Some will. I think you still need to do some sort of joint venture. It's important in most Asian countries to have some local knowledge with you, so you are not a 'white knight' and you have people with local experience knowing the way their system works.

Is there a single issue you think is going to drive the Australian sharemarket higher or lower over the next few years?

That's a hard one and it depends on cycles. We need to be very careful here in that we have had such an extremely good run where it hasn't been uncommon for companies to report 20 to 40 per cent increases in profits, and some of that has been done two or three halves in a row. Particularly, the younger people in the market are not accustomed to companies reporting more normal earnings growth. In normal times, if a company produced profits that were up 8 to 10 to 12 per cent each half, you would jump up and down and pat yourself on the back. Coca-Cola at a recent Macquarie Bank conference said it was going to have low double-digit profits. To me, that's fantastic. If you do that twice a year, your shareholders should be very happy. But the market slammed the shares down around 6 per cent. I think we need to get back to a bit of reality here. Things can't go up and up forever. The PEs are pretty stretched.

I have always been a great believer — and we were brought up in the old school — that if anything had a PE of twenty or above, it was getting pretty expensive. If you look through *The Australian Financial Review* or IRESS [Market Technology], a lot of companies are trading at PEs of more than twenty times.

I think it's a time for caution.

But are you generally optimistic about the sharemarket over a long-term horizon?

Unless something bizarre happens to the western world. Australia's economy has been well managed. The 2.5 to 3 per cent growth forecast being talked about is quite reasonable in the western world. Obviously, we don't get the growth that the Asian economies do. They grow by 7 or 8 per cent, but if we can grow by 2.5 to 3.5 per cent, that will be acceptable — we have some issues such as debt and you have to remember we have been through an horrific drought, probably the worst drought in history, and it's still continuing. We have some rural interests and so does David Fairfull, who sits on the board of Souls. We all have rural interests and it's been frightening in the past four or five years.

I have heard of people in the West Wyong/Condoblin area who haven't had a wheat crop in three years — how much longer can they keep going? I have an irrigation block of my own and I haven't had water for two years.

At the end of the day, we are a commodity-exporting country and primary production is a part of it. It's not only iron ore and coal, it's primary production.

Do you see similarities between the current resources rally and the resources boom of the 1960s?

It's the most sustained commodity price rise since the 1960s and early 1970s. The profits that New Hope are generating for Souls at the moment are unbelievable and are locked in for another twelve months.

You are getting US$52 a tonne for coal whereas two or three years ago, it was US$25 or US$27. The price has doubled in the last twelve months — that's thermal coal. Coking coal has done even better than that. Some of the coking coal boys have been getting over US$125 a tonne. That's been a wonderful thing for both the family companies and Soul Pattinson. As I mentioned earlier, our exposure in the family companies is probably not as big as it once was because some of the family companies need to pay dividends to family members. They, like shareholders, like to get an increased dividend every year.

When you talk about the family members, how many are there?

On Jim's side, he had two brothers, including my father. Jim doesn't have his own family. But there's my father, and with Michael's side, there's six children. The six have all gone on and had two or three children, so it's expanding. That's the way we run the family companies. We give them dividends rather than give them big handouts in cash. Unfortunately, if family members get their hands on big wads of cash, they will often go out and buy a boat or a car and the next minute their inheritance is gone in one bad investment. So we have been great believers in paying some good dividend income so we can do a few things and we can go on a few trips or pay off some loans. I know it's old-fashioned.

Do you look after all of the family's affairs?

Jim used to do it. He was the governing director but now I have taken over that role. It takes a reasonable amount of my time.

What does the role of governing director involve?

Obviously, we need to sign proxies and things like that and decide whether to be involved in rights issues or placements. It's easier to have one person making the decision rather than have all the family members signing things. It's all for the sake of ease really. They are all shareholders of the family company.

You have been actively spinning off Soul's big investments into separately listed companies — examples being SP Telecommunications, New Hope Coal and Brickworks Investment Company. Why have you done this?

The main reason why we have done this is we have been criticised for a long time within the Soul Patts/Brickworks group for being too conservative and not doing enough for our shareholders.

With the higher market and confidence in the industry, we thought the best way of creating shareholder value was to spin off some of these assets into the public arena. The first one we did was Clover

Corporation. We offered that to shareholders at 30¢ each and they also got a free one-for-ten option. Those shares have traded up to a high of 66¢ so there has been plenty of opportunity for Clover shareholders to do well out of that. Unfortunately, the shares are trading below that at the moment but shareholders had the opportunity if they want to cash out of them.

The next one we did was SP Telemedia. It has gone from strength to strength. It now has a market capitalisation of more than $650 million. Again that was floated at 25¢ with a one-for-ten option. Those shares rose to a high of $2.40 and at the moment they are about $1.80. They have been paying dividends twice a year. That company has done extremely well. We sold the NBN assets into that company last year, which created a $100 million profit for Soul Pattinson. Souls was then able to use some of that money to pay special dividends to its shareholders.

Again, we had been criticised and I shudder to think how many times we had been asked what we were going to do with our franking credits. I said to them the time will come when we can utilise those franking credits and that was one of those times. We announced two special dividends out of that NBN sale. One was paid in November last year and the another will be paid in November this year. So that's been a wonderful investment for Soul Pattinson shareholders.

Can you explain why NBN ended up as part of the SP Telemedia business rather than you selling the business to another media organisation?

Going forward, you are going to find in the media game that you will receive a bundled package through your telecommunications provider. NBN was virtually run by the same management that was running SP Telecommunications [which became SP Telemedia], so it was commonsense to put it together. We have been able to do a joint venture with WIN Television. They are also the largest Nine Network affiliate. So it's a wonderful way of advertising your product. Even during the Olympic Games in Sydney, Seven did not have 100 per cent rate cards. When you have empty spots, you are able to put a Kooee ad[2] or a SP Telemedia ad in, so it seemed commonsense to put them together.

---

2   Kooee is a telecommunications company owned by B Digital, which formed an alliance with SP Telemedia in late 2004.

Going forward with this Voice over Internet Protocol [VoIP] and all these other products coming onto the market, you will be able to bundle products for the customer a lot more. They have also gone onto buy the Comindico network, the second largest [broadband] network in Australia, and just done a deal with B-Digital that provides us with mobile phones. We can now offer the full package to corporates and government whereas we couldn't before. That's been a wonderful investment.

The other one was New Hope Corporation, which spun out. It was the most recent one. There were 40¢ shares with a one-for-ten option. Those shares have been up to $1.70 and the company paid dividends and we have had an offer for our Indonesian operations. That will give New Hope $500 million cash. It's a consortium of buyers out of Singapore. Some of the shareholders in that operation are going to stay in. Temasek, the Singaporean Government superannuation vehicle is there, as is Robert Kuok and Favalon, a large US fund manager. Obviously, New Hope won't need that cash but Soul, with 64 per cent of New Hope, will probably get their hands on a large chunk of that. Again, Soul shareholders can expect another special dividend in one form or another.

Why did you sell?

We own around 41 per cent of the operations up there and we have a very good relationship with our shareholders. Some of them wanted to take profits at the top of the market and we didn't want to get locked into a minority situation with someone we didn't know and didn't trust in a place like Indonesia. The company has no debt up there and we have very little capital gains tax to pay.

You're not worried about getting out too early?

Who knows?

What is the future for the rest of New Hope with its remaining Queensland coal mining operations?

We developed a new mine called Acland two years ago. We have approval there now for two and a half million tonnes, which we are mining to capacity. We now have approval to take that to four million. We are exploring for other deposits in Queensland. We have been for some time. We are going to have $200 million to $300 million sitting in our back pocket.

These commodity prices won't last forever so we will be in a very strong position to do something (if they fall). At this stage, we will concentrate on Australia. We own our own port in Brisbane. Our Queensland coal operations will grow and grow and grow going forward.

You have also created your own listed investment company called Brickworks Investment Company.

We spun that out of Brickworks after we took over Bristile. Again that portfolio was made up of surplus cash over the years so we utilised that to give Brickworks $120 million in cash, which we put towards the Bristile takeover. We also offered opportunities for Brickworks and Souls shareholders to participate in that and it has done very well. That was listed at $1.00. The shares have been up to about $1.20 and they are paying a fully franked dividend. Brickworks still owns a percentage of that.[3]

So if you go through and add it all up, I think the shareholders have done very well.

Despite these spin-offs, you have still maintained an interlocking shareholding between Brickworks and Soul Patts. Do you anticipate that continuing over the long term?[4]

Well, at this stage I can see no reason to change. If you look at the performance of both companies, they are up 15 and 16 per cent per annum. I don't know where else you would get an investment like that.

It is complicated and it makes it hard for people but they have been good investments. And it will show through in their next set of results. Brickworks makes about two-thirds of its earnings from clay products and it is now the largest clay producer in Australia by some considerable distance. When there are downturns, it has income from Soul Pattinson to still be able to pay increased dividends to Brickworks' shareholders. I think that's very important. You will see, when some of the other building companies are struggling to maintain dividends, we will still be able to increase dividends.

---

3   Brickworks owns 25 per cent of Brickworks Investment Company, a listed investment company.

4   The interlocking shareholding structure is such that Washington H. Soul Pattinson owns 49.8 per cent of Brickworks, while Brickworks owns 42.85 per cent of Soul Patts.

I think at the end of the day if we all got bored, we could probably sit down and look at whether there are advantages for both companies in breaking the shareholding up, but at the moment we are very happy. We are creating more value for shareholders by keeping it all together.

SP Telecommunications has been another successful investment for you — in fact, it is one of the few smaller telecommunications companies that is making profits. Why has it done so well?

We are regionally based. You don't have the same competition that you have in the large capital cities. We are in the capital cities, but not to the same extent as others. Once you get into regional Australia you only have Telstra as a competitor. Optus is there in a small way but you don't have Vodafone, Virgin, Hutchison Telecoms and other players that are tinkering around the side. It's virtually only us and Telstra. Comindico spent $400 million building their network but we bought it from the receivers for $27 million and it is the most modern network in Australia.

Overall, you seem quite confident about the long-term investment environment.

Having cash is always important and, as we mentioned last time, we bought Commonwealth Bank at $23 or $24. We topped up at a time when no-one wanted to own banks and if you look at it now, it's up to $35 and in four years we have probably picked up $4 to $5 worth of dividends. Those sorts of examples highlight what we do when the market falls.

Something else we are concentrating on in the Soul Pattinson group, and it is important for our employees and our shareholders, is the superannuation market, which has not been successful for a lot of investors. I think people need to focus more long term, particularly our children. Ours are in their early twenties and they couldn't care less about what happens to sharemarket indices in the next three months or so.

We need to get some sort of stability into the superannuation market. For example, one of the superannuation funds of a large insurance company only earned 3 per cent last year, when the sharemarket returned 22 per cent. How can someone only get a 3 per cent return? It's not right because people are playing with other people's money. It's a poor return. How are they going to fare in a downturn?

I am showing my interest here as chairman of listed investment companies, but I think LICs are going to have a large part to play in the industry because they are run at a very low cost. There's no great outperformance fees. They pay a fully franked dividend. Their fees are 0.2 per cent or 0.3 per cent. If you look at some of the funds, their fees are much higher and if you look at some of these new investment companies, they have come out with ridiculous performance fees. At the end of the day, it's people's money and it should be cared for and fostered carefully because when they retire they want to see a nice amount of money.

A lot of people only have a few thousand or less to invest each quarter so if they go to a broker or a fund manager, they are not going to get exposure to a lot of different stocks. If you go and buy shares in Milton, Argo Investments, Choiseul or Brickworks Investment Company, you are going to get exposure to a spread of resources and industrial stocks — and you know you are going to get a fully franked dividend twice a year. In a super fund, that is a great way to reinvest. That's something I am keen to focus on. We have 3500 employees in the Souls group. I am concerned for them.

We have established Souls Funds Management, through which we are running the Souls super fund. It's not rocket science. It's simple long-term investing. The money shouldn't be churning every quarter or every half because it doesn't fit in some index — to me it's not right. I know it's an 'old fogy' way of thinking but, at the end of the day, people are playing with other people's money, and not terribly successfully at times.

If you or I had money in a fund that earned 3 per cent, you wouldn't be happy and you would be looking for other options.

Jim can't join us for the interview but can you tell us how he is?

He's in his eighty-sixth year — he was born in 1919. His mind's still very good. He reads the newspaper every day and *The Economist* every week. But he's not too good on his pins. His mobility's not too good. I guess when you consider what he's been through, though, he is very tough. He doesn't smoke anymore.

When did he give up smoking?

He gave it up a couple of years ago when he was crook.

What do you put his strength and longevity down to?

Genes, I suppose. Both my grandfather and my grandmother — on Jim and my father's side — lived to their hundreth year. I can remember my grandfather in his nineties used to smoke and I never heard him cough.

In terms of your stock selection, do you meet with management of the companies before you invest?

Things have changed in the last couple of years. Obviously, I get a lot of broking research and, being chairman of Milton and Choiseul, I meet with the investment committee most weeks. Also Souls Funds Management, which I am chairman of, manages Brickworks Investment Company and has $500 million in funds. I keep up to speed there. I get updates from them and when the reporting season is on we have people running around everywhere going to company presentations. If I can, I try to go as well.

How many people are involved in investing the group's funds?

I still do Soul Pattinson's investing on my own and I talk to the directors each month. We have what we call the bible, which each director gets with all of the stocks and what we have bought or sold. We talk about that at each board meeting. In the funds management company [Souls Funds Management], I think they have far too many people servicing the amount of money they do. I look after more money than they do on my own. I probably get a better return because there are no performance fees. But you need to have people in place before the gatekeepers give you money. At Milton, we have analysts there.

Most of the companies we want to invest in we know anyway. On IRESS, I have a list of companies I look at every day.

Given the way your business has changed in recent years, do you trade more regularly rather than buy and hold?

No. We have a small trading portfolio. Sometimes it doesn't go well. In Soul's trading portfolio we have probably got $2 million to $3 million to play around with. We do well sometimes but not always.

But that's trading. You need to have some sort of trading portfolio and when you are dealing with brokers all the time, sometimes you may need to take some stocks you might not like to get the good ones.

This year we have made $300 000 out of share trading — last year we made $197 000.

I must admit I am not a very good trader. I may not sell as quickly as I should. In trading, you should sometimes sell a stock for $1.10 rather than wait and try to get $1.15 out of it.

In trading, you should sometimes sell a stock for $1.10 rather than wait and try to get $1.15 out of it.

Washington H. Soul Pattinson retains all the trappings of an enterprise from another era. Despite this, it has managed to combine investments in its long-held traditional businesses like brick-making with new-age businesses like telecommunications, while at the same time maintaining a large and diversified share portfolio. The Millners are not averse to a flutter but the trading portfolio only ever represents a small part of their overall portfolio, such that there is never significant capital at risk.

The Millners have developed an appreciation of what a good business is — often with what seems like a fairly simple assessment of its prospects — while being extremely opportunistic in buying these assets from distressed sellers or at times when the general investment climate is poor. Once they have got their hands on these assets, the Millners have shown a canny knack of adding value by identifying growth opportunities that previous management may not have contemplated.

Our basic philosophy hasn't changed at all. Our approach to investing is still fundamentally based on a value investment approach. We look at the fundamentals of the business, focus on management and make an assessment of where the company could go in its market. If we think companies have the characteristics and the aspirations to go a long way, those are the companies we choose to back.

7

The chief

Alex Waislitz

Alex Waislitz is perhaps best known as the son-in-law of Richard Pratt, the cardboard box king and Melbourne's richest man. The 2005 *BRW* Rich 200 rich list estimated that Pratt was worth $4.2 billion, equal second in Australia with Westfield's Frank Lowy. What is not commonly known is that a large chunk of Pratt's burgeoning wealth in recent years has been achieved by Waislitz and the investments he has made through the Pratt-owned Thorney Group.

Thorney was established on a part-time basis in late 1991 when Waislitz convinced Pratt to seed a sharemarket investment company with $1.15 million. The seed money was ironically the direct result of Pratt selling shares his family owned in his great cardboard box rival Amcor. In the first year, Waislitz's trading managed to grow the original investment to $4 million — $7 million by the end of year two. While building a capital base, Waislitz honed his own investment style. Given the relatively small amount of capital he was managing at that time, he focused on small companies that had reasonable track records, good growth prospects and, above all, good people. Unlike institutional fund managers, Thorney is prepared to put its own representatives on the board of investee companies and back management by taking large equity positions. This approach is different from most fund managers because the

Pratt family is putting only its own money at risk, not managing external funds. As a result, there are no management fees, leaving Thorney to concentrate solely on absolute returns.

Waislitz has latched onto numerous success stories. Thorney hit the jackpot when it backed Simon Rowell and his team at the junior food company Dollar Sweets (later renamed Snack Foods). Thorney helped Dollar Sweets purchase Pepsi's snack food division by underwriting the purchase and taking a 32 per cent stake into the company. Thorney's average purchase price was around 40¢, eventually selling out when Snack Foods was taken over by the Arnotts/Campbells group for $2 a share. Waislitz had delivered a profit close to $80 million on the deal.

Today, Thorney's net worth is reportedly in excess of $600 million, a testament to Waislitz's success and Pratt's confidence in his son-in-law's investing ability.

Waislitz is the son of post-Holocaust Jewish migrants. He was born in Australia and his parents worked long hours to establish themselves in Australia. His father, David, eventually found success in property and is now a wealthy man in his own right. For the last five or six years, David has worked with Alex to build Thorney's burgeoning property portfolio.

Alex graduated as a lawyer but decided against a career in that field. While travelling overseas in his early twenties, he managed to snare a job with Bell Group, the investment vehicle of Australia's most famous entrepreneur of the 1980s, Robert Holmes à Court. The position, based in New York, saw Waislitz help Bell Group become a player in the world's largest economy. Waislitz worked closely with Holmes à Court and his right-hand man Alan Newman from 1985 until after the 1987 sharemarket crash. In that time, Waislitz watched Holmes à Court mastermind his daring raid to gain control of Australia's largest company, BHP. After the crash the Bell Group was forced to wind back its operations and virtually close down. Waislitz returned to Australia when Holmes à Court died in 1990, and it was then that Waislitz starting working for Pratt and his cardboard box company, Visy. Not long afterwards Waislitz was dating Pratt's daughter Heloise and they were soon married.

Waislitz actively supports Heloise in her role as chair of The Pratt Foundation, one of Australia's largest sources of private philanthropy. Two years ago, the couple launched another program specifically designed to undertake charitable activities in partnership with the organisations and individuals with whom Thorney does business. Outside of business and philanthropy, Waislitz has held a number of community positions, most notably board membership of the Collingwood Football Club.

When we last spoke to Waislitz in 2003, the Thorney group was riding high on the success of several highly profitable investments such as in the caravan manufacturer Fleetwood and in publishing and homewares group McPherson's. Two years on, with the Australian sharemarket enjoying its strongest bull market since the mid-1980s, Waislitz is still buoyant and optimistic about Thorney's future.

For the most part, he has not changed the group's investment style despite significant growth in recent years. Waislitz concentrates on emerging companies with a decent track record and good growth prospects. This time around, he emphasises above all else the importance of backing good management with time, resources and, of course, capital. We spoke with Waislitz in July 2005.

How have you faired in the bull market of the last two years?

We have comfortably outperformed the market.

What has been your best investment of the last two years and why did you make that investment?

Baxter is probably one of them. I think we bought in at $2.35 and it reached a peak of around $6.00 a share, but has recently come back to around $5.00 a share. We recently exercised some options and own about 13 per cent of the company.[1]

Baxter had and still has good prospects. It has a major resource being a landfill site in the south-east Melbourne corridor, which is a high growth area of Melbourne. The company has the appropriate licenses to operate the landfill and those are very difficult to obtain

---

1   Baxter, a waste management company, has a market capitalisation of approximately $200 million.

and are a scarce commodity. We think the whole area of how we deal with our waste is a growing challenge.

One other stock that has performed well for us in recent times has been one of our longest held companies — the mining services group Monodelphous (up 240 per cent in the last two years). We've been supporters of Monodelphous for almost ten years and have had an excellent relationship with management. We like their business model, strategic approach and ability to attract and retain good people. We also like the fact that its founder and CEO, John Rubino, owns a sizeable amount of the equity and is committed to the company's success. We increased our holding in Monodelphus going into the resources boom. At current prices our stake is worth about $30 million on an effective cost base after dividends of zero.

Other strong performers have been Caltex (up 479 per cent), traffic light operator Redflex (up 412 per cent), Consolidated Minerals (up 370 per cent), conglomerate Washington H. Soul Pattinson (up 61 per cent) and caravan manufacturer Fleetwood (up 70 per cent).

We have also managed to identify certain sectors that have performed extremely well in this period. We saw structured finance as a great growth area to be in. Australia has proven to be a world leader in technically advanced financial structures and this has been supported by a growing appetite from superannuation funds for new asset classes, particularly infrastructure. We have identified the entrepreneurial skills of the team at Macquarie Bank, David Coe at Allco/Record Investments, Phil Green at Babcock & Brown, Bill Ireland at Marriner and Mike Tilley at Challenger, and have taken advantage of this part of the market and made some excellent profits.

An area where we have taken a contrarian view and performed well has been in the coal sector. Coal is a very cyclical business and a few years back was terribly out of favour and valuations were historically cheap. In the last two years, the cycle has changed with the emergence of China and India as industrialising countries. Among other impacts of this have been huge purchases of coal. For us, Centennial Coal, Gloucester Coal and Austral Coal have delivered great returns.

What has been the worst investment?

Our worst investment has been the direct marketing home shopping network company TVSN chaired by Ron Baskin and run by CEO Rob

Hunt. At first we thought it was a good story as the business model had been very successful overseas. Initially we believed TVSN was much further advanced in its restructuring and turnaround than it turned out to be.

The experience underscores how important it is to not only get the thematic right but to go beyond that, to do deep due diligence into the organisation and not rely just on what a few people who are promoting the story are saying. You must get right down into things like stock controls and looking at the debtors and creditors, closely analysing the cash flow and all the basics of the business. Whenever we have researched things to the utmost degree, we've had more success than the other way around.

> *The experience underscores how important it is to not only get the thematic right but to go beyond that, to do deep due diligence into the organisation and not rely just on what a few people who are promoting the story are saying.*

We're trying to recover our loss of around $6 to $7 million through the receivers. We believe we have grounds to recover a fair amount of this money but it's still a painful lesson and will be a painful process.

Is the current environment a good one for investing?

I think what we've seen in the early part of 2005 is a realignment of the market after a couple of very strong years. The market and the analysts were pricing companies and putting price/earnings multiples on a perfect economy going forward for another few years and that, obviously, is not sustainable.

What has been interesting to see is how easy it is for prices to come off, particularly in the medium- and small-cap range, as liquidity dries up. Usually what happens is it gets overdone and it can present buying opportunities. The price falls can be exacerbated if any of the small-cap fund managers find they have redemptions in their funds and are required to raise cash in a less than orderly fashion [such as through selling shares to raise cash].

This could be particularly opportunistic this time around because most companies' balance sheets are in very good order, their gearing levels are modest and therefore their ability to pay dividends and undergo capital management initiatives such as stock buybacks and special dividends is quite robust — probably more so than at any other time in the last decade.

While being interviewed, Waislitz adds a story that he likes to tell people when they ask him how the sharemarket operates. Waislitz's grandfather was an actor and the tradition of storytelling has been handed down in the family.

A tribe of Indians in Canada went to their chief to ask how cold the upcoming winter would be so they could prepare by collecting the right amount of wood. The chief told the tribe that it would be a cold winter and so the tribe went out and starting collecting wood to keep them warm when winter arrived.

The next week the tribe decided to again ask the chief whether the winter would be cold and again he said he thought it would be cold. So the tribe went out again and collected more wood. About this time, the chief thought he would call on the local meteorologist to find out if in fact his feeling about it being cold was correct. The meteorologist told the chief it was indeed going to be a very cold winter.

Another week passed and winter was fast approaching. The tribe asked the chief a third time if he thought it was going to be a cold winter. For a third time he said it was going to be cold. Off went the tribe and collected more wood.

In the meantime, the chief went back to the meteorologist to ask how cold it would be.

The meteorologist said he thought it would be the coldest winter on record. The chief asked him why he was so sure and he said, 'You know it's going to be cold when the Indians are collecting as much wood as they can'.

There is probably more than one lesson to be learnt from the above story but, in essence, Waislitz is saying that much of what is in the market is simply hearsay (often self-generated) and rarely based on facts. Listening to such hearsay can bring you undone. Instead of listening to market whispers, it is far more fruitful to do your homework and come to your own conclusions. Back to the interview.

Has Thorney's investment style changed since we spoke two years ago?

Our basic philosophy hasn't changed at all. Our approach to investing is still fundamentally based on a value investment approach. We look at the fundamentals of the business, focus on management and make an assessment of where the company could go in its market. If we think companies have the characteristics and the aspirations to go a long way, those are the companies we choose to back.

That said, we did modify our tactics over the last few years to take advantage of the bull market. The bull market resulted in a tremendous number of initial public offerings and placements and other types of capital raisings. There has been a lot of momentum and we made sure that we participated in this momentum-driven activity, and that has been a very successful initiative for us.

> *We look at the fundamentals of the business, focus on management and make an assessment of where the company could go in its market.*

The problem with that approach over the long term is that you must be careful not to 'shoot first and ask questions later'. We did not get carried away with the momentum and were careful to act when we saw some small-cap multiples getting too high. Just as we had previously done in the tech boom, we took some profits in the small-cap sector and reinvested in some of the larger cap stocks that represented better comparative value at that time. We also took advantage of higher prices to trim the portfolio a little and use cash raised to lower our gearing. For example, we reduced our holding in Fleetwood, which we have held for many years, but we remain long-term supporters of the company.

So while we may have modified our approach through the bull market, fundamentally we are long-term investors and we will continue along that path.

If we delve back into your past, is there one experience, whether it be when you were working with Holmes à Court, that typifies how you approach your investing?

I recall an incident when I was in my early twenties that taught me many things about values and hard work, and added to my investment philosophy.

In the summer of 1982, I undertook a project on behalf of my father who had subdivided some land near Sunbury, a suburb on the western outskirts of Melbourne. He was having trouble selling it. We decided to try to offer an additional element to one of the blocks of land by putting a house on it. We could not afford a new house but discovered that we could buy an old weatherboard house for not much money and relocate it.

I set about the task and identified a house in inner-city Coburg that I managed to buy for $1800. I organised to take the roof down, have the house sawed in two and then have each half transported on a long-loader trailer to the site in Sunbury. For the next four months we re-stumped the house, attached cladding, reconnected the two halves, replaced the roof, re-plumbed, re-wired and refitted the entire house. I worked on the house every day with a builder and we completed the job for about $8600.

As we were nearing completion, I recollect driving along the freeway with a trailer load of timber to a sky covered with black soot. As I approached the house, I saw the glow of what became known as the Ash Wednesday bush fires on the hill not far away. Fortunately for me, unlike many others who had suffered, the fires did not quite reach us. I certainly learnt, and have always remembered, that no matter how much work and preparation you put into a transaction there is always the unexpected or unpredictable that can potentially wipe you out, which therefore requires you to have a degree of diversity and spread of risk. No matter how smart or diligent you think you have been, you must avoid the classic risk of having all your eggs in one basket.

We went on to sell the block of land with the house on it with an effective uplift for the house to a value of $35 000. All of a sudden the subdivision had changed its character and before long the rest of the lots in the subdivision were sold and the sale prices were quite good.

The lessons? Firstly, investing is not a static game. It is dynamic. You must adapt to uncertainty or problems. Secondly, look for the value-add that might change or unlock a situation. Bravely pursue initiative or innovation. Thirdly, the more you roll up your sleeves and get involved, the more you will ensure success. Fourthly, study the market you are in. Finally, don't overexpose yourself to any one investment. You don't have all the answers. Spread your risk.

Do you believe the bull market in the small-cap companies is coming to an end and, if so, how does that affect Thorney?

I think we are seeing capital move out of small-cap companies that are listed on the Australian sharemarket and I think it will be some time before money flows back into this emerging space. Investors will only return to the small end of the market when they are convinced that earnings have stabilised and are sustainable.

Thorney in the last period has diversified away from just being an investor in emerging companies. We have moved into property, and are trading a derivative book around larger companies and taking part in some private equity plays. However, we still think the best way to achieve long-term performance comes from the stock market and, in particular, the emerging sector of the market.

In recent years, Thorney has made tremendous gains in consumer-related stocks such as McPherson's and Fleetwood. These types of stocks have suffered big corrections in the early part of 2005. Does this create a buying opportunity or are consumer-dependent stocks set to underperform for a long period of time?

As I've said, no business is static. For the last few years, consumer-related stocks have performed well as the public spent their new-found wealth. That is probably in the process of adjusting back to normal levels.

At some stage, this adjustment will see these types of companies, if their business model is robust enough, represent good value. Not unlike the coal stocks three years ago. I think you always have to be prepared to look at stocks that are unpopular at a particular point in time and if the business model is strong enough, there is an opportunity to invest.

In recent years we have seen the emergence of China as an industrial giant. This has helped drive the Australian sharemarket, particularly the mining sector. Do you see China being the key theme for the Australian sharemarket in the coming years?

My own trips to China to see the growth and talk to a number of industrial and other companies only confirm that the appetite for growth is immense. Australia is, and will continue to be, one of the global beneficiaries of the China phenomenon. Consequently, at Thorney we have been an aggressive participant in the resource sector over the last year and a half. We employed a resource analyst with a background in geology to provide more detailed industry knowledge.

Again, we took the time to visit a lot of the mines around Australia. We visited coalmines, goldmines, coppermines — the same fundamental approach that Thorney adopts in any sector we invest in. We see the operation, meet the management, understand the dynamics of the business, ask the 'what if' questions, examine movements in the exchange rate and other elements of the matrix that make up the economics of the business.

I must say it was a quite fascinating journey to do that in the resource sector. I've enjoyed it and I made sure I made the journey with people who have insight that they can share. We've quite often chartered a small plane and, together with our own analyst, external resource analysts and other investors with experience in this field, have headed off to make the visits.

Having everyone together on the plane enables us to chat in a lot of detail about the companies and what we see and how they compare to other companies. I think that's been part of the reason why we've been successful in some of our investments. This may seem extravagant but it turns out to be a very cheap outlay because you get to have the dialogue that develops from being all together in a confined space.

What about China itself? Why is it so important?

I think without a doubt anyone who wants to be serious about the investment game needs to make several trips to China to get a sense of what is going on there.

When you see the scale of projects undertaken, the sense of urgency, the entrepreneurial nature of the Chinese people, the massive urbanisation program where more than 100 million people are being moved to cities, you see that the Chinese economy is flexing its muscles. Again, there will probably be some hiccups but I think that China will be an ongoing theme for Australia and the world over the next several decades.

If China decides to float its currency, what do you think the impact would be on Australian companies?[2]

There are many large external themes that influence the stock market, including the ones we can't avoid like industrial relations and currencies. Clearly, a revaluation of the Yuan [official Chinese currency] is one of the most topical of these. Anyone who has tried to second-guess what the Chinese will do next is usually left wanting.

2   The Chinese Government allowed the currency to rise 2 per cent in value against the US dollar in July 2005 (after this interview was conducted) but stopped short of a full revaluation.

Having said that, I think fundamentally a float of the Yuan, if it happens, will have a great impact including helping create other opportunities. Hopefully, our approach of investing with a very stock-specific basis will help us come through that transition. We would hope that we are backing companies with management who can cope with changes. We would also expect that a good business leader would deal with uncertainty of matters out of his control by running his business as efficiently as it can be. We are constantly searching for those type of qualities to back with our capital.

I suspect that many Australian businesses have become reliant on a strong Australian dollar and cheap Chinese production and if the float occurs, those businesses will have to deal with a significant disruption that will challenge the efficacy of their model.

What do you think will be the best performing asset class over the coming two to three years?

I think if you are a believer in the growth story in China, and also in India, you'd have to have some exposure to the resource sector, including oil. Even though most of the commodity prices are at highs, the insatiable appetite of those two economies will enable the Australian companies to export significant amounts of their output, unless there is a major economic setback. That should underwrite record profits for those companies with the appropriate investments for exploration and greater capacity in their mills.

So despite their enormous price increases already, resources stocks can continue to outperform?

I think so but, of course, growth in economies usually don't run smoothly. There may be some overcapacity and there may be some bumps along the way. However, I suspect they will be small bumps in what will be a very strong growth trend. So I believe that's a sector that's worth having some exposure in.

Do you think the traditional 'bogyman' of equity markets, inflation, is again a major concern in Australia given the rise in commodity prices and shortages of labour?

I think the concerns that the market was showing earlier in the year now point to these issues being of significant concern. They, obviously, affect some companies more than others, and we've seen that with retailers being hit and consumer-related organisations suffering. There is the ability to short sell those stocks and other stocks that are seen to be sensitive to inflation issues and rising interest rates. This allows us to make money on the downside.

Having said that, we still need to bear in mind that, even though interest rates have gone up, they have done so from historical lows and remain close to those levels. The interest cover and servicing ability of many companies is still quite comfortable. So even if there is some decline in earnings, there are still many companies that can handle slightly higher interest rates and a degree of inflation.

What do you think is the biggest issue driving the Australian sharemarket in the longer term?

I think the Australian market is still very sensitive to the US economy. Like in Australia, in the US there are concerns about inflation and the possibility of rising interest rates. While China is the biggest new influence, the US still is the key to world growth and equity markets. Notwithstanding what I said earlier, there are concerns about the Chinese economy and the impact that will have on the US economy. I see that issue as the critical factor for the Australian market and it could create a certain amount of volatility in the medium term.

Nevertheless, the Australian economy has been a standout economy over the last five or six years in world terms and so I think we are well-positioned to withstand some global volatility.

> *The Australian economy has been a standout economy over the last five or six years in world terms and so I think we are well-positioned to withstand some global volatility.*

Well enough positioned to continue to outperform global peers?

I suspect when you're looking out over five years we probably will, although we've already got ahead of the pack in the immediate short term.

At Thorney, you are prepared to put representatives on the boards of public companies, something most institutional investors steer well clear of. What are the pros and cons of being on boards?

We have a lot of discussions about this as we take strategic stakes in companies. Our approach is to limit the number of boards that we go on but to help those companies find quality independent directors, so that we're comfortable the chief executive has a group of people who can help in the development of the strategy and mentor him or her through the relevant issues.

The restrictions of being able to invest in the stock or divest the stock where you have a board representative are real. The authorities are increasingly tougher on the ability of directors to trade within certain windows of information flows. We take our responsibility in relation to that very seriously. But we will go onto a board when we feel that a company is in a development or mentor stage and can use our help.

We may also choose to go on a board if we see a need to protect our investment by working with the company to help solve problems and help redirect the corporate strategy, and develop the game plan in a constructive way. That's what we've done on a number of occasions and that's what we'll continue to do going forward.

I think what we also need to do is be more disciplined about the time we exit boards once the company is back on the right track. Once it has built a more solid institutional share register and its path forward is clear, more professional and experienced board members may be able to do a more serviceable job than we can.

Where do you get most of your investment ideas?

We generate most of the ideas internally. This has always been the case for Thorney and comes from our discipline of pouring over information and data from a number of sources — magazines, papers, research reports and so on. Furthermore, we continue to have direct contact with many companies and have a dialogue with the chief executive or chairman to understand the insights and the direction the company would like to go in if it had the means to do so.

Over time we have also developed a network of advisers who we trust and believe in and who generate an 'ideas pipeline' for us. We tend to lean towards those advisers who have done their own research and a thorough examination so that when they are putting an idea towards us, they have an informed opinion from which we can start our own research.

Is there one particular sector in the market where you can see good opportunities in the future?

One area that still quite intrigues me, although it's not for the faint-hearted, is life sciences and medical innovation, or biotech as it's more commonly called. There have been a lot of false dawns in biotech in recent years. However, the fact remains that Australia has a very well developed and cost-effective research base, and has universities that have produced one of the highest ratios of PhDs in the biotech area of any country.

The research and technology that comes out of Australia is world standard and has global application. Unfortunately, this technical expertise has not been matched by commercialisation expertise. This has been exacerbated by a general lack of venture capital and early-stage funding. But I remain convinced that the convergence of computer power, robotics, nanotechnologies and biotechnology, coupled with the impact of the human genome project and similar work, is going to change the world forever.

Many vast wealth creation opportunities are starting to emerge from this and so the biotech sector is beginning to attract a much better calibre of businessperson. Indeed, in the US, many multi-billion dollar organisations exist in this sector that were not even conceived of a decade ago. If you could identify early-stage technology in the Australian market with similar potential, the returns could be significant.

Two companies I like in this area are Amrad, which has a great pipeline of research technology with real commercial potential, and Messoblast, which is a company focused on adult stem cells. We have shares in both.

I stress again, the area is not for the faint-hearted. It requires considerable patience but it is a sector I would definitely keep some exposure to.

How big can Thorney get before 20 per cent or above annual returns become difficult to achieve?

I don't believe that there are restrictions on us still being able to grow. There's a lot of money in the system at the moment looking for a home, mainly coming from the growing superannuation pool. We are, for the most part, operating in the niche of the emerging company market. We're still seeing a very good pipeline of deals and so I think there is still plenty of capacity to grow. Our focus on due diligence means we probably only proceed with one in twenty of the deals that are put to us. One area we have toyed with is expanding into funds management of external (non–Pratt) money.

It has both attractions and drawbacks, and we won't be rushing in just for the sake of it.

We also have a property portfolio that has been active in residential development, retirement villages and several commercial projects.

We think there are opportunities for our style of investing in other countries, not just in Australia. To some extent, we have started down this path with a small amount of money invested in European, American and Asian markets. Those investments, obviously, come with their own risk profile and so we would look to do them in alliance or partnership with experienced players.

However, we will take the same approach no matter where we invest or what we invest in. We are value investors.

———————●———————

The second interview with Alex Waislitz shed some new insights into the way he invests. When we spoke to Waislitz in 2003, his Thorney group had big shareholdings in many consumer-related companies. In early 2005, many of these companies were floored by the downturn in consumer spending. But to think Waislitz was caught flat-footed would be to underestimate him. He was quick to identify emerging areas of the market such as resources and allocate large percentages of the group's money to those areas.

What do we learn from this? Without doubt the initial lesson is to have an open mind. Not disheartened by the tough period in early 2005, Waislitz sought to identify new opportunities. As the mining sector began to pick up, Waislitz and his team were quick to get on a plane and travel the length and breadth of Australia to find the right companies to invest in while they were still cheap. At the same time, he ventured to China to see first-hand the industrialisation of the world's most populace country.

Waislitz is a driven man and continues to drive his Thorney group and its employees very hard to generate superior returns. Who knows? One day Thorney may be the jewel in the Pratt empire's crown.

*In a sideways, drifting market, you have to look to invest in equities
that will be re-rated through a structural change or a regulatory
change that could lead to a consolidation of an industry.*

8

The media mogul emerges
Tim Hughes

Tim Hughes has been incredibly busy since 2003. The boy from Dubbo, plucked from obscurity in 1983 by Australia's game show king Reg Grundy, has completely overhauled his investment portfolio. At the time of writing, Hughes was in a prime position to be an important figure in any media shake-up resulting from possible legislative changes by the Federal Liberal Government.

RG Capital Radio, the business controlled by Reg Grundy but overseen by Hughes, was surprisingly sold to Macquarie Bank in 2004. Hughes accepted the job of executive chairman for Macquarie's latest fund, a media fund. Soon afterwards Macquarie snapped up rival regional radio group DMG, combining it with RG Capital Radio to become the clear leader in regional radio in the country. Now Macquarie Bank is planning to re-float the group for an estimated $500 to $600 million in preparation for the proposed changes to media rules. Macquarie Bank, with Hughes, could easily branch out into regional television or regional newspapers. Whatever the case, the plans will undoubtedly be big.

All of this must have a touch of deja vu for Hughes who, as a young gun in the 1980s, orchestrated a plan for Grundy to become a major player in regional media at the time of licence aggregation.

Back then, Grundy made a killing on the exercise and Macquarie is no doubt hoping to replicate this success.

During the past two years, Hughes has also managed to float his pet project — marketing/communications services group Photon, which Hughes founded in February 2000. Photon Group Limited listed on the ASX in May 2004 with an issue price of $1.80. Since then, the shares have risen to $3.20 a share and at the time of writing Photon has a market capitalisation of $185 million.

RG Capital also exited its shareholding in online stockbroker E*Trade Australia in September 2004, selling its remaining 15 per cent in the company. Under Hughes's guidance, RG Capital (Reg Grundy's Australian investment vehicle) invested $12 million in E*Trade in 1999 and over the last five years has slowly sold out for a profit of approximately $56 million.

Despite Hughes's move to executive chairman of Macquarie Media, he still manages a share portfolio, a job he convinced Reg Grundy he could do as a twenty-one year old back in 1984. Hughes turned $20000 into $100000 for Grundy back then and has been an active fund manager ever since. Hughes, who leads a dual life as a company builder and sharemarket investor, labels his investment style as contrarian. He does not spend hours and hours pouring over company annual reports, trying to find an edge over other people. He is not a value investor who seeks out oversold stocks. Instead, Hughes concentrates on market sentiment. Like human beings, the mood of the market can swing from depression to euphoria and back again within short time periods. Hughes has made his investing fortune by investing against the crowd — while also ensuring he reduces the risks by mainly sticking to businesses he understands intimately, like media and finance.

When Rupert Murdoch's News Corporation hit hard times in 1990 and most investors were predicting a financial collapse, Hughes was buying News Corp shares. His faith in media and in Murdoch paid off and he tripled his money in a short period of time.

In a similar move, Hughes, on behalf of RG Capital, pounced on a 5 per cent stake in the Seven Network in 1995 when the stock tumbled following an advertising bungle by then management. When Seven shares fell from $4.20 to $2.70, Hughes invested around $25 million as institutional and retail shareholders rushed to the door. Within days, another buyer in the form of billionaire

Kerry Stokes appeared as a substantial shareholder. Knowing they would be in for a fight to gain control of Seven, RG Capital sold its stake to Stokes for around $4.10 a share, netting a tidy profit of around $14 million in a matter of weeks.

Nothing much has changed for Hughes. The bull market of the last two years has provided great opportunities for the contrarian. A net buyer of stocks in late 2002 and early 2003, Hughes could smell fear among the investment community as the US market led world equity indices lower. However, two years on he is a seller into the current euphoria. As he told us in the first edition of *Masters of the Market*, 'When the institutions are panicking, we look to buy into the market. When they are booming, we sell … It is brave but generally most rewarding if you swim against the tide and get it right'.

We caught up with Tim on 24 June 2005 at his old digs in Macquarie Street in Sydney. His energy (some would say nervous energy) is ever-present and his manner disarming, like any great salesman.

———————●———————

Tim, how as an investor have you handled the last two years of extreme market optimism?

I was a buyer throughout 2003 and right up until early 2004. This meant that I was fully invested by March 2003. To be fully invested is a rare occurrence for me. Generally, I like a lot of liquidity [cash] in my portfolio so I can take advantage of short-term overreactions in the market. I do, however, have a bit of a history of being fully invested by the later part of a bear market.

> *Generally, I like a lot of liquidity [cash] in my portfolio so I can take advantage of short-term overreactions in the market.*

I should say that I did not pick the bottom of the bear market, which finished in March 2003, because I started my buying spree in 2002. The good news, though, is that I was fully invested when the market decided to turn around in 2003. As a result, I enjoyed a great run and finished the financial year to June 2004 up 37 per cent. Since June 2004, my portfolio is up another 20 per cent. A true contrarian view is to buy when the market is falling and sell when it is rising. That best describes the last couple of years for me.

What has been your best investment call during the past two years?

Given my history and my liking for media, you would probably think it was a media stock. Well, it wasn't. It was a stock that benefited from the emerging trend of rising commodity prices. In early 2003, I started purchasing Western Areas, a nickel stock, at around 40¢ a share. I bought it all the way up to around 80¢ a share. The stock went up to $2.00 a share in October 2003 and my last sale price was $1.96 a share. The trade range gain was 500 per cent but, based on my average entry and exit price, my gain was about 240 per cent.

I got into the China story early. The nickel market went ballistic from early 2003 due to the demand for commodities from China and its booming economy.

What has been your worst investment in this time?

That is a better question. You tend to learn more from your duds. I got sucked into a health care stock called Nova Health. It was an initial public offering of a number of private hospitals. Private hospitals are recognised as a huge growth area in this country. However, this was an aggregation of a number of private operators and it floated for the wrong reasons. The company was looking to get cost savings from putting all the companies together and not looking for growth, which should be the reason for going public.

Due to terrible management and an overpriced issue, it bombed. My average buy price was 78¢ a share and my average sale price was 24¢ a share. A 70 per cent loss.

Given the strong Australian market during the past two years, do you think the current market is a good one for investing?

I think after such a strong rally it is time to be cautious. I think we will track sideways for the rest of the year. I have been a net seller of equities during the last six months and I have raised my cash levels to about 40 per cent of the portfolio, which will be really handy should the market tip over.

What, if anything, have you learnt during the past two years and have you changed any aspects of how you might invest?

The turn in the market in early 2003 after a couple of tough years reinforced my view that falling markets will eventually turn as sure as rising markets will in the end tip over. I never forget bear markets and am constantly monitoring the market trends. I must say, nothing in the last few years has changed the way I invest.

What do you believe will be the best performing asset classes over the next two to three years?

In a sideways, drifting market, you have to look to invest in equities that will be re-rated through a structural change or a regulatory change that could lead to a consolidation of an industry. A good example of this situation could be when John Howard's federal government takes over control of the senate later this year [it took control in July 2005]. I think sectors of the stock market to watch as a result of a change of power in the senate will be media, transport and finance. Media companies (such as PBL, Ten, Seven, Prime TV and Austereo) could be winners with the cross and foreign ownership restrictions due to be watered down. Transport and infrastructure stocks such as Patrick and Toll Holdings will benefit from industrial relations reform and the opening up of our ports and rail. The finance sector could also be a beneficiary with a possibility that the laws governing takeovers and mergers in the sector will be loosened. In other words, we might see big bank mergers and a general rationalisation of the market.

I'm looking in these areas because I don't believe you can just invest in the general market and watch it rise.

> *In a sideways, drifting market, you have to look to invest in equities that will be re-rated through a structural change or a regulatory change that could lead to a consolidation of an industry.*

As for other asset classes, I don't have much of a view. I do think cash will be a decent alternative to the equity market given my view it will trade sideways for six months or more.

After being considered a poor investment for more than a decade, resources stocks are back in vogue. Do you believe

*that resources stocks can continue to outperform the broader
market in the medium to long term?*

A lot of good news is factored into the current prices being paid
for the resources sector. Resources stocks are very cyclical and they
don't go up forever. If interest rates continue to rise in the US or
there is a hiccup in China that slows down economic growth, the
resources sector might pull back really quickly.

*Does that mean you are not really a believer in resource-base
companies or are you just adopting the contrarian view again?*

It is a contrarian view. Why would anyone recommend resources
stocks today after the run they have had over the last few years. The
one exception to this could be oil, where I feel the oil price may
remain high for quite some time.

*We seem to be in a period of rising interest rates on the back of a
thirteen-year economic boom and the emerging fear of inflation. Even
though rates are only rising gradually, what is the best way to make
money in this environment?*

It is time to preserve capital and raise cash. There is nothing wrong
with compound interest rates in a period of rising interest rates.

*Is the fear of inflation and rising interest rates a primary reason for
you taking your portfolio to a position of 40 per cent cash?*

In many ways it is irrelevant what I believe in regards to where
interest rates and inflation are going. What is important in regards
to those two issues is how the market reacts if interest rates go higher
than expected and if inflation does raise its head up. Early this year,
around March and April, these issues seemed to be of concern to
markets both here and in the US and markets started to go lower.
So that tells me interest rates and inflation beyond expectations
would be a negative in the market. Having cash levels at around 40
per cent, I have total flexibility until the picture becomes clearer. If
inflation and interest rates remain in check and the market starts
to trend higher, I can invest the money. If, on the other hand, these
factors see the market fall quite sharply, I may be able to pick up some
bargains. I see having this much cash as a big plus at this stage.

*China and its growth rates has been a huge focus for the investment
community during the past two years. Do you believe China will*

continue to be a key theme in the coming years for the Australian
sharemarket?

I don't get hung up on it like a lot of people. Once it was a booming
Asia (we had the Asian meltdown in 1997), then it was Latin America
and the third world countries and they went bankrupt, then a
couple of years ago everyone was raving on about Russia. Sorry, it's
too late to be talking about China.

Look at China Fund's share price on Wall Street. In December 2002,
it was US$14. A year later in December 2003 it closed at US$47.
It drifted down all through 2004 to close in December 2004 at
US$34. Now it is about US$30. The China Fund is listed on Wall
Street, representing a basket of Chinese stocks, and is fundamentally
a barometer of how US investors view China. If you believe that, I
think you have missed the boat.

I think the real money is made by buying today what they will be
talking about in two years' time and it isn't China. It could be India.
Just remember — markets lead and people follow.

What about energy costs — especially the soaring oil price? Are
high oil prices a problem for markets or, like China, is oil yesterday's
story?

It's interesting that you ask this question because from what I can
gather the high oil price may have longer term implications. It
seems fairly clear that the price of oil will stay at these types of
higher levels for quite some time. If we don't come up with a genuine
alternative means of energy to oil, it may feed through into higher
inflation. The problem with oil feeding through to inflation is that
the regulators around the world would need to raise interest rates
to keep inflation in check. Higher interest rates slow economies
and that's bad for company earnings and, as a result, for equity
prices.

As a contrarian investor, how do you identify what people will be
talking about in two years and pick those trends early?

You just tend to pick up on things, especially when you are running
companies. For example, our marketing company, Photon, was
recently assessing the development and production of new software.
After a fair bit of work it was suggested that India might be the best
place to achieve the result.

Coincidentally, India is looking to deregulate its media industry and may issue new radio licences. That is obviously interesting to me. The Macquarie Media Fund might see an opportunity to branch overseas.

These two insights, gained through the two companies I am involved in, tell me that India may be the next potential investment fad. Time will tell.

What is the single issue that will drive the Australian sharemarket higher or lower in the coming five years?

An old saying is that a rising tide lifts all boats. During the last two years, everyone has made money. The next leg will be the stockpickers' domain. The market will most likely track sideways so it will get back to good old-fashioned stock selection. I recommend that you use your research and follow your gut instincts. Filter, screen and rotate. I think complacency and comfort will drive the market, causing a dull drift. In such a market, it will be much harder to make money. It will get back to the best managed companies in the right sectors of the economy.

Do you believe the Australian sharemarket will outperform its global peers over the next two years?

I must answer no. If I said yes, you would strip me of my moniker. We have outperformed incredibly the last three years. I think we will shift away from a commodity-driven market like Australia and back to service-driven markets such as the US and the UK, and emerging markets like India.

Is this view based on fundamental analysis or are you applying your highly successful contrarian view?

Once again, it is my contrarian view. I feel that Australia has been the best performing equity market among western countries for the last three years. In fact, its relative outperformance has been the best I've seen of any country during my twenty years of investing. So, as I said in my previous answer, I would be looking for the reason why we won't have such a strong performance going forward. At this stage, I am not sure what that reason is but history and experience tells me you can't outperform other markets like Australia has done during the last three years forever.

As a contrarian investor, what do you recommend we should do regarding our exposure to the Australian sharemarket at this stage in the cycle?

Easy — reduce.

What have you been doing to take advantage of this contrarian view?

Raising cash. Weighting my positions towards sectors such as media, transport and financials. I am also being patient and waiting for the right opportunities to present themselves.

In the first edition of Masters of the Market *you said that normally you sold out of positions too early. Do you think this might be the case again, given your selling of late?*

No doubts about it being too early — the Australian market in particular has been stronger than I would have expected during the last six months. By now, I would have expected a major correction in share prices but that hasn't happened. So I am wrong at the moment. Having said that, I am quite comfortable with my position — history tells me I will be right at some point and that will create an opportunity. Normally there is some short-term pain when you truly are a contrarian investor.

Since the first edition of Masters of the Market *in 2003, you have been extremely busy. You joined Macquarie Bank to run their regional media fund, which no doubt will grow in size, and you have grown Photon at a rapid rate. These companies are cousins in that they are media and marketing organisations. Do you think these two areas are stand-out growth areas for the future?*

Obviously, my positions at Macquarie Media and the Photon float reflect a certain market view. I do think these two areas are heading for major rationalisation. Hopefully, the cross media ownership laws will be lifted and we can expand Macquarie Media further. If not, we will look offshore for opportunities.

The approach by Macquarie Bank to start a media fund came out of the blue and it took me some months to realise the potential with RG Capital Radio as the initial investment. Macquarie Bank is a highly savvy bank and hugely resourceful, so I couldn't resist the opportunity. The ability to combine RG Capital Radio and DMG Regional Radio was a special [Hughes likes to use racing terms given his love of horses]. The synergies between the two companies are massive and we have quickly increased operating margins. My chief executive officer from RG Capital Radio, Rhys Holleran, is running the lot now and he and his team are doing a super job. We are now the largest owner of radio stations in Australia, with ninety-seven in our portfolio. Radio is a great cash flow business and we've had lots of experience in the area. I think we have a good idea on how to extract superior returns while improving the product and getting results for clients. The next couple of years are going to be very exciting.

Photon reflects the changing landscape of advertising and marketing in this country. The consumer is now much more discerning and there are numerous points of contact between companies and their clients. It used to be that companies look to promote their products by using the mainstream media — newspapers, television and radio. Now marketing also involves direct communication and interactivity using computers and phones, both fixed and mobile. This is huge. As the producer or distributor of products reaches out to consumers, they have many options available to them.

At Photon we concentrate on what we call below the line direct marketing and communication. In the advertising industry, above the line refers to the old style of using an advertising agency to place your ads with the old forms of media. Below the line, like in Photon's case, provides opportunities in email marketing, corporate communications, merchandising, consumer research, public relations, mobile phone content, internet distribution, interactive media and direct response SMS, as well as some of the older forms of traditional advertising. I think Photon is well positioned in one of the highest growth sectors in Australia.

Assuming the cross and foreign media ownership laws in Australia do change in the next twelve months, how do you see events unfolding? Will there be mass rationalisation and only a few players left standing?

There will not be mass rationalisation, mainly because of the principle reason behind deregulation — that is, the consumer in today's world has many and varied means of receiving information and entertainment. Therefore, the premium paid for the so called rivers of gold [the term sometimes applied to Fairfax's classified advertising revenue stream, for instance] are not what they were back in the 1980s, which was the last time major rationalisation took place in the industry.

What will occur this time is rationalisation based on economies of scale of media production. This will create the opportunity to provide a better product that sells more because the campaign can be integrated into numerous platforms. For example, you could start a new music-based program because it would have the ability to promote such products as Coca-Cola across a range of medium such as TV, radio, websites and mobile communications.

Is Photon an example of picking how trends will unfold into the future? If so, does this mean Photon was initially a big risk for yourself and your main investor, Reg Grundy?

Photon was us picking the trend. The risk, however, was not so much in starting the company but really in the implementation of the strategy. The problem with the internet boom of the late 1990s was that people overpaid and overvalued assets. Fundamentally, the trend was right but the implementation was wrong. So with Photon I have made sure that we have bought the right companies at the right price. I have little doubt the strategy of concentrating on alternative marketing formats is the correct one.

I think change creates opportunity.

If you strongly believe that the advertising and marketing worlds are changing, what does this mean for the old mediums such as radio, which is obviously your other area of major interest?

The old mediums don't have a problem. It just means those businesses have to recognise changes and embrace them. They have to place themselves in a position to benefit from the changes. I think all smart media operators will move, and look to come up with more integrated and interactive ways of selling products for clients. I think change creates opportunity.

In the long term, do you think you will continue to play a dual role of professional sharemarket investor and company creator and executive?

I can't see why not. As long as I enjoy it and I'm making a quid, I will continue to do both. I find my investing and corporate roles very complementary.

One thing is for certain, Tim Hughes will never be criticised for sitting still. His fertile mind seems to be ticking over at a million miles an hour. But what does our contrarian teach us this time around? He leaves us with very little doubt that what has happened over the last two years will not repeat itself during the upcoming two years. There is a high chance resources stocks are past their best, China will fade as a focal point and the Australia market will not continue to outperform the rest of the world.

Hughes believes the best way to take advantage of this scenario is to be ready. Have some cash on the sidelines ready to pounce on the opportunities. He saw big opportunities in 2002 and, after pain for a few months, the rewards started to come his way. In Hughes's eyes, it is better to be early than too late.

He also leaves us with the impression that if you are going to succeed in the investment game, you must look forward and try to work out what will deliver the goods — rather than look backwards to those stocks that performed last year.

Who knows? Hughes, with Macquarie Bank behind him, could in the future be in charge of a multibillion-dollar media group that stretches across Australia and to other parts of the globe. It seems he might be just the visionary to pull it off.

We believe that an environment where share prices are rising strongly is generally an unfavourable one for value investors as it implies paying ever increasing amounts for the same forecast future earnings streams. The longer such a scenario is sustained, the greater the risks become and the more potentially damaging the outcome to investor wealth.

9

Making money, not just spending it
Erik Metanomski

The last two years have not presented the easiest investment environment for the Adelaide-based Erik Metanomski. As he is a strict value investor, the rocketing sharemarket has severely limited the number of companies in which he has been able to invest. Metanomski and his team have continued to hold around 60 per cent of their portfolio in cash while the market has hit record high after record high. But he has never relented from his philosophy and is unlikely to do so. Metanomski is determined to adhere to an approach that has delivered average pre-fee returns of 24 to 25 per cent per annum to his investors over the last twelve years.

Metanomski cut his teeth in funds management in the 1980s, managing funds from Melbourne and then London. By his own admission, Metanomski struggled in those early years to find an investment discipline that he could adopt and feel truly comfortable with. It wasn't until the late 1980s that his approach to investing in the sharemarket changed forever. At the time, Metanomski was working with new *Masters of the Market* entrant Phil Mathews in London. Both men discovered books written about Warren Buffett, Benjamin Graham and Phillip Fisher. They read these books several times and then tried to apply the lessons to their day-to-day work.

Metanomski didn't stop here, though. He followed up the changes with a fact-finding tour of the US, the home of boutique funds management. He talked to many fund managers around the country, hoping to pick up any crumbs of wisdom that might help in the formulation of his own investment philosophy. On his tour he met with investment greats such as Charles Royce, Abe Nicholas, Randolph Updyke, Julian Robertson, David Dreman and Charles Dreifus of Lazard. By the time he had completed his tour, it had become clear to him that there were very few managers around who had outperformed the market over long periods of time. Of the managers who had, all, with the exception of Julian Robertson, were deep value investors. These managers were very stock specific and rarely, if ever, got caught up in the day-to-day machinations and 'noise' of the sharemarket.

The US left a lasting impression on Metanomski and to this day he is a deep value investor. When he returned to Australia in 1992 after six years in the UK, he set up his own management company and strictly adhered to this style. Fundamentally, he focuses upon management and free cash flow and does not place undue emphasis on what a company may earn in the distant future. In other words, he looks to invest in companies that he believes are cheap relative to their current and immediate (one to two years out at the most) valuation, rather than attempting to justify an investment based on what can turn out to be very fragile long-term assumptions.

We met with Metanomski, now forty-seven, in a café in Sydney in June 2005, during one of his many investment trips around the country. Despite the poor investment environment for his style of investing, MMC has continued to perform strongly. While Metanomski is not happy with current company valuations, he is as pleasant and helpful as always.

———————⬤———————

Since March 2003 the Australian sharemarket has rallied close to 60 per cent, not including dividends. In the 2004 calendar year alone, the market rose 22.5 per cent — the best year since 1993. How have you faired in this significant bull market?

In the second half of calendar year 2004, the MMC Value Growth Trust [Metanomski's VGT fund is the group's benchmark fund] was up around 20 per cent before fees. This was quite pleasing given this fund held an average of 60 per cent of its funds in cash during that period, thus reducing the risk exposure of our investors. In addition, it is very rare for the Value Growth Trust to hold resource stocks. This placed us a considerable distance behind the starting line, given the major contribution to the market's performance that came from the resources sector.

Over the last two years, the VGT fund has risen around 20 per cent each year before fees.

> **I place a lot of importance on investment calls that save us money and I believe that such calls can be important in determining the long-term success of an investment strategy.**

What was your best investment call during the past two years?

I place a lot of importance on investment calls that save us money and I believe that such calls can be important in determining the long-term success of an investment strategy. Not being seduced by the promise of a never-ending period of consumer, retail and housing expansion has saved us from the recent rout that has occurred in those sectors.

I would like to think that we will be rewarded in a similar way for our current steadfast refusal to believe that the resource sector will forever be underwritten by uninterrupted expansion in China and/or India.

We also continue to question the commonly and strongly held notion that the banking sector represents a defensive investment. We have had an incredibly protracted favourable economic cycle and it is tough to believe that the major Australian banks, which carry around 95 per cent or so of debt with 5 per cent or so of equity, are not incredibly leveraged and vulnerable to a downturn. An increasingly questionable reduction in provisioning[1] at such a mature stage in the economic cycle — when banks should

---

1   Provisioning is taking a loss now based on an expectation of future losses. In the case of banks, this usually relates to bad debts.

arguably be doing just the opposite — has provided a regular, albeit somewhat artificial, boost to earnings. This coupled with an ever-increasing affection for capitalisation of expenses (followed by subsequent 'non-recurring' write-offs of these same assets — for example, IT systems) only adds to the vulnerability of this sector going forward. As Warren Buffett once famously said, 'You only find who has been swimming naked once the tide has gone out', and I suspect that in a tougher economic environment these sorts of machinations, which obviously contribute strongly to short-term reported earnings, can have a tendency to come back and bite you very hard.

With respect to our winners, we have gone close to doubling our money in IOOF, a company that is one of the last remaining major independent financial services icons in the country. When it floated a couple of years back it was initially poorly followed by the market. Its cost structure was far too high compared to its competitors and being a funds management business its earnings were enormously leveraged to a lower cost base. At the time of the float, the company had around $70 million in net cash and its resultant enterprise value really reflected some very good long-term value.

We have also made significant realised gains in IBT Education and Health Communication Network[2] and meaningful unrealised gains in Burns Philp, Prime Infrastructure Fund and UnderCoverWear. I would hasten to add that in the latter group of companies the gains to this point remain purely quotational. Our ability to realise these gains at some point will obviously be a function of the ongoing performance of the underlying businesses. In other words, while the short-term rise in their share price may be modestly reassuring, it will be the underlying performances of the individual business that ultimately prove or disprove our longer term thesis on these companies.

Conversely, what has been your worst investment during the last two years?

In percentage terms, our worst loss has been in a niche advertising/ placement business called Adcorp. We underestimated the full extent of this company's leverage to the economic cycle and the legacy issues pertaining to previous acquisitions. We also missed a couple of shorter term issues and made some analytical errors of omission. It has again reinforced to us the importance of continually

---

2   HCN was taken over by Primary Health Care in 2004.

revisiting and questioning conclusions with regard to the businesses you are invested in. We continued to increase our holding in the company as the share price fell without adequately re-checking our numbers and underlying assumptions. This is normally something we are extremely fastidious about. Our average price into Adcorp was around $1.10 and it is currently [June 2005] trading at $0.65. So the paper loss has been around 40 per cent. Having said that, I now believe the company has overshot on the downside. It carries net cash of around $5 million, generates strong free cash flow and the dividend yield is now more than 10 per cent fully franked.

Compared to our average cost price of around $1.65, we are also currently underwater in our investment in printing and direct mail group PMP.[3] However, we continue to believe in the quality of this company's management and the very significant potential uplift in earnings, improvement in business quality and substantial lowering of the fixed cost base that should accrue from its current very significant capital expenditure program. The historically poor economics of printing businesses are well documented but in this case we believe that PMP could establish itself as Australia's lowest cost printer with a direct mail business that deserves a higher market rating.

Once the capital expenditure plan is completed the business has the potential to generate very significant free cash flows for the next three to five years. This should see debt levels substantially decrease and the equity value of the business rise commensurately. The jury is out and only time will reveal whether these recent major initiatives will prove successful — we are currently comfortable with that probability.

Since we last interviewed you the structure of your business has changed and the funds under management have grown. Can you explain how and why that has occurred?

When we last spoke in April 2003, we had about $185 million in funds under management. That has increased to approximately $550 million, of which $235 million is in the listed vehicle MMC Contrarian, which floated in December 2003.

Unlike our unlisted managed funds, MMC Contrarian is managed in conjunction with the highly successful and listed HGL Group,

---

3   PMP was trading at $1.31 at the time of writing.

which is an experienced manager and owner of operating businesses. Contrarian would ultimately like to become more active in companies that need ongoing management support. This is where HGL comes into play with their 'active' management style, as opposed to MMC's traditionally 'passive' role. Unfortunately, current valuation levels in the market have provided little opportunity so far to put this strategy into action.

With the growth of funds under management, the size and quality of the investment team has also expanded. Peter Constable, who has run a highly successful small companies fund for some years, is now chief investment officer and is based in our Sydney office with Charles Dalziell who joined us from Maple-Brown Abbott [see chapter 4 on Robert Maple-Brown]. HGL's representative is Kevin Eley and Sam Le Cornu is also becoming an increasingly important part of the team.

Given the current strong sharemarket do you believe the environment is a good one for investing?

We believe that an environment where share prices are rising strongly is generally an unfavourable one for value investors as it implies paying ever increasing amounts for the same forecast future earnings streams. The longer such a scenario is sustained, the greater the risks become and the more potentially damaging the outcome to investor wealth. While the market may appear to be reasonably priced today, at around sixteen times prospective earnings, the maintenance of these historically high earnings and the way above average profit margins that support them is in my view highly questionable. In other words, multiples of earnings need to be related to perceived maturity levels in economic cycles in order to paint a fairer picture of their quality and sustainability.

An environment where share prices are rising strongly is generally an unfavourable one for value investors as it implies paying ever increasing amounts for the same forecast future earnings streams.

Investing in the current market [June 2005] at current prices implies a very optimistic long-term view with respect to earnings. This is at a time when it could reasonably and perhaps forcibly be argued that the long upward economic cycle that we have experienced has a higher probability of turning south than continuing north.

Having significant equity exposure at this point in the cycle could involve significant future opportunity cost penalties or worse. We would certainly prefer a weaker environment where pessimism with respect to equities becomes more pervasive. This tends to manifest itself in lower share prices and therefore lower risk and higher potential future returns, providing you are willing to take a medium- to long-term view.

In a nutshell and from a general investment perspective, we believe that shares, fixed-income, residential and commercial real estate, and equity-linked convertibles and bonds are currently overvalued relative to any reasonably conservative estimate of intrinsic values.

On average over the last dozen years or so, we have held cash at around 30 per cent of funds under management but at the moment it is a bit over 60 per cent spread across all our funds.

Can you explain in more detail your concept of risk and return and why it is important?

I tend to approach risk from the perspective of what is probably the most important principle of investing. That is, it is the 'price' you pay for any investment that will be the ultimate determinant of the return you achieve — it's certainly not how fully invested you are. Long bull markets concentrate people's minds much more on how much money can be made, with very little emphasis being placed upon the risk of significant capital impairment or wealth destruction should the virtuous cycle come to an end (as it always does at some point). I get the strong impression these days that the average investor and most financial professionals are far more pre-occupied with the fear of missing some potential upside than they are with avoiding downside risk and focusing upon capital preservation.

We look at it fairly simply. If our appraisal of the potential upside in a stock is not significantly greater than the potential downside, we won't go there. There aren't many stocks that stack up to us on this basis right now.

More specifically, I have always believed that a stock should deliver an earnings yield of at least 4 per cent above that of the risk-free ten-year bond. So if a risk-free bond is offering a 5 per cent yield, I would be loathe to pay much more than eleven times earnings or a 9 per cent earnings yield for a business, notwithstanding the potential capital growth factor. Having said that, it is extremely important to distinguish between early-cycle earnings and late-cycle earnings. At peak earnings — at or close to the top of an economic cycle, which is arguably the case for many companies now — an investor should demand a higher return above the risk-free rate, while at the nadir of an economic cycle it might be somewhat lower.

If earnings appear to be at or nearing a cyclical high, they are more at risk, so it stands to reason that you should require incremental compensation. But markets are renowned for their unpredictability and sometimes cycles both on the upswing and the downswing phase last longer than you would expect. Momentum can be quite deceiving. It's like an ocean liner — when the Captain turns off the engine, the ship keeps gliding along for quite some time … until it stops.

What do you believe the best performing assets will be during the next two to three years?

At current prices for shares, property, convertibles and just about any other asset class I can think of, I would have to say that a strong weighting to cash is probably the best option. I would argue that if you can't purchase an asset at a fair or discounted price, it is better to hold cash regardless of its yield. This is preferable to paying too much for an asset that could take many years to provide you with a satisfactory comparable return or, even worse, involve loss of capital. I think that there are periods in markets where the extra bit of return that people always crave comes at the expense of a disproportionate level of risk.

Showing discipline and patience when valuations are far from compelling, such as through a willingness to hold larger than average levels of cash, may place you in a very advantageous position at some stage in the future. That is, you will eventually be rewarded by being in a position to buy assets at far more sensible valuations. Such opportunities are lost if you do not have the cash to take full advantage. I guess it comes back to that old chestnut of what is more important to a fund manager — his own business risk or the long term welfare of his investors

Warren Buffett once closed his investment partnership at a time of high valuations that he couldn't reconcile. That is a bit extreme for us but the compromise is to maintain our valuation disciplines. It is one of the great paradoxes that money tends to be freely and increasingly available to chase assets as they become more and more expensive but very tough to come by when opportunities are more abundant as prices fall.

After being considered a poor investment for a decade, resources companies are back in vogue. Do you believe that resources stocks can continue to outperform the broader market for the medium to long term?

It is our view that the vast majority of mining companies, when viewed over an extended period of time, have been serial wealth-destroyers. They are highly cyclical, highly capital intensive and highly commoditised in that long periods of pricing power tend to be very much the exception rather than the rule.

Other than oil, where there appears to be a sound argument for the long-term demand exceeding supply thesis, most commodities generally only experience relatively short-term windows of excess demand before new sources of supply are quite quickly brought on stream to redress the imbalance.

The way to make money and keep it in any environment is to first and foremost be obsessive about preserving what you already have.

It seems the pundits are extremely bullish about this particular resource cycle with the often-repeated refrain that, due to China and India, 'this time it's going to be different' — that is, sustained. Maybe, but things always look at their very best right at the top and as the old saying goes, 'the more things change, the more they stay the same'.

We seem to be in a period of rising interest rates on the back of a strong economy and the fear of higher inflation. Even though rates may have only moved marginally higher, what is the best way to make money in this environment?

At the risk of sounding repetitive, the way to make money and keep it in any environment is to first and foremost be obsessive about preserving what you already have. And secondly, insist on only buying assets when the prospects and the price are working strongly in your favour.

There are times when transactional inactivity represents sound commonsense. Major losses play terrible havoc with long-term compound returns and attempted wealth creation. It is far better to be the consistent carthorse than the one-in-five-year wonder.

As far as interest rates go, they are only one variable in a very complex equation. Japan has experienced interest rates of between 0 and 2 per cent for close on ten years now, and that has been accompanied by a remorseless downward spiral in that sharemarket. Relating interest rates to the earnings yield of stocks is fine, providing you are highly confident in your ability to project earnings. I am very dubious when it comes to the market's long-term track record in this endeavour.

China and its staggering growth rates has probably been the number one talking point among the investment community during the last two years. Do you believe China will be a key theme in the coming years for the Australian sharemarket?

I think we will all be experts with regards to this question with the benefit of hindsight. There are many valid arguments for the China phenomenon continuing, but there are also persuasive reasons for why this has been more representative of an extremely strong cyclical (and to a degree speculative) phenomenon that will revert back to more constrained levels of growth over time.

Undoubtedly, China and India will continue to be of great importance — not only to Australia, but to the entire world economy in the future. The tough part is being objective and realistic about the degree to which this will be the case and not just a way of justifying inflated asset valuations. Having said that, the cycle is alive and well and I imagine that will prove to be the case in China and India — if not even more so, given the inevitable adjustments that tend to follow on from unusually strong growth phases.

The potential problem here is that financial markets, particularly in Australia, appear to have priced in a continuation of the linear growth pattern in China and, to a lesser extent, India. But history tells us that uninterrupted linear growth is a fantasy rather than a reality. There will be hiccups along the way and these will certainly affect countries like Australia, which has been a major beneficiary of the growth in China. The question seldom asked is whether risk is being adequately priced into the whole China equation, and this is where I have some doubts.

If you go back fifteen or twenty years, I think many of the same assumptions were being made about Japan and its ongoing growth, and we now know how that has panned out. I'm not saying that China is going the same way as Japan, but it is a good lesson for overly optimistic investors to ponder over. Put another way, if China keeps growing at 9 to 10 per cent a year, it will represent a staggering proportion of world GDP in a very short period of time. That would imply a shift in the manufacturing bases of many other countries to China, so it's not the gross gain to China that is all important, but rather the net world gain.

What single issue is going to drive the Australian sharemarket higher or lower during the next five years?

I do not believe there will be one single issue. Valuations will continue to be driven, as they always have been, by the level of risk that the investment community feels comfortable taking at any point in time and by the underlying performances of individual businesses. However, I do suspect that people's focus on risk is likely to make a strong comeback at some point. If this does occur, valuations should reduce commensurately. I don't believe the current potential reward for risk is anywhere near sufficient.

Do you believe the Australian sharemarket will outperform other markets during the next two years?

Given the very significant level of outperformance achieved by the Australian market over the last few years, I would have to say no. Looking at the role that the resources boom has played in driving the market higher and the fact that individual markets rarely sustain long-term levels of relative outperformance forms the basis for this belief.

Like some other 'Masters of the Market' you have raised funds since 2003 by establishing a listed investment company. Why is this a good vehicle for you and your investors?

A listed investment structure allows a manager to manage an investment portfolio without having to deal with fund inflows and outflows. As a result of not being faced with a situation where fund redemptions potentially force the sale of such securities in opportune times, such as in market downturns, the manager has greater confidence in building long-term positions in companies.

From MMC Asset Management's perspective, a listed company provides a more predictable revenue stream. This has greatly assisted us in attracting some extremely capable, but often expensive, investment professionals to the organisation.

Your stockpicking skills have been outstanding in recent times, picking such companies as Burns Philp. Why do you think you continue to be successful in picking companies with share prices that have doubled or tripled over time?

We have a history of trawling the market for companies that are either poorly followed or are out of favour for one or more reasons. Our objective is to uncover companies that are out of favour for short-term reasons such as a temporary blip in short-term earnings prospects, being a victim of the market's pre-occupation with headline versus underlying earnings, or being the subject of press hysteria and/or mis-reporting.

Generally, share prices that are falling are doing so for a very good reason. Therefore, if you are to adopt a contrarian approach, you need to be very selective and thorough in your research and, above all, patient.

You must also be prepared for short-term setbacks as companies with issues one day are rarely the overnight success of the next day. In fact, many of our most successful investments have caused considerable pain before the more than compensating gains.

So a patient and long-term approach is vital, as is having investors who are not going to slavishly overemphasise your three- and six-month results.

It is very much a matter of attempting to identify areas of disconnection between the way the market is pricing a business and what we consider to be the long-term underlying value of that business. It comes back to the pretty obvious statement that popular asset classes and popular companies tend to trade at prices reflective of that popularity and are therefore seldom attractive to us.

Given you tend to invest in very few companies, how much work goes in before you make the investment?

Without labouring the point too much, we put a huge amount of time and effort into selecting and then monitoring our investments. Does that make us immune to error? I wish. But, sadly, it doesn't.

All we are trying to do via our research and analysis is to assess whether the probability of success is sufficiently high enough to allocate capital to the opportunity.

Investing in businesses brings with it myriad factors and risks that can render the best thought out and researched theses undone. All businesses are subject to varying degrees of risk — whether it be through exchange rates, interest rates, the behaviour of competitors, government regulations, technological change, movements in profit margins, changes in labour and raw material costs, managerial change or just about anything else that can come out of left field and shock the hell out of you.

You need to question whether it is more risky to hold a whole bundle of stocks where you have limited knowledge of each one, or to hold a more finite number of companies that you know extremely well, have researched thoroughly and feel relatively comfortable with.

When certain commentators attempt to justify contracting risk premiums for stocks over risk-free rates available from long-term government bonds, one does need to be a little cynical. It is certainly my view that investors should always seek significant additional compensation well above the risk-free rate when investing in businesses.

Many fund managers shy away from putting more than 5 per cent of their portfolio into an individual stock. You, on the other hand, are prepared to go much higher, possibly to triple that level. Why?

I think to give yourself the opportunity to outperform over time you have to have the courage and confidence in your own research and convictions to back yourself. We are paid management fees by our investors because over a reasonable time frame they expect us to add value on a risk-adjusted basis. So you need to question whether it is more risky to hold a whole bundle of stocks where you have limited knowledge of each one, or to hold a more finite number of companies that you know extremely well, have researched thoroughly and feel relatively comfortable with. To me, providing you are willing to put in the effort, the latter seems the more logical option.

It also needs to be related to what the general expectations of your investor base are. There are many investors who prefer indexing, and that is fine and it will no doubt produce perfectly acceptable results. Our approach is far more concentrated and as such can produce outperformance, providing you get it right.

The undeniable risk, or downside, to our approach is that, because of its concentrated nature, we pay a very high price if we get it wrong. Having said that, show me an easy approach that provides higher than average returns for no increase in risk and I will forever be in your debt.

Can you share with us your biggest holdings at the moment and what they represent as a percentage of your portfolio?

At the moment we have a couple of stocks, including Burns Philp, that represent about 7 per cent of our portfolio. We did have 12 per cent of our funds in Burns Philp when it was cheaper but it hit some of our price targets and we have reduced our holding. But if the price declined for some reason and the fundamentals of the business remained intact, we wouldn't be concerned about increasing our holdings to 10 per cent and higher again.

Many of the recently floated listed investment companies have been criticised for holding too much cash in a bull market. Your contrarian fund has held a high proportion of cash. Do you think, in hindsight, that has been a wise move and should managers be paid to simply hold cash?

Firstly, I would like to respond very strongly that we are not being paid to hold cash. We are being paid to invest our clients' or shareholders' funds prudently and responsibly in companies that meet all or most of the criteria outlined in our prospectus. Spending the money and buying a portfolio spread of stocks for the sake of it requires little effort — this is what we should not be paid to do! If we are unable to isolate sufficient opportunities that meet our strict criteria at any given point in time, it would be dangerous, foolhardy and irresponsible of us to invest in companies at valuations that could, ultimately, seriously threaten the capital of our shareholders.

We are not relative value investors. To say that a stock is cheap relative to an extremely expensive stock does not necessarily mean it is anywhere near cheap enough on an absolute value basis. It may, in fact, still be downright expensive.

We are not paid, and nor should we be, for the quantum of our transactions. In fact, there is a strong argument to suggest that the two should be inversely correlated.

What we are paid to do is to work hard, but sensibly, with the objective of identifying companies that are available at a price that offers our investors considerable potential upside without placing their capital at undue risk. Advocating that fund managers should always have most of the capital at their disposal invested really has shades of *Yes Minister* about it. It seems to me that the same minority criticising managers for holding cash now are likely to be the same people who would be the first to criticise managers who are highly invested at the top of the market should the market experience a sharp reversal. As Warren Buffett very recently stated, we get paid for 'making' the money, rather than just spending it. Berkshire Hathaway has approximately $45 billion in cash.

What, if any, investment lessons have you learnt during the past two years and how has that influenced your style and approach?

I know it is a cliché but every day you learn something in this game. I suppose the main learning over the last couple of years has come with the introduction of more capable people into the MMC business. They have added insights and perspectives, and they challenge your conclusions. That introduces an additional layer of discipline and emphasis. For a long time I was based in Adelaide, primarily by myself, and working with other people has been a good learning curve for me. It has helped my thinking, given that the HGL people bring operating company knowledge to the table and not just investment know-how, and the new investment team brings significant additional expertise to the table.

How long can you keep going in such a mentally taxing job?

In some form or another, I will be investing in companies as long as I can. It might not be at this intense level but I won't quit just because I'm older. When you are so involved and passionate about an industry like this, you don't just take your gold watch and leave.

I have been at it pretty much full on for twenty or so years now, so at some stage I think it would be appropriate and beneficial to take a three- to six-month break, just to do some uninterrupted thinking and reading and to recharge the batteries. Because of the demands of this occupation, you do miss a lot of very important family time so this is something I also look forward to making amends for.

There can be little doubt that the last two years have been stressful for Metanomski. After raising $200 million in his listed investment company in 2003, the environment has been poor for those looking to implement a deep value approach to investing. As the local stock market has roared ahead, Metanomski has kept a big portion of his new fund in cash, in the belief that there will be a better time to buy stocks at the right price. While in the years to come Metanomski will more than likely be proved correct, the pain of sitting on the sidelines is immense.

Metanomski remains defiant, however. He continues to search long and hard for the types of companies that will deliver the 20 per cent plus per annum returns he has managed during the last decade or more. Of all the points during the interview this time around, Metanomski's most passionate reaction came when we asked whether it was prudent to hold cash instead of investing all funds. He responded very firmly that he was not being paid to hold cash but to simply make the best risk-related decisions he could for his investors. This yet again shows that for long-term investors there can be some very painful shorter periods.

Despite the adverse circumstances, Metanomski has performed admirably since we last spoke to him in 2003. His returns of 20 per cent per annum, while also holding large amounts of cash, speak volumes for his stockpicking abilities. Moreover, he is still enthused by the market and hungry to achieve future success. For the authors, he was very helpful and in good spirits.

Australian investors will have to stomach the fallout from any major market disruptions globally. Investors will have to use more than darts and stock tips. The next few years will reward the careful and punish the lazy. Investors need to actually do some research and at the very least it may be an idea to actually know what the company they are investing in does.

10

The warrior returns
Brian Price

After the first edition of *Masters of the Market* was published in 2003, many people said to us, 'Who is this guy Brian Price? He sounds incredible'.

The quirky Canadian-born, Sydney-based Price captured the imagination of many readers because he was in a league all of his own. He did not just trade the Australian equity market. He was not a pure value investor. Above all, he was prepared to take extremely big risks and leverage his position. Add to this a penchant to stay up most nights to trade global markets and you have a highly unusual and rare character.

Price started trading futures on the Sydney Futures Exchange floor back in the mid-1980s, working first for Transcity Holdings and Irving Trust and then Brian Yuill's Bisley Group. They were tough days. The floor took no prisoners and only the toughest personalities survived in the noisy, dirty and aggressive environment. Price excelled in this environment.

After doing his tour of duty on the futures floor, Price traded for himself in the late 1980s, which he still does today. However, the floor is closed now and Price trades primarily from his home office, working for himself and a select group of clients. Those clients, as Price puts it, are looking for more sophisticated 'insurance' or 'macro-offset' strategies to diversify away from their significant investment positions both in Australian and offshore markets.

Over time, Price's bets have become bigger and bigger. During the 1990s, Price daringly took a short position (a trading position that allows you to profit from a falling market) on the US Nasdaq and S&P 500 indices. But the bull market at that time (which Price in his own idiosyncratic way refers to as 'the market of golden fluffed peacocks ready for the slaughter of equilibrium') showed no signs of reversing. Price's unrealised losses grew larger and larger. Late in 1999 and as a result of a threefold increase in margin requirements, Price was margin-called out of his position and crystallised an overall cumulative loss of $30 million. That's an unfathomable loss for all but those with the deepest of pockets. But, as he has today, Price had other trading positions and by leveraging them as well, he made money elsewhere and kept on trading.

Price also finds time to invest in Australian shares. Although the Australian sharemarket is not the market in which he predominantly trades, here he adopts a precise methodology and has generated a very good return from it. Price tries to find stocks where he can identify tangible asset backing — his core belief is that value is created in focusing on basic investment fundamentals and remaining fixated on these. In these cases, Price is investing for the medium term and is prepared to take a controlling position or a strategic stake in a company.

Price has the ability to adapt to market conditions. It is a matter of policy that his investments are not passive positions. Price works proactively as a contributing shareholder to add value to the investment. His big plays have included investments in the diversified agribusiness group Tandou and in Kerry Packer's cash box CPH Investment Corp, which eventually morphed into Challenger Financial Services.

Price, always thinking and never shy in making a call on the future direction of markets, has also had time to help write the story for the successful movie *The Bank*, starring Anthony LaPaglia and David Wenham. He has now moved onto writing his first novel — a stock market insurance-fraud thriller.

For the second edition of *Masters of the Market* we visited Price at his home and trading bunker at Neutral Bay, on Sydney's lower North Shore. Noticeably, Price had framed and hung his military style trading jacket from his Bisley days in his lounge room for visitors to see. The jacket had faded but the lines of battle could still be recognised. Also in his lounge room was a wide-screen TV, on which Price watches the global markets, and a blanket draped over a lounge, sunken from Price's body after a night's trading. His mother, who suffers paralysis due to polio, lives in a cottage on the same block of land.

As usual, Price was in an up-beat mood after just playing a game of morning tennis. Price provided a lesson in some of the more sophisticated aspects of trading shares and derivatives on global markets and, as always, was extremely forthright and confident in his views.

———————————●———————————

How have you performed against the Australian bull market of the last two years?

The primary emphasis of my trading activities is on the European and US markets. The Australian bull market is not of major significance to me.

I must make the point that it is very hard to measure my performance against a single market. I tailor my investments to each individual client. I provide insurance for many of my clients using futures and options to offset their main investment position. For example, a client might have had a large exposure to the rising Australian equity market over the last two years and want insurance against a falling market. They might invest money with me after a lengthy discussion whereby a specific strategy is designed to match their requirements and expectations. In the event the market turns against their long position at least they have some 'non-correlated' investments.

What has been your best investment call during the past two years?

This is a tough question in that a good investment call may differ from a good investment result. A coin toss may result in a favourable outcome yet the methodology involved is inadequate. My most profitable trade during the last two years was running a long bias[1] Nikkei

A good investment call may differ from a good investment result. A coin toss may result in a favourable outcome yet the methodology involved is inadequate.

[Japanese sharemarket] futures position where, with leverage, the return has been about fivefold. The reason for taking this position was not based on extensive fundamental or macro-economic study but simply an observation that sentiment towards Japan by large global investors was turning positive. This was particularly so in the case of the large American funds. The basic story they believed was that, despite stagnant growth, Japan was still one of the gatekeepers to growth in greater Asia.

What has been your worst investment call during the past two years?

In terms of investment calls, in March 2004 there were clear indications of an extraordinary imbalance in the volatility of global stock indices. When measured by expected and implied volatility, new record lows were continually being breached. The Chicago Board Options Exchange (CBOE) VIX Index[2] and the Australian Share Price Index's volatility were at record lows.

The press at the time was saturated by commentary about how quiet the global markets were. The Australian market was on a steady upward trend that just got steeper as 2004 continued.

My strategy was to make a pre-emptive strike against the low volatility by getting set for an increase in volatility in global markets. As well as being a volatility strategy, it might also have been viewed as an insurance strategy as volatility usually accompanies market disruption.

The basic premise was that the market had it wrong and its excessive complacency would be shattered. Clearly, for the

---

1   By 'long bias', Price means the portfolio is positioned to benefit from a rising Japanese market.

2   The CBOE VIX index is the barometer of stock index volatility and an oscillating indicator. The Australian Share Price Index (SPI) is the Australian equities futures contracts index.

strategy to be profitable, the market needed maximum volatility with frequent directional changes. Conversely, low volatility, no gap trending, grinding markets would create the least profitable scenario. When you have low volatility and the market is heading in the one direction, you have no opportunity to use the directional protection that you have bought through the use of options. If the market heads one way, your option value slowly but with certain mathematical accuracy decays as time passes.

The behaviour of the market between May 2004 and November 2004 was diametrically opposed to the optimum conditions required for my strategy to be profitable. The SPI was in particular the least co-operative to statistical expectations. During a seven-month time frame all of the following occurred. The DAX [German market] volatility reached record lows of 12.5 per cent after spending most of the past five years above 18.5 per cent. The SPI volatility dropped to record lows of 7.5 per cent after spending the past five years above 17 per cent. Out of the 153 days, the SPI only closed on its lows five times. During the same period, the SPI had forty-one days of record highs and just traded steadily higher in a quiet manner. Option volume and liquidity dried up. Market shocks were virtually non-existent. Market gapping was virtually non-existent. And by November 2004 the CBOE VIX was at a new low of 12.56 per cent.

During this period — due to the low volatility premiums — even a 5 per cent gap by the markets would have returned my investors a greater than 80 per cent return in one day and a subsequent direction reversal would have delivered a similar result.

During that seven-month period, there were many reasons for the market to be volatile, including constant US terror alerts and upgrades to US homeland security, battles in Afghanistan and the war in Iraq, the power handover in Iraq, six Federal Open Market Committee meetings with three US rate hikes and warnings of more to come, severe weakening in the US currency, interest rate hikes in Europe, interest rate increases in China and talk of currency revaluations. There was also the instructions by the People's Bank of China to stop lending to certain industries [the Korean market dropped 14 per cent on the news]. There was an oil price explosion with extreme volatility, and a US election, which even to the last days was a close call — a Kerry win would have brought certain volatility. There was a damaging strengthening of the Australian dollar, and the targeting of Australia by Jemaah Islamiah and

Al-Qaeda — any attack would have caused severe volatility in the Australian market. Finally, there was Arafat's terminal illness and huge suicide bombs in Israel.

Despite all of this, volatility remained at historical lows. Of course, the volatility that was experienced in March and April 2005 has more than compensated those investors who remained resilient to the strategy and held their positions. Losses realised by investors who quit the strategy in November 2004 reached 45 per cent of capital invested.

Given the bull market in Australia during the past two years, do you believe the current environment — domestically speaking, that is — is a good one for investing?

The Australian market has certainly been strong. The April volatility caused some disruption. Having said that, the Australian rally in a global context is actually not historically or statistically that significant.

I still consider Australia, even at these levels, to be materially less vulnerable to a fall than, say, the American markets. Unfortunately though, Australian investors will have to stomach the fallout from any major market disruptions globally. Investors will have to use more than darts and stock tips. The next few years will reward the careful and punish the lazy. Investors need to actually do some research and at the very least it may be an idea to actually know what the company they are investing in does. Again, I think avoid the US market completely on a macro basis.

What do you believe will be the best performing asset class over the next two to three years?

Given that I trade on a global basis, I will go through each continent and rank assets on a risk/reward basis.

In Australia, the best assets classes in order will be: sharemarket, cash, bonds, property.

In the USA: cash (but denominated evenly in foreign currencies), bonds, property, sharemarket.

In Europe: cash (but denominated evenly in foreign currencies), bonds, property, sharemarket.

In Asia: sharemarket, property, bonds, cash.

But in the 1990s, you took a big bet against the US bull market and it burnt you! Despite this, you are still prepared to bet against the US sharemarket?

Yes, each new decision can only be based on the information currently available. Apart from gaining experience, the past has no relevance.

To me, the US has peaked as an economic power. The decline of the US may take years — twenty years perhaps. I think the US is spread too thinly around the globe, both economically and militarily. There are another 5.7 billion people who have their own dreams and aspirations. All empires collapse.

If the USA is declining, who is going to fill the void on the world stage?

As the US declines I think the economic void will be filled by China, India and South America — primarily Brazil. Economically, the prospects for Australia are excellent.

> The China rhetoric is interesting and very valid but, as in the technology hysteria, those of us with children should be practising the game of 'hot potato'.

Do you believe resources stocks can continue to outperform the market in the medium to longer term?

The interesting aspect of the resource market is that it has that wonderful ability to be the place where dreams can be dreamt and tales told around the camp fire. Resources stocks have the capability to deliver the euphoria of investment victory but also the potential to drive home the agony of defeat. The China rhetoric is interesting and very valid but, as in the technology hysteria [in the late 1990s], those of us with children should be practising the game of 'hot potato'.

The issue with resources is the expected volatility and the difficulty in timing your investment. Equilibrium will sneak in one night and raid the pantry.

After virtually no inflation during the 1990s and the early part of this decade, there seems to be a concern out there about inflation on the back of rising raw material prices and to a lesser extent wages. What is the best way of dealing with inflation?

Economic students know that with inflation, cash and cash-type securities lose 'value'. In this situation, an investor should own real assets and protect geared investments. Short sell interest-bearing securities or futures. Divest debt securities. Buy inflation-linked investments. Buy puts in long-dated interest-rate instruments. Buy selected commodity indicies.

China and its staggering economic growth rates has been a key theme in financial markets in recent times. Do you think that will continue in the coming years?

Yes. Both China and India will continue to be important. But I think we must be aware that the Chinese and Indian people are very, very clever (surprise, surprise — as smart as us!). They know the game and I guarantee they won't be the bountiful carcass that some believe.

As we sit here, the price of crude oil is surging and is currently around US$58[3] a barrel. Do you have a view on where oil is heading given all the talk about peak oil and looming oil shortages?

From what I can tell traders are continuing to short oil, which suggests in the short term the price of crude is probably going higher. Once all these shorts are taken out, you might just get a fall in the price of oil for some time despite the predictions of demand outstripping supply. Humans are very resourceful and excellent problem solvers. Oil is an emotional and strategically important raw material. The answer [to oil shortages] exists but is yet to be identified. There seems to be an awful lot of power in those waves that slam the Australian coasts with statistical regularity.

What single issue is going to drive the sharemarket higher or lower over the next five years?

Sentiment. Take a poll of ten of your friends as to where they believe the market will be in the next two or three years. If more than 75 per cent believe the market will be strong, sell and stand aside. If they are depressed about or uninterested in the market, buy stocks.

Which global market presents the best investment opportunity for you now and over the next few years?

The most significant (as opposed to best) opportunity is in short selling the US S&P 500 index and maintaining resilience of strategy.

---

3   At the time of publication, the oil price had reached more than US$67 a barrel.

Then build a buy strategy globally around this protection from global 'market risk'.

When we last spoke in 2003 you were very critical of the US authorities and how they had managed to inflate the value of their equities market through policy intiatives. Is this still the case?

I believe very strongly that the US government has the apparent health of the stock markets and other financial markets as major policy objectives. This is a country fighting substantial financial and military battles and the morale of the general public is crucial in promoting the 'success' of these objectives within the investing community. This [the US market] is an equity market that remains overvalued and vulnerable. I think, ultimately, it will be the general public who suffer the consequences by being trapped by debt levels and falling asset prices.

Of all the 'Masters of the Market', you are one of the few who short sells markets and stocks. Are you actively shorting now and, if so, where?

As I've said, I am short the S&P 500. As for specific Australian stocks, I am short Billabong, Wesfarmers, Great Southern Plantations, Perpetual and Multiplex.

Could you make some predictions on which direction some of the major financial markets in the world will head over the next few years?

In the US, I see the US dollar weakening against the Japanese, South American and Asian currencies. Interest rates will be finely balanced with the pressures and expectations building from cost push and demand pull variables in conflict with currency stability maintenance and open market operations. I see the S&P 500 index down, Russell 2000 down, Dow Jones index down and the Nasdaq steady.

In Europe, there is slight bias towards increased interest rates and, obviously, decreasing bond prices. Stock markets will be relatively weak, especially the FTSE and DAX.

In Australia, the dollar will be stronger against nearly all cross rates in the developed countries. Interest rates will be relatively stable, property markets will fall and the sharemarket will have a stronger bias.

In Asia, stock markets should head higher. Currencies will be stronger against the US dollar and the euro, and interest rates should remain relatively stable.

Overall, outperforming sharemarkets will include India, China and South America.

Turning to the second part of your investment strategy — buying Australian companies at or below their tangible asset backing, has this task proven difficult given the bull market over the last two years?

The problem with a market like the one that occurred in the second half of 2004 is that the public begins to believe that they are invincible as investors and chase stocks to unrealistic levels, much like pyramid building. This makes finding value more difficult. However, as in life, there are always opportunities available to those prepared to work and do their research. Forget for one moment the hot potato, leave the tour group and explore the woods on your own.

I have just purchased 16 per cent of [wine and intensive irrigation company] Tandou, for example.

This is your second crack at trying to realise the asset-based value in Tandou.[4] It worked well the first time, but why have a second go?

Tandou fits the profile for the value investor. It has been seven long years in purgatory. I want to practise the art of value-add investing — to be a contributing shareholder so to speak.

Will this mean that you will no longer concentrate on trading global markets?

Only in Australia will the focus be on individual company investments. I could never even pretend to have the jump on individual stocks in overseas markets. My offshore investing has been and always will be index-based, concentrating on macro-strategies designed for global risk management.

Can we expect to see your name pop up on the Australian equity scene more regularly then?

Definitely.

---

4   In the late 1990s, Price invested about $4 million buying 19 per cent of Tandou. His entry price was 80¢ a share and he exited for a tidy profit at $1.55 a share.

In our first interview in 1998 and again in 2003, you talked a lot about looking after yourself, given the lifestyle you lead — staying up most nights and trading — was sure to take its toll. What has happened to your lifestyle over the last two years?

My mother says that continuing to chase unsuitable women is stressful but on a positive note, improved technology and more reliable software allows for greater relaxation.

I can travel more freely. Last year, for example, I spent three months abroad in places like Israel, Jordon, Colombia and the UK. The whole time, I was fully able to focus on the market without undue stress related to location.

I continue to attempt to achieve the improbable without shame and that in itself brings an element of peace to my life.

———————●———————

Brian Price was a warrior on the floor of the Sydney Futures Exchange in the 1980s and he is still a financial warrior trading from his home in Neutral Bay twenty years later. He still bets against the pack and does so at high risk with enormous leverage. The US debacle in the 1990s when he lost an estimated $30 million of his own money could have rattled him a little but Price is unfazed. Yet again, he is betting big time on a fall in the US sharemarket. Indeed, as time has gone on, he has learnt to cope better with highly volatile returns. He keeps on taking big bets, knowing that not all are going to pay off and that big losses could be incurred at different time intervals.

Ever the entrepreneur, Price is now looking to make big investments in Australian companies as he continues the search for great returns. The size of the companies involved doesn't worry him. It will be interesting to see if Price can achieve as much success as a corporate warrior on the Australian sharemarket as he has achieved with his often intricate but highly rewarding global trading strategies.

In the medium to longer term, I believe that small companies will outperform the broader market given their higher earnings growth profile. Despite a lot of attention at the small end of the market during the bull run of the last two years, many companies with great growth profiles have not been identified and the opportunity is there for those prepared to keep digging around.

11

Good things come in small packages
David Paradice

In April this year (2005) David Paradice celebrated the fifth birthday of his company, Paradice Cooper, at a function on the sixth level of the Museum of Contemporary Art at Sydney's Circular Quay. The 300 attendees included stockbrokers, company executives and even some fellow fund managers. Initially, there were to be 1000 invited but the company decided to have separate functions in Sydney, Melbourne and Brisbane. The market was abuzz about the elite gathering for days afterwards. Attendees were shocked that the usually frugal (in the money sense of the word) Paradice would indulge his colleagues. He even joked in his speech during the evening that most people waited until their tenth anniversary for such an event but that he wanted to have a function to thank everyone now, just in case he wasn't around in ten years.

Paradice's fifth birthday bash was certainly a worthwhile celebration. Since its inception in 2000, the small-cap funds of Paradice Cooper have grown from zero to $1.2 billion. The fund was closed in 2003 with $450 million committed, while the rest of the money, close to $800 million, has resulted from the fund's performance. But don't hold your breath for a second bash on the harbour. Paradice is by nature anything but a big spender, both in his personal life and when looking for stocks to buy.

When we interviewed him for the first edition of *Masters of the Market*, it was clear that he was a person who had little or no time to buy new shoes, new suits or any of the extras that would normally impress investors and asset consultants.

Despite his continued success since our first interview, nothing much has changed. Paradice is still a bit dishevelled, with his hair for the most part uncombed and his shirt unironed. His investment style has not changed either. In the 1990s while managing money for Mercantile Mutual (now ING), Paradice delivered returns of 28 per cent a year, twice the average of the market. His basic philosophy was to buy growth companies at a reasonable price. Paradice transferred this same philosophy across to his own company, only investing in companies outside the top 100 on the Australian sharemarket. Partner Peter Cooper has a team based in Melbourne that concentrates on top 100 companies and is managing $2.3 billion at the time of writing. Their performance has also been very good, delivering 21.7 per cent per annum return over the last three years (the index was up 14.7 per cent per annum) and ranking them as top quartile managers over every time period.

One thing that has changed since our last interview is the personnel working underneath Paradice. David Smith has departed after taking a job in Hong Kong, while Alan Crozier has used the strategy of his old boss and started his own funds management business. To help run his portfolio, Paradice decided to seek out the best people in the market, hiring Matt Riordan, ex-head of small caps at BT, and John Harbot from stockbrokers Austock. More recently, he has taken on Adam Harvey as his dealer, while Kylie Barns keeps the office running smoothly.

In the five years since starting his own company, Paradice has managed to deliver an annual return of slightly above 30 per cent — compared to an annual return from the S&P/ASX Small Ordinaries Index of just 7.2 per cent.

The second edition of *Masters of the Market* came at an interesting time for one of Australia's most successful investors in small-cap stocks. After two years of a raging bull market, the small companies index was shaken in the first half of 2005 as economic growth appeared to slow and raw material prices rose.

During his birthday bash, Paradice remarked that it was probably the top of the market for now. It was perhaps more of an insight into

Paradice's state of mind rather than a specific forecast. He avoids excess. To wrap up his speech, Paradice wrote a poem. The final two lines said, 'I hope you have a good night. Drink as much tap water as you like'.

Every time Paradice visits a company he may want to invest in, he is on the lookout for management extravagances that may be a sign management has taken their eyes off the job at hand. That is never a problem for Paradice — he lives and breathes the market, seven days a week. He spends every spare moment talking to companies, stockbrokers and other fund managers in the hope of finding an edge. His family is used to waiting in the car outside as he discusses with the proprietors of corner stores or bike hire shops the dynamics of their businesses.

We met again with Paradice at his latest office headquarters on Bent Street, Sydney on 21 June 2005.

———————•———————

For the two years since March 2003, the S&P/ASX Small Ordinaries Index (the benchmark your company uses to measure its performance) has risen a staggering 75 per cent. How have you performed during this bull run?

We have managed to keep ahead of the market with a gain of approximately 107 per cent, which is an annualised gain of about 44 per cent compared to the Small Ordinaries Index's return of 32 per cent a year.

What has been your best investment call in the last two years?

We started buying Caltex at $1.75 in August 2002. The stock is currently around $18.00. There were a number of reasons why we bought the stock. Based on historical long-term cash flows, the stock looked cheap and the introduction of the clean fuel legislation created higher barriers to entry. This new legislation would also make it more difficult for weaker players in the industry to compete, which would probably lead to those weaker competing oil refineries closing down, reducing capacity and increasing margins for the remaining players. Refining margins were trading below long-term averages and the Australian market looked similar to the one in California, where the industry had already rationalised and the stronger companies were prospering.

Stocks that we have held for over two years that have averaged returns of over 100 per cent per annum include Worley Parsons, ABC Learning, Monadelphous Group, Reece, Transfield Services, Colorado Group, UNiTAB, Metcash Trading, Healthscope and Ramsay Healthcare. The common component of all these investments is that they have excellent management.

What has been your worst investment in this time?

Possibly our worst investment was Intellect Holdings, which among other things makes EFTPOS machines. We participated in a placement at 45¢ in November 2003 on the belief that they could make machines cheaper than their competitors and that they had superior distribution. Three months after the placement they released a profit downgrade, based on information that was not forecast by management. This caused us to have concerns about management and the fundamentals of the business. We subsequently sold the stock from 45¢ down to approximately 21¢, with an average exit price of 27¢. The stock is now trading at 2.6¢.

We find that if we make a mistake and the fundamentals of the business have changed, it is usually best to sell the stock out and look from the sidelines.

Given the strong market in small-capitalisation stocks, do you believe the environment in June 2005 is a good one for investing in?

As a general comment it is getting hard to find value at the moment, with many stocks looking fully priced given their current growth outlook.

On the one hand, there are companies that are exposed to the non-residential side of the economy and look expensive, but have a considerable growth outlook. I suspect that a lot of the expected growth to come is anticipated in these high-PE stocks. For example, UNiTAB is a great company with great management and has a reasonable growth outlook but it is hard to expect the price to earnings ratio to expand significantly from current levels.

Where you tend to get your big winners is when there is good earnings growth combined with price to earnings multiple expansion.

Then, on the other hand, there are the consumer-related stocks such as retailers and building materials companies that look cheap, but their sectors have slowed down fairly dramatically, and the outlook is uncertain. These companies look cheap on just about every measure, with not much growth priced in. But in the medium term, I can see many of those stocks that trade on nine times earnings trading again at, say eleven or twelve times. Where you tend to get your big winners is when there is good earnings growth combined with price to earnings multiple expansion.[1] So our preference over time would be to move towards those cheaper stocks that have all the bad news priced in. I hate buying high PE/growthy stocks.

There is less risk in buying cheap stocks that have no growth expectations in the price than in buying expensive stocks that have to hit high growth expectations to justify their price.

What sectors of the small-company market do you think will perform over the next two to three years?

I think one of the key sectors for the next few years will be health care. It is a growth area that should perform well despite the ups and downs of the economy. Another key sector is non-residential or infrastructure construction. This area should be fuelled by increased government spending on infrastructure, and ongoing spending in the resources sector. Finally, financial services. This high growth area does not require high levels of capital investment, which leads to higher than average incremental return on capital.

---

1   Price to earnings multiple expansion is where a company's price to earnings multiple rises significantly. For example, if a company has historically had a price to earnings multiple of twelve times but is trading at eight times because of a poor economy, there may be an opportunity. In time, as the macro-economic environment improves, the company's earnings may again grow at 12 per cent; however, the share price could double that growth rate over the next two years as the price earnings multiple expands from eight times to its historical average of twelve. Paradice warns, though, that price earnings multiples can sometimes contract for company specific reasons or a structural change, and the multiple may stay low for a long time. Only thorough research will tell you if this is the case.

After being considered a poor investment for more than a decade, resources stocks are back. Do you believe the resources sector can continue to outperform the broader market for the medium to long term?

It appears reasonable to assume that growth will continue to come from China and India, which should see commodity prices stay high in the short term. That said, it is very hard currently to invest in companies in that sector. At the moment, most stocks and commodity prices are historically high. They are priced for a perfect scenario of strong world growth over a long period of time, with valuations currently being supported by forecast commodity prices way above long-term historical averages. I think you will find there will be some hiccups along the way and that will cause prices to adjust. If that scenario plays out, you could see some buying opportunities.

In the small company end of the market, there have been many earnings downgrades in the first half of calendar year 2005. Many of the companies have downgraded their earnings as a result of sharp rises in costs — both labour and raw materials. Do you see inflation being a threat to the current bull market and, if so, how are you coping with it?

Rising costs have become an issue again after being quite benign over the last decade or so. We tend to make our judgements on what is happening on the economic front by talking to the companies that tend to be at the coalface and know first-hand what the economy's strong and weak points are. One of the questions we always ask companies, and their competitors and customers, is whether or not they have the ability to absorb higher costs by increasing the prices of their goods and services. We try to avoid companies that do not have the potential to pass on higher costs by increasing prices themselves. We also try to avoid companies that have highly concentrated customer bases that constantly want their suppliers to reduce prices. Those companies that depend on one or two major customers like Woolworths, Coles or Bunnings may find it hard to pass on price increases.

Do you see China as the key theme driving the market higher or lower in the medium term, or will another issue dominate?

Most of the time, it is the issues we can't see today that affect the market the most in the future. However, I do believe two themes will continue to have a big impact on the market.

Firstly, China and India. At the moment these two countries are industrialising and growing strongly. However, if the US has a hiccup on the growth front or goes into recession, it is reasonable to believe that China, and to a lesser extent India, may have a problem. China depends largely on US consumers buying many of the cheap goods it makes. If demand for these goods slows, China will also slow and that will have a negative impact on demand for Australian products and commodities. In addition, if demand in China and/or India increases, oil prices may continue to rise (along with inflation in China), placing stress on global growth.

Secondly, it appears that governments around Australia, both federal and state, need to spend money on improving infrastructure. That will be on roads, water, ports and the like. If they spend as they currently indicate, a number of companies will benefit. However, many of the big infrastructure contracts will be won on price and it is therefore important when investing in the sector to seek out the most efficient operators in their field. Companies with above average costs who tender too low end up being hurt by winning too much work at low margins.

In early 2005 the S&P/ASX Small Ordinaries Index traded on similar price to earnings multiples to the S&P/ASX 100 Index. Historically, the small companies have traded at around a 15 per cent discount to their bigger colleagues. Do you think small caps will again trade at a similar discount?

I think Australian small-cap companies as a group are currently overpriced and will therefore underperform in the short term. In the medium to longer term, though, I believe that small companies will outperform the broader market given their higher earnings growth profile. Despite a lot of attention at the small end of the market during the bull run of the last two years, many companies with great growth profiles have not been identified and the opportunity is there for those prepared to keep digging around.

Despite a lot of attention at the small end of the market during the bull run of the last two years, many companies with great growth profiles have not been identified.

In the top 100 stocks, every piece of information is digested, scrutinised and factored into the share price. I still think that is not the case at the smaller end. High returns will be achieved by finding companies that have good growth prospects combined with the capacity for price to earnings multiple expansion.

We understand that there are periods when small caps outperform big caps and vice versa. As a result (besides many other reasons), Paradice Cooper has combined these two areas — big caps and small caps — to offset the volatility of being exposed to one area.

Between 2003 and 2005, Paradice Cooper almost tripled the amount of money under management in small companies to $1.2 billion. Is this too much money for someone looking to outperform in the small company area of the market?

We closed the fund to new business in 2003. At that stage, we had raised $450 million. We have made about $800 million for our clients, taking total funds under management to over $1.2 billion. However, over that period the small company index has increased by about 62 per cent. In addition, there has been a considerable number of large floats in the small-cap market that have further expanded the market. As a result, running $1.2 billion at this end of the market is quite manageable. Currently, our funds represent 0.7 per cent of the total value of the companies outside the top 100. I think if you got to about 1.5 per cent of that market, you might run into some problems trying to get set in stocks and finding opportunities to keep performing.

The first half of calendar year 2005 has been a volatile one for the market, especially small companies. During March and April, the S&P/ASX Small Ordinaries Index fell about 12 per cent — only to bounce back strongly, approaching new highs by mid-June. Have you been surprised by the dramatic bounce back?

I have been surprised by the bounce back. Reasons provided by market commentators for the bounce include increased liquidity, lower interest rates and comfort on longer term economic growth. Once again, we tend to be more bottom-up and just look at how the stocks in our universe are travelling. Over the last few months, we have been highly active in visiting companies as we search for investment possibilities and the direction of the economy. Currently, there are not many cheap stocks out there for our style of investing. Over the years this scenario has told me the market is getting ahead of itself.

Are there any particular small companies that you see as having good longer term prospects that are worth investigating and thoroughly researching?

As I said earlier, you have two types of companies at the moment — cheaply priced earnings multiple stocks, such as those exposed to the weak consumer discretionary market, and those stocks that appear expensive like those in non-residential or infrastructure construction.

Over time, we have tended to do well in companies that are trading below historical valuation averages. Once the outlook for those companies starts to clear, they should achieve not only earnings growth but, crucially, price earnings multiple expansion. If you can get that combination, you will get a good return out of a company. At the moment, there are a bunch of retailers and wholesalers, like David Jones, Colorado, GUD and Housewares, as well as building material companies, such as Crane Group, that are all trading on franked yields of more than 7 per cent. Sure, the growth in the sector they operate in is questionable at the moment, but at some stage that should improve.

You are known to have a great adviser network in the financial community. Where do you get most of your investment ideas from?

Most of our ideas come from continually talking to the companies in our universe of stocks — asking how things are going, and talking to their competitors, suppliers and customers.

I talk to other fund managers — who normally tell you the stocks they have already bought, and so you have to take that with a grain of salt — but overall that is a good source of ideas. I also talk to not only big brokers but also the small brokers, especially in regional areas.

———————●———————

Despite changes in personnel, David Paradice is still performing incredibly well in the small company end of the market. With more than $1.2 billion under management, he has been able to continually beat the index. The reason seems to be that he sticks to his investment style and scours bombed-out situations, buying stocks with growth for a reasonable price. This has worked in the past and continues to pay dividends.

From the authors' point of view, Paradice has several unique qualities. Firstly, he is enthusiastic and never tires of the market — he regularly comments that he couldn't do much else anyway. He is always talking to a company or broker or customer, or whoever might have some quality information. Secondly, he seems to be able to distil very quickly the crucial two or three elements that will see a stock perform or, conversely, not perform. Usually this is based on fundamentals. Finally, Paradice understands what delivers investment performance. He is not only looking for growth but companies that look cheap and have the potential to deliver price to earnings multiple expansion.

Some of the cyclicals look cheap on this year's earnings, but the big question going forward is whether the cycle still exists. And we're believers that, yes, the cycle does exist. The cycle will have a downturn just as much as it has had an upturn and today is not the time to be buying cyclical stocks.

12

History repeating
Anton Tagliaferro

Anton Tagliaferro looks agitated and frustrated. His voice, normally high pitched, hits a new octave. He is fidgety and finding it hard to concentrate.

Before we can start our interview for the second edition of *Masters of the Market*, Tagliaferro insists that we go into a room in his offices that houses a whiteboard so he can explain why he believes parts of the market are full of froth and bubble and a correction is not too far away. He interrupts a meeting that his colleagues Andrew King and Simon Conn are conducting and starts scribbling notes on the board at a frantic pace about a listed infrastructure company. At the end of the short lecture, he says, 'Can you believe the level of borrowings in some of these companies and the fees being charged? And people say there are no excesses — ha!'

When we met Tagliaferro for the first edition of *Masters of the Market*, he gave us some great stories about the emotions of investors during times of peaking markets. When the tech boom reached its peak in 2000, Tagliaferro could not understand why companies with no profits, and very little prospect of ever making profits, were being valued by the market at hundreds of millions or billions of dollars. Having just started his own funds management business with an investment philosophy that avoided those very companies, he would visit the Sydney Aquarium at lunchtime to ease the stress of his early underperformance. When the tech boom inevitably ended with the sharemarket crash in April 2000, Tagliaferro didn't need to watch fish any more. His business didn't look back, winning awards and regularly topping league tables by delivering consistently high investment returns.

Five years later and with the market again at record highs, Tagliaferro says he feels like visiting the aquarium again. He simply fails to understand why investors are prepared to award highly cyclical stocks such as mining companies massive valuations. Similarly, he is baffled by the sharemarket's willingness to support, virtually without question, the new generation of investment vehicles spawned by fee-generating investment firms.

Tagliaferro, like many of our Masters, started his career as an accountant. After moving to Australia, from his native Malta via the UK, he began to get interested in the sharemarket. Auditing was just too slow-paced for someone so ambitious. To feed his growing addiction to the sharemarket, he would spend many a lunchtime in the mid-1980s in the viewing gallery of the stock market floor, watching brokers ply their trade. In the gallery, he met some great characters like Billy the Bear, who warned the market boom at the time would end in tears for investors. Billy was right but Tagliaferro was hooked.

After a stint at Prudential, Tagliaferro landed his first job really managing a share portfolio at Perpetual Trustees. Perpetual was a minnow by today's standards and really only managed money for trustee clients. Tagliaferro set about carving out a reputation following the 1987 crash that saw Perpetual shoot to the top of the charts and gain deep respect in the funds management community. Initially by himself and then with the help of fellow Master Peter Morgan, Tagliaferro developed a valued-based stockpicking style that worked famously. In 1992, he moved from Sydney to Melbourne to work for County Natwest Funds Management. County used a different style of investing that focused mainly on picking growth stocks through identifying sectors or themes with good prospects.

This didn't fit with Tagliaferro's preferred style of picking stocks. He moved back to Sydney in the mid-1990s and successfully brought both philosophies together at his next employer, BNP Investment Management. In 1998, Tagliaferro felt the urge to control his own destiny by starting his own business, Investors Mutual.

Testament to its success, Investors Mutual now manages about $5 billion in funds.

While Tagliaferro has been lucky enough to experience various investment styles, it is fair to say he is a value-based investor. Put simply, he is not interested in stocks that trade on high price/earnings multiples. But while this was a good recipe for his funds from 2000 through to 2003, this style has not been as rewarding in the buoyant markets of 2004 and 2005. Even though his stress levels are rocketing, Tagliaferro is determined not to get sucked into the latest bull market and the darling resources stocks.

We interviewed Tagliaferro at his Spring Street office in Sydney in August 2005. Despite his obvious irritation at the market's staggering rise, he was polite and always informative.

———————●———————

Since March 2003, the S&P/ASX 200 is up about 60 per cent; in 2004, it rose 23 per cent — its best performance since 1993. This represents the market's strongest run since the bull market in the lead up to the 1987 crash. How have you fared in these conditions?

Well, we've made pretty good money for our clients, although it's a bit hard to keep in touch with the market and generate returns similar to what the market is getting, and it's getting tougher every day as the market keeps climbing. It's only certain sectors of the market that are running. In our view, they don't represent very good long-term value, so we just have to sit and take the pain at the moment.

I think up to June 2004 we matched the index, but to June 2005 we were five per cent behind the index. So we did about 20-odd per cent to June 2004 and just over 20 per cent again to June 2005 but that was behind the index, which did 26 per cent.

What cash levels were your funds holding during that period?

We've had cash levels of between 10 and 20 per cent so it has been reasonably high I guess.

So what you've invested in has done a little bit better than the market.

We've done okay considering we're quite cautious of sectors such as the resources sector and stocks with highly leveraged financial structures. In our opinion, many of these are excessively priced, so considering we're not fans of those, we've done okay.

I wouldn't say it's been the best period of my life because it's always frustrating when you underperform the index by a significant amount. You know how I get very upset and emotional. It affects my whole outlook on life. But it's okay, we're holding on.

In the last two years, what was your best investment call?

I think the last time we spoke, we spoke about MIA [Medical Imaging Australasia], the radiology group that was trading at about 50¢ or 60¢. It was taken over by DCA Group in a scrip bid for the equivalent of $1.10 then. DCA is now trading at four bucks, so I guess our old MIA shares are worth well over $2 a share.

So you made four times your money over that period. Have you held your DCA shares?

Actually we sold them very recently. We thought they were getting too expensive, but we enjoyed most of that gain.

And can you elaborate on why you bought those shares to begin with?

We bought shares in MIA because it was Australia's largest radiology company. We thought it had many of the attributes we look for in a company — competitive advantage, predictable earnings that could grow   and we thought it was trading at a very cheap price. Everyone disliked it greatly at the time because MIA had missed their earnings numbers a couple of times. Everyone also disliked the radiology industry as a whole because the view was that it was a very capital-intensive industry. And, given that 50 per cent of revenue goes towards salaries, why would you want to own MIA when nurses' and doctors' salaries are going up all the time? But in our view the stock was trading at about nine or ten times, which we thought was a good price to be buying at. Funny how views change — today DCA

Group, which is 80 per cent radiology, is trading at a multiple of more than twenty times earnings. So apparently the capital intensity and the labour cost as a percentage of sales is no longer a problem for most investors. It's funny how companies don't change, but perceptions can change so drastically.

Conversely, what's been your worst investment?

One very disappointing stock over the last couple of years has been Amcor — in fact, it's probably been one of the worst performers in Australia's top fifty. I have followed Amcor for a long time — since the 1980s — and what is it really? It's a producer of bottles and boxes. It's not a very complicated or high-tech company — you needed someone twenty years ago to produce bottles, boxes and cartons, you need them today and you'll need them in twenty years' time. It's not a company that's going to go away.

> *It's funny how companies don't change, but perceptions can change so drastically.*

The reason we like Amcor is because over 90 per cent of its earnings comes from packaging for the food, beverage and pharmaceutical industries, so it has a pretty stable, predictable earnings rate. They've had a couple of hiccups over the past few years with some parts of their overseas operation, as well as the ACCC inquiry that happened last year[1], which was a bit negative. But the company still looks pretty good to us from a long-term point of view. It's trading at eleven or twelve times earnings, so it's one of the cheapest stocks in the top fifty.

But everyone hates it. I've followed Amcor for a long time and it's very difficult to find anyone to say a good word about the company, which is interesting considering the simple steady business that it is — especially in a market where people keep saying there's no value. And here's a stock like Amcor that is a multinational, a leader in packaging around the world, trading at eleven or twelve times earnings with a dividend yield of over 5 per cent on a payout ratio of only 55 per cent.

We have about 5 per cent [of the portfolio] in Amcor.

---

1   In late 2004, the Australian Competition and Consumer Commission (ACCC) announced it was investigating Amcor's involvement in an alleged cardboard box cartel.

Since 2003, by how much have you grown funds under management?

We had $3 billion in 2003 and we have just over $5 billion now.

So you've got 5 per cent of that $5 billion invested in Amcor?

More or less.

So you're prepared to stay with that investment?

We've bought more. Every time the shares dip well below $7, we buy a few more.

And it's purely on a valuation argument?

Well, it's at eleven or twelve times earnings, everyone hates it, it's on a yield of over five and the dividend payout ratio is 55 per cent so the dividend is maintainable. It's in the top fifty stocks and we can't find another of its type. Amcor is almost an annuity type of business that is trading very cheaply. It has a few issues, but that's why it's cheap.

At the moment, you're paying well over fifteen times for Rinker; you're paying record prices for stocks such as BlueScope Steel and Boral and many of these types of companies. I think people have forgotten that cycles do exist. You've got to be very cautious because a lot of these types of companies are now trading at close to the top of the cycle for earnings. So their PEs will look a lot higher when these cycles fall back to reality.

And there's Amcor, which operates in a cycle where their volumes don't get huge volatility, but it's trading on ten, eleven times.

Is the current market a good one for investing?

There are some parts of the market that offer reasonable value if you are prepared to be patient. As I mentioned earlier, we think Amcor is okay; Tabcorp is another stock that is reasonably priced. There are some companies where the dividend yield today is over 5 per cent and the PE is ten to fourteen — in our opinion, that's generally a good time to buy.

Then you've got companies like CSL trading on forty times; or Macquarie Bank, where if you strip out performance fees and profits on asset sales, it is trading on fifty times, and there are a lot of other companies trading on twenty to forty times earnings.

Some of the cyclicals look cheap on this year's earnings, but the big question going forward is whether the cycle still exists. And we're believers that, yes, the cycle does exist. The cycle will have a downturn just as much as it has had an upturn and today is not the time to be buying cyclical stocks.

What do you think will be the best performing asset class over the next two to three years? Cash or equities?

At this stage, I would say cash and some high-yielding industrial shares. Quite frankly, in the next two to three years I think there will be a much better time to buy many shares. Our preference has always been to buy good solid industrials on good sustainable yields. That's definitely what I would stick to now.

I think in the next two or three years — either because interest rates will surprise on the upside or inflation will go higher than we think or consumer demand will falter — there will be a catalyst where we get a downrating in the equity market. I think for the time being one's got to be patient but in the next two or three years, I think there will be very good opportunities to buy a lot of good companies cheaper than what they are today.

Is your view based on a belief that interest rates are going to go higher and investors are going to receive a better yield from cash, or is it based more on a belief that equities are overvalued?

Well, it's a belief that there will be a better time in the next two or three years to build a portfolio of good quality shares and today is not the day.

We're effectively in a rising interest rate market with inflation expected to rise. Historically, inflation is the 'bogyman' of the market and interest rates can rapidly dampen the market. How do you make money in this kind of environment?

I think one has to be patient, because what we're seeing are asset bubbles. You've got an asset bubble in the housing market and you've got asset bubbles in financial markets. There's a lot of excess liquidity at the moment, which tells me interest rates are too low and have to go higher in the next few years. So one has to be patient.

We're sticking to our current portfolio, just buying boring companies like the Amcors, the Tabcorps, and Telecom NZ, where the yields are high and the PEs are reasonable. At the moment, that's where we are comfortable being.

Hopefully in the next two or three years there'll be more opportunity to venture out. In the small-cap market, which is traditionally where one can make very good returns, we can hardly find two or three stocks today that we think are attractive. The best you can say about most of them is that they are fair value or that the price is high because they are very high quality companies. But there's very few we can find today that are actually very cheap.

That's telling me that there will be a better time in the future to buy small- to mid-caps.

So if you didn't have a mandate to invest, would you hold a lot more cash?

Yes, we probably would. As I said, the market is two-tiered. There are stocks that we are quite comfortable to hold because of their reasonable PEs and attractive dividend yields, but they're not the ones performing very well at the moment. You can have as many Amcors and Tabcorps as you like but you're still going to lag the overall sharemarket. What's performing in this market at the moment are the stocks enjoying all this sort of pro-growth 'things will be good forever' and 'the resources boom is going to last forever' sentiment. Stocks like the ASX, Macquarie Bank and Computershare are reaching new highs every day because apparently the equity markets are going to keep rising forever and they have leverage to a rising equity market.

It's nonsense really.

In our first interview two years ago you described the period of the tech boom — the late 1990s into 2000 — as a very difficult period. You talked about going to the aquarium and buying a full-year membership to calm you down. Does this period match that kind of frustration?

It's very close.

But not as bad yet?

I'm not going to the aquarium yet but I'm close to going there again! I am trying to keep a straight mind but maybe I'll tell you about aquarium visits in your next book if the sharemarket keeps behaving as irrationally as it is today!

But I have to admit that I am finding it pretty tough going at the moment. When you look at some of the infrastructure vehicles being listed now and some of the excesses, the gearing in a lot of the vehicles in the market, the gearing in the LPT sector — the risks are there but nobody seems to be paying attention.

> *There's no view on risk/reward anymore. It's all a bit skewed toward the seeking out of the best return and no-one is that concerned about the riskiness of the sharemarket.*

The sharemarket doesn't appear to be assessing risk well. There's no view on risk/reward anymore. It's all a bit skewed toward the seeking out of the best return and no-one is that concerned about the riskiness of the sharemarket.

Going back to the market in general, the China theme has been an important part of the market in the past two years. Obviously, the Chinese economy is growing strongly and is generating a lot of demand for a lot of products. Do you think China will continue to be a common theme in the next two years and, if so, do you think it will be a positive thing?

China has already had a big impact on commodity prices and resources shares so our view is that a lot of the good news is now priced in.

You've also got to watch what the US economy does in terms of where it goes for the next couple of years, given higher US rates and an overleveraged consumer. On balance, I would have thought most of the good news in commodities is already priced into resources stocks.

So what does that say about China?

China's growing and it's a large market. Everyone knows that, but we believe a lot of that news is already factored into resources companies' earnings and share prices. Any negative news on China will have an immediate negative impact on the resources market. We've had this huge leap in commodity prices over the last twelve months because the US economy has been pump-primed with very low interest rates and huge budget deficits. At the same time, you've had Chinese demand coming through, so you've had this demand surge that has led to prices jumping.

At some stage, both or either the US and China will slow to more sustainable growth rates. The other thing (which is already starting to happen) is that we will get a supply reaction from commodity producers responding to high prices — such as copper at US$1.70 a pound, up from 60¢ just a few years ago. At 60¢ a pound, one of the biggest copper producers — BHP, I think — was writing off its Magma copper assets, which they bought not that long before for $3 billion. Back then, they were saying that, on all their modelling and calculations, the long-term average price for copper was 90¢ a pound. Here we are now, when the copper price is $1.70, and they're off paying $9 billion for WMC Resources.

One's got to put the current market into the context of where we've come from. We've come from a situation where copper was 60¢ a pound. Only a few years ago, the experts were saying 90¢ to $1 for copper was an appropriate long-term average. Today, at $1.70 many of these same forecasters are saying that the copper price is going to stay there a long time. It's just gone from one extreme to the other, so I think one has to be very cautious buying resources stocks on the current consensus.

What do you think will be the key theme that will drive the Australian sharemarket in the next few years?

Any changes to demand from China and the US will have an immediate effect on the resources sector. What will really drive the market in the next few years is how interest rates, consumer demand and inflation pan out. There is a lot of leverage in the system. You've got leverage in household balance sheets and you've got leverage in a lot of companies.

There's not so much in 'normal' industrial companies, but if you look at sectors such as the listed property trust [LPT] sector, you're lucky to find trusts on three times interest cover, which is not that comfortable. And the thing about LPTs is their debt levels never go down because they're paying out 100 per cent of earnings [in the form of distributions to unitholders]. So you've got all these LPTs as well as many infrastructure vehicles that are geared up extremely heavily on the expectation that interest rates will stay low and the economy will be steady. I think we've just got to see how it pans out. If these assumptions turn out to be overly optimistic — if interest rates do happen to go up a bit more than people expect, for example — it will be very bad news.

I think interest rates will be the key issue because there is so much leverage.

As we sit here, oil is trading at around US$65 a barrel. Besides China, it's the other big talking point in the market. What impact do you think high oil prices will have on the market?

I think we probably have to get used to a higher oil price going forward — maybe not $65 a barrel, but maybe around the $40 a barrel mark. How will it play out? I guess the key will be inflation — how it affects consumer spending and how it passes on into price inflation.

It's quite amazing that the sharemarket can continue to go up in its own merry way when you have so many uncertainties. It is quite staggering really. Normally sharemarkets pause or get worried when there's uncertainty, but at the moment no-one seems to be worried, which in itself is a concern.

Do you think the Australian sharemarket will continue to outperform its global peers over the next two years?

There's a weight of money argument and a view that at the moment commodity prices are at an all-time high and will stay at these levels for some time. Can that continue to allow us to perform better than the rest of the world? I doubt it.

So is the weight of money argument — that is to say, the impact of our superannuation structure — a short- or long-term thing?

Weight of money itself has never been a medium- to longer term sustainable reason for markets to trade above fair value. In the short term, it will help but in the medium to long term, markets always come back to what is the right price.

And why is that?

Because it's called gravity. I don't know [laughs].

I've heard the weight of money argument so many times in my career. The one that really sticks in my mind was in the early 1990s when the Japanese stock market continued to rise and rise, despite high valuations. The Nikkei went from 24 000 to 30 000 to 38 000 until finally everyone concluded that it would never decline because of the weight of money. The whole argument was based on the weight of money because Japanese interest rates were extremely low and because of their high savings rate.

The whole world knew the Japanese market was expensive but no-one forecast a downturn because the view of many experts was that weight of money would keep it above fair value. When markets get above fundamentals, the weight of money argument doesn't work because markets always track back to fundamentals.

Why do you think oil is different to any other commodity?

I think oil is a bit different because there's not a lot of new supply coming on stream. It's a commodity where there aren't a lot of new large discoveries being made and it appears that reserves are slowly depleting.

The trouble with sharemarkets is that they do go to extremes. Once the market gets onto a theme, it can take share prices a lot higher.

Commodities like copper or coal are quite different. There is heaps of supply still in the ground. Oil is a bit different in that there does not seem to be much new supply yet to come on stream. Additionally, when you look at most of the places where oil is produced, unfortunately, it's in places that are either economically or politically very unstable so the guarantee of supply will be disrupted from time to time.

Given those dynamics, have you been happy to invest in oil stocks?

We have held Woodside for many years — since it was $7 — and we still hold them, although at $33 I would have to say that a bit of blue sky is beginning to be priced in. The trouble with sharemarkets is that they do go to extremes. Once the market gets onto a theme, it can take share prices a lot higher than its fundamentals.

But we still own Woodside. We've been buying a few Origin Energy. While their base business is as a utility, they do have some oil exposure and they haven't moved in line with other oil stocks.

We're trying to look for things in the oil sector that look like reasonable value, but there's not much there at the moment.

So oil is the exception in the commodity market?

Yes, I think so — only because there is not a lot of new supply of oil that's been mothballed or that's sitting there waiting to come to market. With every other commodity — be it coal or copper — there is ample supply once it gets to market. Having said this, the oil price, like other commodity prices, would be affected by a slow down in China or the US.

$5 billion used to be a large amount of money for an institution to manage, but these days it's not that uncommon. How difficult is it to successfully manage $5 billion?

I don't think it's a big issue. I think what's hard is finding value in the current sharemarket. As value managers, that's the bigger issue for us. To be honest, whether we had $300 million today or $5 billion, I don't think our portfolio would look that different. I mean there's not a lot in the small-cap sector that we look at and think, 'Oh gee, I wish my fund was smaller because I'd love to buy that'. So I don't think size is an issue today because there's nothing in the small- or mid-cap areas that are particularly attractive.

So $5 billion in funds under management is not a huge amount of money whereas it was five or six years ago …

But neither is a million dollars for a house!

And why is that?

It's due to asset inflation. While the official stats will tell you that there is not much price inflation for goods (at around 2 per cent), a million dollars today is worth a lot less than a million dollars five years ago. Can you explain that to me?

Because of asset inflation.

And is it sustainable? I remember when I bought my first house in Sydney a few years ago for around a million dollars and everyone went, 'Whoa, gee, a million dollars!' (As I did, by the way!) Today, people buy a house for a million [in Sydney] and it's seen as quite normal … I just don't understand what's happened to the value of money in a supposedly low-inflation environment.

So what's a good amount of money these days for you to manage? Would you be happier with $10 billion?

$5 billion is fine. We just need market conditions that better suit our style. We need some sort of reality check in the market. I think many investors buying shares today have forgotten about downside risk and how quickly the market can turn. We just need a bit of a sobering period to get people back to fundamentals, to looking at things like PEs, yields and balance sheets. I don't think too many people are focusing anymore on things like interest cover, sustainability of dividends and balance sheets.

Given the longevity of the bull market, which is in its third year now, are we at risk of a crash?

I think there will be a correction, yes, at some stage.

But not an 1987-style crash?

It's difficult to predict but anything's possible. I still think that if you look at the market you'll find some parts where there is reasonable value.

Amcor, Tabcorp, Qantas and even Telstra — I mean, if you look at the cash flow and the dividend yield on these companies' underlying operations, it is difficult to argue that any of these are overvalued. But then if you look at other sectors of the market, the infrastructure funds, some of the leveraged players to the market — such as the ASXs and the Computershares and those types of companies — I think you definitely need a good pull back in their share prices. I can see 20 to 30 per cent corrections in the latter type of company on the cards at some time in the next two years.

> *I don't think we need a crash. We just need a sobering reality check. We just need a cleanout … We just need people to focus back on what the important fundamentals are.*

If we have another six months or twelve months of 25 or 26 per cent growth, would a crash be at the forefront of your mind? Would you say that's your biggest fear?

I don't think we need a crash. We just need a sobering reality check. We just need a cleanout — because we're getting excesses in some parts of the market. We just need people to focus back on what the important fundamentals are.

You're a very emotional character. It's not an ideal market for a value investor, so how do you behave in this type of market?

I get very consumed and worried when we don't perform that well. I don't know, I just retest all these things and see if we've missed anything and just try to convince myself that we're still doing what we've always done. I don't think we've missed anything. It's just the way the market is viewing things is quite different to [how it will] when the cold light of day reappears.

So over the last two years, what have you learnt?

With the benefit of hindsight we probably sold a few stocks too early; but then again, hindsight is a wonderful thing.

So, for example, we bought stocks like Coles Myer, CSL, ASX and Brambles two years ago at the right price. After much analysis, we bought heavily into these companies when they were trading at what we thought were reasonable PEs at twelve to fifteen times. When on our analysis these stocks got to around twenty times earnings, we sold into strength — only trouble is, these stocks have all kept rising. So I guess the moral of the story is, in a bull market, be greedy! Not really greedy, but you just have to be optimistic on how you price stocks.

It's very easy to underestimate momentum in a bull market and how high this wave of optimism can take certain share prices. I mean, look at Coles Myer — it was $6 and no-one wanted it. Today the same company, despite an impending slowdown in consumer spending, is trading at $10 and the PE has gone from thirteen or fourteen times to around nineteen times.

So people will talk about how this has all been an earnings-led bull market, but that's not completely true. You've had some very big re-ratings in the PE as well. If there's one thing I have learnt, it's that you shouldn't sell too early because PEs can get to levels beyond your imagination.

Look at Brambles. In 2003 and at $4, Brambles was seen as a company with a business that was 'broken'. They'd lost eleven million pallets and sentiment was very poor. As a result, the stock was trading at around $4 — it was on a PE of thirteen times with a dividend yield of five. Two years later the stock is almost $9, the business model is apparently very attractive again and everyone is happy to pay over twenty times earnings and receive a yield of two.

We bought millions of Brambles at $4. We thought at $6 they were starting to get up there a bit and by $7.50 we'd exited the stock.

So you've learnt not to sell too early especially in a bull market, but how has that changed the way you invest? Will you take that lesson and implement it or will your fundamental value judgment get in the way of that lesson?

It probably won't change the way we invest as we will probably always buy a bit too early and sell too early — that's what value managers tend to do. Having said this, we have refined a few internal tools to help us better assess when to exit companies.

That's what you've done historically?

Yeah. We bought our CSLs at $16, Brambles at $4 and Coles at $6 as we thought they were great value at these prices. With hindsight, we sold all those companies too early as they've kept going. But hindsight is a wonderful but quite useless tool!

On the other end it looks like Amcor was bought too early, yet you still believe it's good stock.

> *I'm looking forward to the day when the market is more sober … where fundamentals count and you can sift through things and look at balance sheets and find things that are trading below intrinsic value.*

The fundamentals are intact. The cash flow is strong, the dividend is pretty high and sustainable so we're still happy with Amcor.

You've been investing in the market for eighteen years. It's a very tense game, especially when you're battling against the index. How long can you keep at the top?

Well, at the moment we're nearer the bottom of the surveys than at the top so you're asking me the right question at the wrong time! Anyway, I enjoy what I do. I like to win rather than to lose and at the moment I don't feel like we're winning too many innings in the market. But I'm looking forward to the day when the market is more sober, when it's more our style of market, where fundamentals count and you can sift through things and look at balance sheets and find things that are trading below intrinsic value — which we did only two and a half years ago. Things like MIA, Coles Myer and Brambles.

But today we can't find too many opportunities like that.

When it comes to having a high profile and managing a lot of people and having to answer to a lot of people, do you feel it will shorten your life?

[Laughs] Maybe I was destined to have a short life. But, yes, it is quite stressful as I take our performance quite personally. I know a lot of people think fund managers don't care, but I actually take it very personally.

I don't enjoy lagging the index but then again I don't tend to boast about it when we're doing well either. You've got to take the ups with the downs and I hope and pray that in the not too distant future the market psychology will change so it's more in line with the way we do things.

One person who has succeeded in investing for a long time is Warren Buffett and he's in his late seventies. Do you see yourself at seventy-five running billions and billions of dollars in this kind of business?

Well, if you're in this industry and this is what you enjoy doing, what else would you do with yourself? Go hiking? Drive fast cars? I haven't been into much else in the last twenty years apart from the stockmarket! I've built a team of very good people around me at Investors Mutual. We have worked together for many years now, through ups and downs in the market.

My model of who I think has done a terrific job in this industry is Robert Maple-Brown. He is now in his sixties and is the non-executive chairman of his own company, Maple-Brown Abbott. As I understand, he still goes into the office two or three days a week to overview things and make sure his team are on track. But he also has time to do more of his own stuff as well. I believe Rob sits on quite a few charitable institutions' boards, which for me is something to aspire to.

I plan to always have some involvement with Investors Mutual. My kids will have grown up in ten years' time and I look forward to spending more time with my family, as they have always been very supportive of me. So I guess that's what I am aiming for — to have that balance where you're still quite involved but perhaps not at the coalface every day. I've got people who I've worked with for a long time and who I trust to do that job, so I can eventually devote some time to other interests.

Most good fund managers eventually make a reasonable amount of money and, for quite a few of them, that is enough. Would you say you've made enough money or is it still about performance?

I think when I first started in this industry financial success was one of the most important factors for me. Today the challenge for me is about building a sustainable business in what is a highly competitive industry. The only way you can do that is by performing well over the long term as fund manager. So that's what I want to do, improve our performance.

Hopefully, the market will move in our favour in the not too distant future and our performance will be back to where it should be — that's what I'm really looking forward to at the moment, and hopefully this will justify the faith clients have placed in us.

———————•———————

For the average investor who has forgotten or was not active during previous periods, it is easy to be seduced and believe that today's market darlings are infallible.

Anton Tagliaferro reminds us to be incredibly sceptical of markets and stocks that have enjoyed stunning and seemingly unstoppable share price rises. Having experienced first-hand several booms and busts, Tagliaferro has seen it all before so he knows that extended rallies in the sharemarket cannot last forever.

In a market that is more uneven, Tagliaferro's skills shine but in the conditions that prevailed at the time of our interview, he was clearly in an agitated state. As far as he is concerned it is a matter of when, not if, he will be proved right.

We live in a dynamic world that is experiencing a huge growth in wealth, and the Phil Fisher 'long-term growth/franchise' approach is going to deliver higher returns than the Ben Graham 'used cigar butt' approach in that environment.

13

Survival of the fittest

Peter Hall

Peter Hall has built a fortune since starting his own funds management firm in 1993; however, the last two years have not been kind to one of our most unconventional and straight-talking Masters. Always refreshingly upfront, Hall admits this has been the toughest period of his investing career, with the momentum-driven and resources-based market rally testing his undoubted stock-picking talent.

His firm, Hunter Hall, has still delivered positive returns for investors. The average annual return over ten years for Hunter Hall's biggest fund, the $750 million Value Growth Trust (VGT), is 10 per cent above the benchmark sharemarket index. And Hunter Hall's funds under management have more than doubled to $1.3 billion since we spoke to Hall in 2003. However, in the year to 31 July 2005, the VGT's 12.1 per cent gain has been left behind by a 27.5 per cent return from the All Ordinaries Accumulation Index.

Hall has always been an extremely confident and driven person and this is reflected in his investment style. Hall's strength of conviction is evident throughout his investing career, which is distinguished by the occasional falling-out with colleagues and, prior to starting Hunter Hall, his employers. He is not one to suffer mediocrity in others, which must have made the difficult period facing his funds at the time of writing even tougher to stomach. But Hall's confidence is such that he is not one to pretend to his investors that all is well when it isn't. The underperformance from several of his funds in early 2005 has prompted Hall to undertake a complete reassessment of the way Hunter Hall manages money and picks stocks.

In mid-2005, Hall sent a letter to investors in Hunter Hall's Australian Value Trust (a $160 million fund) explaining what went wrong and how he would fix the problem. Hall identified four factors behind the underperformance. Almost half of the underperformance, according to Hall, could be attributed to 'meaningless price fluctuations'. However, Hall also blamed mistakes by his fund managers, including a failure to forecast downward profit revisions by companies such as PMP (which had been a great investment for Hunter Hall until then). Hunter Hall has since significantly scaled back its position in the printing group.

Hall adopts a Darwinian perspective on Hunter Hall's future, arguing the firm must keep evolving its investment style if it is to continue to prosper. While Hall still makes a lot of the investment decisions, his concern during the latest period of underperformance was that an unhealthy, committee-style decision-making process had developed in the firm. According to Hall, this slowed down the investment decision-making process and meant the Hunter Hall portfolio had become too diversified, with fewer 'high conviction' bets.

Hall also became worried that Hunter Hall had become too much like an 'owner' of certain companies, potentially compromising a dispassionate assessment of a stock because of loyalty towards the company involved. Hall now prefers each of his fund managers to be fully responsible and accountable for their investment decisions, and has implemented what he calls a 'federation of portfolio managers' approach. This means that Hunter Hall's fund managers will now be given the freedom to identify opportunities and individually take responsibility for them, within agreed-upon risk parameters.

Hall, another disciple of the Warren Buffett school of investing, continues to be an activist shareholder and favours the small-cap end of the market. Hall also invests internationally, particularly in the UK where he spends half of his year. Hunter Hall tends to invest in 'turnaround' stocks in the search for factor gains and invests heavily in individual companies, often taking a substantial shareholding. Hunter Hall will insist on board seats where necessary to represent its interests and aid management. Reflecting Hall's own preference and interest in broader social agendas, Hunter Hall will only invest in companies that don't harm the environment.

Hall was interviewed in August 2005 — a time when the Australian sharemarket was trading at or near record highs. One of Hall's great loves is travelling (his childhood saw him live in a number of different countries), and, typically, Hall was globetrotting at the time we caught up with him. While he bases himself in London for half of the year, he was visiting Brazil when we finally managed to track him down. Hall was clearly frustrated with some his investment calls, but he is extremely determined to make amends.

———————●———————

What has been your best investment call in the last two years?

There are different ways of measuring 'best investment call' — greatest dollar return, greatest percentage return, greatest time-weighted percentage return, and so on. PMP is by far the greatest dollar contributor to the Value Growth Trust[1] over the two years to 31 December 2004 and has a sound percentage return over that period. PMP rose from 41.5¢ on 31 December 2002 to $2.12 on 31 December 2004, a return of 411 per cent. We purchased shares for prices up to 46¢ to the end of February 2003, sold a few for 95¢ in August–September 2003, bought again at $1.25 to $1.30 in February–March 2004 and sold in July at $1.63 and $1.77. We bought again in September–October 2004 at $1.68 and sold in November at $2.05. [Mining contractor] Macmahon was another good one — up 18¢ to 48¢ (up 167 per cent), although we started buying at 11¢. [Blinds distributor] Kresta was up 178 per cent (but has subsequently fallen by half).

Conversely, what has been your worst investment in this time?

Sirtex Medical has been my biggest disaster, having fallen from its high of $5.31 to a recent low of $1.20 (down 77 per cent). It has

---

1   The Value Growth Trust is Hunter Hall's biggest fund with $754 million under management as at 31 July 2005.

been absolutely agonising for Hunter Hall and has caused our team a lot of soul-searching and personal friction. I think the investment was one of the contributing factors behind Kim Tracey's departure from Hunter Hall. To be quite honest, I believe the Sirtex experience has caused a significant erosion of the respect my colleagues have felt for me. A lot more is at stake than money — although the money involved is no small matter!

We have averaged down and recently bought 1.5 million shares at $1.25. Our average cost is now $3.99 for 11 million shares or 19.9 per cent of the company. We have invested a total of $44.2 million and earlier this month when the shares hit $1.20, we were looking at an unrealised loss of about $30 million. That was the biggest mistake of my career thus far.

However, I am not convinced it is a mistake! I still believe Sirtex has the potential to rise to over $10 and maybe to $50 over the next three to five years. The company is commercialising a treatment for liver cancer, which has been used in about 1000 treatments in the US. The US market has about 200 000 cases of primary and secondary liver cancer each year. The gross margin on each treatment is about $15 000 so for each 1 per cent of market share, Sirtex could make gross margin of about A$30 million, equal to 50¢ a share. If Sirtex gets to 5 per cent market share and is valued on a PE ratio of 15 (quite low for medical device companies), the share price would be about $25. A 10 per cent share means $50.

> *The world economy is looking good, with relatively low interest rates and encouraging growth prospects.*

There is a lot of work to do in terms of building clinical trial evidence for the efficacy of the treatment and a management and sales team to roll it out, but the potential is great.[2]

Given the strong market, do you believe the current environment is a good one for investing?

The world economy is looking good, with relatively low interest rates and encouraging growth prospects in a number of important economies. The oil price rise is a threat as is the leveraged nature of

---

2   Sirtex shares were trading at $2.21 at the time of writing. Further information on this is provided in a letter to investors on Hunter Hall's website <www.hunterhall.com.au>.

the global financial system combined with relatively high valuations in some areas, but I think there is good value in various pockets of the world.

Japan looks particularly interesting if Koizumi is successful in reforming the Post Office. Continental Europe is still producing at below its capacity and both areas have underfunded pension systems, high fiscal debt, undergeared consumers and an investment culture that favours bonds rather than equities. So there is great upside in both markets. Longer term, great wealth will be generated in developing economies such as Mexico, Brazil, Turkey, Russia, India and China.

What do you believe will be the best performing asset class over the next two to three years?

I am an equities man so I think selected equities will outperform. Gold could also be interesting. Property seems a bit wobbly but some areas seem very cheap such as Europe and some developing economies. Bonds could get crunched if inflation and interest rates increase.

After being considered a poor investment for more than a decade, resources are back. Do you believe that resources stocks can continue to outperform the broader market for the medium to long term?

To be honest, I have never successfully invested in resources so my response is not particularly well informed. I think one should be careful — although, clearly, we are in the middle of a gold rush and (like almost everybody else) we missed a major opportunity to invest in the sector three years ago.

I don't think resources can outperform over the medium to long term, apart from the oil and gas sector. It seems to me that there is no shortage of the main materials, so current price rises are of the nature of a spike driven by bottlenecks that will be ironed out in the next two or three years. Then pressure to grind down prices will resume.

When I was a rookie analyst at New Zealand Insurance I was lucky enough to be able to go through the files of Savage River Mines, which was a direct investment we had in a Tasmanian iron ore mine that Jim Wolfensohn had been an architect of. The Japanese just ruthlessly ground the price down and squeezed the profitability to nothing. Iron ore is a commodity but it requires major capital investment. I think an interesting game may be under way with the big consumers encouraging producers to make major capital expenditure to lift production by paying higher prices for a few years. Once production capacity has been increased, pressure to drop prices will resume. The projects will have long lives but I doubt they will earn excess returns over their economic lives.

However, companies providing services to the resources sector can do well as production volumes are increasing to new plateaus. So let's make hay for the next year or two. That's the way we have been playing it with investments in service companies such as Macmahon, Downer, Clough, RCR Tomlinson, Ausdrill and PCH.

We are also interested in the oil sector and our second largest holding is Statoil, the Norwegian oil and gas producer that has been a huge winner, thanks to my colleague James McDonald.

We seem to be in a period of slightly rising interest rates on the back of a strong economy and the fear of higher inflation. Even though rates are rising only gradually, what is the best way to make money in this environment?

It's the same as it always is — invest in selected good businesses at low valuations.

China has probably been the number one talking point among the investment community over the last two years. Do you believe China is a key theme in the coming years for the Australian sharemarket?

Certainly it will be important as a major market for our food and materials. I worry that China still has an inefficient system for allocating resources and no loyalty to the concepts of the market mechanism, honest reporting, individual rights, property rights, free expression, democracy and so on.

I think it is highly likely that its banking system is bankrupt and that it faces huge environmental, social and political pressures. At some stage, this will lead to a bust of some sort so I think Australia needs to spread its bets. Jared Diamond's excellent recent book *Collapse* has a sobering chapter on the outlook for China. And Australia!

In the long term, if the Chinese civilisation shifts to a liberal, market system, it will have a huge impact on the world and, at the same time as boosting the world economy, will possibly lead to major security problems for us, the US and Japan.

What single issue is going to drive the Australian sharemarket higher or lower in the next five years?

Weight of money, driven by superannuation, will continue to be the major factor as it has been for the last few years. The direction of interest rates is the ultimate factor and their fall has been a major influence over the last two decades. If interest rates stay low, the sharemarket will continue to progress. If they rise, the market will slow its rise.

Do you believe the Australian sharemarket will outperform its global peers over the next two years?

No, I don't. I think Japan and the US economy have good prospects. If Europe starts to improve, as it may do, global markets could rise strongly.

Since our first interview, your company has raised extra funds through a listed investment company called Hunter Hall Global Value.[3] Why do you think this is a good vehicle for investors?

I think LICs can be a good vehicle because they are valued on earnings and dividends rather than net assets. Unlisted trusts and funds trade at net tangible assets. For example, if an LIC consistently generates an after-tax return of 10 per cent a year and pays out 100 per cent of its earnings as fully franked dividends, it will have a yield of 10 per cent. The market is likely to mark the LIC's price up so that the yield falls to, say, 7 per cent, which would mean the LIC price would increase to about a 50 per cent premium to net asset value.

That is essentially what has happened to Platinum Capital[4], which is currently trading at about a 30 per cent premium to net asset value. It has paid a 15¢ dividend for each of the last five years and at $2.16 [at the time of writing] is trading on a yield of about 7 per cent.

With our LIC, our premise was that people would come in at net asset value and that over time we would develop a dividend stream that would allow the share price to advance to a premium to net asset value.

---

3   Hunter Hall Global Value, a listed investment company managed by Hunter Hall, listed on the Australian Stock Exchange in March 2004.

4   The listed investment company managed by Kerr Neilson's Platinum Asset Management.

Another factor to consider is that because LICs do not have to worry about short-term liquidity, they can take a longer term view of investment.

_____

You split your time and investments between Australia and the UK. Which country holds the best prospects in the medium term?

Australia needs to globalise and develop complex service and product businesses that can sustain our society during the periodic slumps in the commodity sector.

As a country and society I think Australia has better prospects because it has a splendid balance sheet (at the government and pension level), great people, social cohesion, a more thorough-going capitalist system and the commodities boom. I think the UK stock market is more interesting because it is a bigger pool to fish in, has a lower valuation and has some interesting and creative global companies. The same is true of Europe, Japan and South Korea.

_____

Australia needs to globalise and develop complex service and product businesses that can sustain our society during the periodic slumps in the commodity sector. What companies like Macquarie Bank (and, in a small way, Sirtex) are doing is a great example, just as it was true of News Corp and Brambles in previous periods.

How do we globalise? I think the best way is to give people personal experience of the wider world so that we develop businesses that can operate in those environments. One scheme I would propose to the government is for it to fund one-year international study programs for young people and businesspeople. Ideally, they would learn a foreign language, immerse themselves in a foreign culture and maybe study at a foreign university, and come back as much more experienced, sophisticated and knowledgeable people.

If such a program cost $40 000 per person and we sent 50 000 people (which I think is about 20 per cent of tertiary graduates), each year the cost would be $2 billion. We can afford that and I think over the long term we would earn a huge dividend in the form of new business enterprises and increased personal capabilities among our people. Of course, before we do that we need to get rid of HECS [the Higher Education Contribution Scheme]!

In our first interview two years ago, you made it clear that you were not interested in making an investment for a small percentage gain.

This aggressive style of investing requires taking some high-risk bets. As you have aged, have you modified your approach?

I am not sure if I agree that it is a high-risk approach. What it requires is an insight into value. Some factor-gain stocks involve recovering from disasters or are highly leveraged plays, such as Reinsurance Australia [now Calliden] and Kresta. But others are situations where companies have grown their profits very solidly over a number of years (such as Macmahon Holdings and PZ Cussons) and are really Phil Fisher–type[5] stocks. I still get excited and interested in those investments and am profoundly uninterested in short-term, low-return investments.

> I am irked that I have never invested in Microsoft, News Corp, Toll Holdings or Patrick, despite being well aware of them. I had an irrational mental block that I am trying to progress beyond.

You have also stated that your investment technique is based upon establishing a company's real cash flow. Have you evolved this idea in recent times or does it continue to serve you well?

It remains the core of my approach but I have become much more interested in growth and its relationship with value. We live in a dynamic world that is experiencing a huge growth in wealth, and the Phil Fisher 'long-term growth/franchise' approach is going to deliver higher returns than the Ben Graham 'used cigar butt' approach in that environment.

I am irked that I have never invested in Microsoft, News Corp, Toll Holdings or Patrick, despite being well aware of them. I had an irrational mental block that I am trying to progress beyond.

---

5   Philip A. Fisher is one of the most influential investors of all time, publishing *Common Stocks and Uncommon Profits* in 1958.

Peter Hall remains extremely confident and prepared to invest large licks of his portfolio in a number of stocks. It is this conviction that has made Hunter Hall one of the most successful independent fund managers in Australia.

More recently, Hall has had to wear the pain of underperformance as this strategy has not paid off during an sharply rising market. This has prompted some soul-searching from Hall and his team, who go to great lengths to understand why they may have made an incorrect investment decision.

Hall is still very confident in his ability to pick stocks that have the ability to produce factor gains, even if the wait may sometimes be a little longer.

It is important for fund managers to stick to their methodology of investing. A lot of people have been caught out following the herd. If you can't find value in the market, stay in cash, because as history continues to show us, eventually opportunities will appear. One of the most important attributes of a successful investor is patience and, unfortunately, a large number of investors don't possess it. We will only invest when we believe the rewards significantly outweigh the risks.

14

A man for all seasons
Geoff Wilson

Bad stockbrokers often make good fund managers. Equally, good brokers often make bad fund managers. This might have something to do with the fact that brokers are more focused on daily trading and short-term movements, whereas professional investing is more about having a long-term view. Conventional wisdom also dictates that a co-author of a book like this one probably shouldn't get his own chapter as well, but Geoff Wilson defies convention in all respects.

Wilson, the founder of Wilson Asset Management (WAM), was a highly successful stockbroker in the 1980s and 1990s. In the eight years since setting WAM up in 1997, he has proved himself equally adept in the realm of funds management. Since WAM began, the firm's funds under management have grown from scratch to $460 million, mainly via the creation of a series of listed investment companies (LICs) and their subsequent growth.

As noted in the first edition of *Masters of the Market*, including Wilson was a difficult decision for the authors to make. The co-authors, including fellow WAM colleague Matthew Kidman, finally agreed that it would be useful for Wilson to share his investment philosophy with readers, given the book was his idea in the first place. At the time, Wilson had already established an impressive track record of gains for his investors. Wilson has found it tougher to outperform in the bullish markets of recent years, but even with a cash allocation of 25 per cent in his portfolios, he has managed to do so.

Unlike many big institutional fund managers, Wilson Asset Management has not been shackled by the endless process and quasi-indexing that many superannuation consultants require from fund managers. This pragmatism has been used to great effect. Wilson is willing to buy growth stocks, value stocks and asset plays, and can switch from being a trader looking for a quick profit to a long-term investor in stocks. He is willing to trade his portfolios aggressively if he believes he will make money for his investors.

Matthew Kidman, who in May 1998 gave up journalism to join Wilson full-time, argued in the first edition of *Masters of the Market* that it would be unfair to classify Wilson as an everyday fund manager. Instead, Kidman referred to Wilson as a 'money-maker', and that description stands. Wilson has a keen sense of what will make money and how companies work. With his broking background, he knows how to execute a trade to maximise the return and has the refreshing attitude of, if something goes wrong, not dwelling on it.

Geoff began his career in the financial markets in the early 1980s as a fund manager with Scottish Amicable. Like Greg Perry, Wilson worked under Don Brinkworth, one of the early pioneers of the funds management industry. It was from Brinkworth and Chris Walker that he learnt many of his skills as a stockpicker. After two years in the funds management game, Wilson switched to broking, joining the Melbourne-based Potter Partners as an industrial analyst. Here he closely followed the deals of some of the great entrepreneurs such as Robert Holmes à Court and John Elliott. Wilson then moved to the sales desk for Potters in London but was at McIntosh in New York at the time of the 1987 crash. In the 1990s he was instrumental in lifting broker Prudential-Bache up the industry pecking order. During this time, Geoff learnt a lot about funds management by broking to such great investors as Perry, David Paradice, Rohan Hedley and John Abernethy of the NRMA. Eventually he was spurred into creating his own funds management firm, encapsulating his broking skills and the lessons he had learned from his funds management clients.

Geoff is a larger-than-life character who always seems to be enjoying himself, although he is also an outspoken critic of companies he believes are failing to look after their shareholders. In much the same way as Anton Tagliaferro and Peter Morgan, this makes him a journalist's dream. He will usually have something insightful and worth quoting to say regarding just about any sharemarket topic and can express himself simply and in a commonsense fashion.

Wilson is a believer in getting out and speaking to as many industry people as possible to glean new snippets of information on how individual companies work and how the economy is travelling.

We interviewed Geoff in August 2005.

———————————●———————————

In two years, the Australian sharemarket has returned more than 60 per cent. In the 2005 financial year alone the market rose 24.8 per cent, the best year since 1993. How have you fared in this bull market?

As the market rallied from its lows in March 2003, the equity portion of the portfolios we manage have performed solidly. Our flagship fund, the Wilson Asset Management Equity Fund, is up 65.3 per cent to 30 June 2005. It achieved this while holding about 25 per cent in cash. Our other portfolios haven't performed anywhere near as well holding higher levels of cash. The return from the cash portion has well and truly underperformed the stock market.

Our focus has always been on absolute performance. The portfolios we are responsible for are managed in a disciplined way. For example, if we can't find the right investment opportunity, we will stay in cash. WAM Capital and the Wilson Asset Management Equity Fund have two distinct styles of investing — research-driven and market-driven. The research-driven approach requires the company to be assessed using our internal research rating process before an investment is made. It doesn't matter what the market is doing, going up or down. In research-driven investing, we use a rating system to determine if a stock is worth buying.

We rate company management, earnings growth, valuation, the industry and the company's industry position. If the rating of the company is high enough, we will buy — but only if we can identify a catalyst or an event that is going to change the valuation of the company on the stock market. Market-driven investing is all about buying shares wholesale and selling them retail. That is, participating in IPOs and placements, sub-underwriting capital raisings or buying blocks of stocks that are being sold at a discount to the current share price. One of our other funds, the Wilson Investment Fund, is a long-term investment fund and doesn't trade. It uses a research-driven approach and an investment-driven approach. The companies we are looking to invest in with the investment-driven approach must have sustainable business models, a track record of dividends and profits, positive free cash flow and a high return on equity.

I have always had a philosophy when managing money to have maximum flexibility and not pigeonhole myself into a particular style. I had a meeting with Brian Ingham [a former fund manager and now stockbroker with Aequs Securities] _____ the other day and he summed up our style. He was writing a report on the listed investment company sector. He said we were a small- to mid-cap value manager. With the research-driven part of our

Value opportunities will always present themselves if you have the patience.

portfolios he is probably right. We are looking for companies on price/earnings ratios of ten times that are growing at 20 per cent per annum. When you spend all your time looking for companies with certain attributes, it can take a long time to find them. It's like looking for a diamond in the rough. It has been very difficult recently to find value in the market. In these circumstances, we will hold cash until the right opportunities arise. One thing we do know is that value opportunities will always present themselves if you have the patience.

What has been your best investment call in the last two years?

One of my best calls was to take my daughter Amelia out of school for a term in 2004 and with my wife, Karen, spend time in England and Europe. While I was in England, I did some detailed research into listed investment companies. In the UK, they call them listed investment trusts, but they also use the company structure. London is the birthplace of LICs. The first listed investment trust, Foreign and Colonial, was formed in 1868. I am a very enthusiastic supporter of LICs as a medium investors can use to gain exposure to the stock market. When you buy shares in a LIC you get exposure to a diversified portfolio of shares and the expertise of the manager of the LIC.

I remember reading some research years ago about LICs. It stated that over a fifty-year period they had outperformed traditional managed funds by more than 1.5 per cent each year. The reason for this outperformance is because LICs are companies — they are closed-end pools of capital. Managed funds are different. They are open-ended pools of capital with a mandate usually requiring them to be fully invested at all times. When the market is very strong, money pours in from retail investors and shares are bought at the top of the market. When the market is weak, money flows out and they are forced into being sellers at the bottom of the market. A LIC is never forced to buy or sell shares because of money flows. The manager of a LIC can invest when he or she believes the opportunities are there. We floated our first of three LICs in 1999. I am currently on the board of five LICs and will help bring as many as I can to the market over time.

On the investment front, one of my better investments has its roots back in 2000–01. Wesfarmers had just taken over rural merchandiser IAMA and was selling a 10 per cent shareholding in Tasmanian rural group Roberts Limited. A stockbroker from Bell Potter, Ross Illingworth, called and offered me the line. He already had buyers for 3 per cent. The stock was trading around $2.10, cum a 10¢ fully franked dividend. It had net assets of about $2.40 and was trading on a price/earnings ratio of about nine times. I did a lot of research, going through all their past announcements and annual reports, and spent time speaking to their managing director Miles Hampton.

From my research, I ascertained it was a well-managed company. It was trading below the value of its net assets, on a low price/earnings ratio with its earnings depressed by the drought, which would break one day. I also liked the idea of buying from a corporate investor that was cleaning out assets after a takeover. Companies usually buy and sell for strategic reasons, not fundamental ones. There is always a chance that they will sell too cheaply. Ross believed he could get the stock for below $2.00. I bid $1.75 and the seller came back late on Friday and offered the shares at $1.85. I said I was going home in half an hour and if the Dow Jones Index was down overnight I mightn't be there on Monday. They accepted my bid that afternoon.

Roberts is the Elders of Tasmania. From my research I knew Elders had recently set up a small business in Tasmania to compete with Roberts. I decided to see if they were interested in Roberts. I rang Alan Newman [managing director of Futuris and owner of Elders] and offered him my stock at $1.85. He declined. Since we bought our shares, Roberts share price has since increased nearly 500 per cent. Recently, they have had a four-for-one share split. In the last two years, they are up 103 per cent.

Another of my better investment calls was the decision to invest $2 million of the fund's money into Powertel at 1¢ a share through a syndicate Sam Gazal had put together. The syndicate [named Roslyndale] was set up by Sam Gazal to take out the main shareholder, Wiltel, and then recapitalise Powertel. The opportunity was a classic 'buy straw hats in winter' play. The telecommunications industry had gone from being the hot place to invest in, to being totally out of favour.

Sam Gazal and Charles Gullotta had put together the syndicate of investors after Powertel's major shareholder had financial difficulties. Powertel had invested significant sums of money building the infrastructure to compete against the other telecommunications companies and was just starting to ramp up its sales revenue. It was a perfect play; unfortunately, after everything was put in place, another player made a partial takeover bid and outmanoeuvred us. Within a few months of the proposal, Powertel's share price had increased 700 per cent.

Conversely, what has been your worst investment in this time?

It's always painful when a company you own shares in goes into administration or liquidation — that is, you lose 100 per cent of your money. Two that come to mind are Gympie Gold and Reynolds Wines. Gympie operated a goldmine and a coalmine, and we invested in it via convertible notes. Investing in convertible notes issued by a mining company is always a high-risk play. I am always suspicious when a company raises money by issuing high-yielding securities (such as preference shares or convertible notes) rather than ordinary shares.

Whenever I invest in a convertible note or a preference share, I ask myself the question, 'What is the risk of the company going under?'

because when that occurs you lose everything and the higher yield isn't worth the risk. Looking at Gympie, I knew that Michael Darling, their major shareholder, was a smart operator. Their strategy looked sound and they had significant earning potential from their coal mine. It looked like a worthwhile investment.

After a great start to production, the company encountered some problems. I was aware of what can happen to single coalmining companies from observing Clutha going into administration after something fell down its mine shaft. I decided this [Gympie] appeared a higher risk play than I initially expected. I started selling the convertible notes. I was bid 91¢ for our holding but instead of accepting the bid I offered at 92¢. I was a few days' late and before a deal was done, the coal in the mine ignited, a fire broke out below ground and the mine had to be closed down. Unfortunately, this led to the company going into administration.

Reynolds was a boutique wine company that had always appeared to have problems ever since it was floated as Cabonne. That in itself should have been worrying enough. A good rule to remember when investing is 'leopards never change their spots'.

The company was going through a recapitalisation. This can sometimes be a perfect time to invest. After spending a number of hours going through the profit forecasts and meeting management, I decided to invest in their high-yielding preference shares. One of the positives was the security — the preference shares were secured over the

The higher the yield, the higher the risk. Make sure you are getting a high enough yield for the risk you are taking.

assets of the company. Another was that the company's banker, which I had heard a few months earlier was trying to get out of the relationship, committed to put in more money. Unfortunately, it wasn't until the company went into administration that I discovered the banker had not put in more money and had insured the debt to remove their downside. Unfortunately, this was never disclosed to the market.[1]

The moral of the above stories of woe is to be very wary when you're investing in high-yielding instruments. The higher the yield, the higher the risk. Make sure you are getting a high enough yield for the risk you are taking.

---

1   An administrator was appointed to Reynolds Wines in August 2003.

Do you believe the current environment is a good one for investing?

The two drivers of share prices are valuation and earnings per share growth. Valuation is directly related to interest rates. When interest rates go up, the price people are prepared to pay for a business (share price) goes down. When interest rates go down, the price goes up. An example I use in my lecturing for the Securities Institute of Australia relates interest rates to price/earnings multiples. A pre-tax interest rate of 7 per cent is equivalent to 4.9 per cent after tax (that is, 7 per cent times 70 per cent, using the corporate tax rate of 30 per cent, equals 4.9 per cent). 4.9 per cent is the same as 4.9/100. To change a yield to a ratio you invert it — that is, 100/4.9 — which is equivalent to 20.4 times. Thus a pre-tax yield of 7 per cent implies a theoretical price/earnings ratio of 20.4 times. In the same way and using the same logic, a pre-tax yield of 15 per cent infers a price-earnings ratio of 9.5 times. Thus, if a company makes $1 million when interest rates are 7 per cent, the company is theoretically worth $20.4 million. When interest rates are 15 per cent, it is theoretically worth $9.5 million, so its value is more than halved.

The second major driver of the value of companies is net profit growth per share or earnings per share growth. Quantitative studies I have seen show that growth in earnings per share has a stronger correlation to share prices than any other measure. Economic activity is a driver of earnings growth. A strong economy usually leads to strong profit growth.

The time to invest is when you believe interest rates are going to fall and when companies will have strong profit growth. Over the last ten years we have had a long period of declining interest rates, and the last two years have seen strong earnings growth in corporate Australia. As always, the challenge with investing is to find the companies that can exhibit strong earnings growth from here on in. The major risk to the market is an increase in interest rates.

What do you believe will be the best performing asset class over the next two to three years?

Each class of asset will over time deliver a return commensurate with their risk — that is, the higher the risk, the higher the return. Of the major asset classes (equities, property, fixed-interest or cash), equities have the highest risk so, by definition, should give you the highest return over the medium term — say, three years.

After being considered a poor investment for more than a decade, resources are back. Do you believe that resources can continue to outperform the broader market for the medium to long term?

I have always found industrial companies easier to analyse and value than resource companies. This revolves around resource companies having an additional variable — the price of the particular commodity they produce. It is difficult to predict commodity prices and a small move can result in a significant increase or decrease in profitability. Also the 'Tattslotto effect' [see the first edition of *Masters of the Market* for an explanation of this effect] tends to overvalue small mining companies, compared with the risk you are taking.

One of the major potential positives with the resources sector is the enormous leverage to moves in commodity prices. The focus for the last few years has centred on the strong demand for commodities resulting from the industrialisation of China. It is believed it will lead to a paradigm shift in demand for a period of time, similar to the industrialisation of Japan in the 1950s. It could take years to play out. One thing you must always remember is we are operating in a free market, where an increase in demand will lift prices, which will eventually lead to an increase in supply and so a fall in prices. History tells us that every boom ends in a bust. So be wary.

> People give me money to manage and in turn I am looking to invest in companies that have exceptional managers.

We seem to be in a period of rising interest rates on the back of a strong economy and the fear of higher inflation. Even though rates are only rising gradually, what is the best way to make money in this environment?

To me, the macro-economic settings are not as important as the fundamentals of each individual company. I am always looking for a company with very strong management, that will grow strongly (by reference to earnings per share), is well priced — on a low PE ratio — operates in a growth industry and is well placed to take advantage of that, and can generate a positive cash flow and a good return on equity.

People give me money to manage and in turn I am looking to invest in companies that have exceptional managers.

China and its staggering growth rate has probably been the number one talking point among the investment community over the last two years. Do you believe China will be a key theme in the coming years for the Australian sharemarket?

The industrialisation of Japan after World War II, and the industrialisation of America before this, had a significant impact on the world economy. China is no different. Australia is a major supplier of base metals and commodities to the world and is a major beneficiary of what is occurring in China. The industrialisation of America took two to three decades from the 1880s to 1910; the industrialisation of Japan took close to forty years and China's industrialisation has been going for less than a decade. Looking at history would lead you to believe the industrialisation phase in China could last for quite a while yet.

What single issue is going to drive the Australian sharemarket higher or lower in the next five years?

I stated earlier that the two major drivers of share prices and values of companies are interest rates and earnings growth. Interest rates will have a major impact on the stock market over the next five years. The biggest risk to the market is always an upward move in interest rates. If interest rates increased from, say, 7 per cent to 14 per cent, the value of companies, or share prices, would halve. I always keep a close eye on inflation, which is a driver of interest rates.

Another of the fascinating dynamics at play over the next five years will be the continued ageing of the developed world's population, which will peak around 2010. It is believed that once this occurs there will be a reduction in demand for equities and a corresponding fall in stock markets. However, the continued strong growth in forced investing through compulsory superannuation in Australia should continue to underpin asset prices over the period and offset some of the reduction in demand.

Do you believe the Australian sharemarket will outperform its global peers over the next two years?

Two significant drivers behind the rise in the market in the past two years have been the recovery in industrial company earnings and strong growth in the resources sector. In the short term, I don't think it gets any better than this and it will be difficult for the Australian market to outperform on a world scale. The risk to the upside is the continued strong performance of the resources sector. The risk to the downside is an increase in interest rates and company earnings not living up to expectations.

Since the first edition of Masters of the Market, *your funds under management have more than doubled. Is this difficult to manage?*

Currently, the Wilson Asset Management Group is managing around $460 million. When we started writing the book [in 1998], we were managing $1 million. When the first edition was finished, we were managing about $280 million. It is a lot easier to perform managing a smaller pool of capital than a larger one. It is easier to manage $1 million than $1 billion. The growth in funds under management has resulted in an increase in staff from one to eight.

If you can't find value in the market, stay in cash ... eventually opportunities will appear. One of the most important attributes of a successful investor is patience.

One of the fortunate things for us has been that the majority of the increase in our funds under management has come from new and very distinct mandates that are different from our original mandate. For instance, the initial pool of money we started managing included Wilson Asset Management Equity Fund and WAM Capital, and is run with a research-driven and market-driven mandate. Both funds were classified as being traders for tax purposes. The next pool of capital was Wilson Investment Fund, which is an investor for tax purposes with a long-term investment horizon. It uses an investment-driven and research-driven approach. Then came Wilson Leaders, which is focused on investing in the top 100 companies and managed by Justin Braitling. More recently, we have assumed management of the International Wine Investment Fund, which has a mandate to invest in wine-related companies around the world.

Since raising the money for the listed investment company, Wilson Investment Fund, in August 2003, you have only invested approximately 50 per cent of the funds into stocks. Why?

The simple answer is we haven't been confident enough with the investment opportunities to invest more. When managing money it is important to stay true to your style. If you can't find companies that exhibit good investment fundamentals, you don't invest. It is important for fund managers to stick to their methodology of investing. A lot of people have been caught out following the herd. If you can't find value in the market, stay in cash, because as history continues to show us, eventually opportunities will appear. One of the most important attributes of a successful investor is patience and, unfortunately, a large number of investors don't possess it. We will only invest when we believe the rewards significantly outweigh the risks.

Do you believe that fund managers should get paid to hold cash?

Fund managers should be paid to manage money. Depending on their mandate, there are three types of exposures they can have to the stock market. They can own shares — long equities. They can sell shares they don't own — short equities. Or they can hold cash, which gives them no exposure to the market.

If you have an absolute return focus with one of your goals being not to lose money, cash is a good place to be if you can't find investment opportunities. It's better being in cash than investing in shares you believe are overpriced. If you are a relative return fund manager, you shouldn't hold cash because your mandate is to perform relative to an index and you are looking for the cheapest companies relative to the other companies. Shares can be very expensive to an absolute fund manager but they can be relatively cheap compared to another company.

We like to manage money on an absolute basis and if you can't find value in the market, we believe you should hold cash rather than buy a stock you believe is overpriced.

You are one of the few managers who has the ability to short stocks. Do you short much and do you believe the outlook for shorting is improving?

When you short stocks you sell shares in a company with the expectation of buying them back at a lower price. The difficulty about shorting stocks is that on average the stock market increases by 7 to 9 per cent a year. If you were short the market, over time you would lose 7 to 9 per cent a year minus the interest on the money you receive from selling the stocks.

Also, shorting stocks is a very different mindset to buying stocks. When you're looking for shares to buy, you're looking for all the attributes that will push the stock up; when you are shorting, you are looking for all the negatives. Over the last eight years, our biggest short position was equivalent to 40 per cent of the portfolio during the Asian crisis in 1998. Since then, we haven't had more than 5 per cent of the portfolio short. It's good to have flexibility to short but it is a difficult skill to perfect. The ability to make and lose money from shorting has increased over the last ten years because companies' share prices react much more violently to new information. This has been a result of an increase in the number of investors being able to short sell, together with a greater focus on absolute performance.

What have you learnt during the past two years and how has this changed your style of investing?

Patience. Remaining patient with the new fund has made me realise the investing public en masse is very impatient. Their impatience has and will continue to provide opportunities. Secondly, don't panic. It's a lesson that I am taught time and time again.

———————●———————

Geoff Wilson seems a little more pragmatic and market-savvy than some of the investors in this book. While others find that sticking to a rigid investment philosophy works for them, Wilson blends some basic principles of value investing with an ability to make money out of short-term trades in companies he might otherwise prefer not to hold for the long term. In part, this reflects his first-hand knowledge of the way in which the broking industry works.

Understanding market flows and who might be buying and selling shares in a particular company is a heavy determinant of a company's share price in the short term. At the same time, his focus on the small-cap end of the market enables him to identify companies that have strong and credible management and good profit growth prospects in industries with favourable characteristics.

This approach explains why Wilson has been able to deliver returns clearly in excess of market indices in most of the years since he started his own funds management firm.

15

A new beginning
Greg Perry

Greg Perry's return to funds management in early 2005 was heralded with a full page dedication by the country's leading business column — *The Australian Financial Review's* 'Chanticleer'. The fact that it was thought worthwhile to spend so much space discussing his supposedly low-key return sends two clear messages to the investment community. Firstly, fund managers have, like their American colleagues, reached star status and, secondly, Perry is a hero among these stars.

Greg Perry took a long time to work out what he could do in life. He attempted university several times in the mid- to late 1970s before deciding to study commerce. After that, he became a stockbroking analyst with establishment firm JB Were, despite coming from the blue collar side of the tracks. Perry, Labor Party to the bone, found it very difficult to express his talents in the ultra-conservative establishment broking firm and in the mid-1980s he made the bold decision to leave the security of a broking job to join the lowly paid ranks of funds management. His first job in the funds management game was for a company controlled by New Zealand entrepreneur Sir Frank Renouf. It was in this period Perry felt the full thrust of the job, riding the 1980s sharemarket boom right into the crash of

1987. After the crash he travelled before landing a job at Colonial First State. In the early 1990s, First State managed the relatively tiny amount of $100 million. By the time Perry left the firm in 2002, First State was the largest equity manager in the country, with more than $20 billion in funds under managment.

The stunning success of First State was built on the back of Perry's philosophy, labelled 'GDP Plus'. Put simply, Perry was looking for well-managed companies that had the ability to grow at a faster rate than the rest of the economy for an extended period. Unlike many of the other Masters, who concentrate on finding value stocks, Perry is an unashamed growth-focused manager. The stockpicking skills that propelled First State from minnow to a leviathan of the funds management industry made him a hero not only to his investors but also his peers, who admired him as a tough competitor. His big calls in the 1990s included media stocks like Kerry Packer's Publishing and Broadcasting, St George Bank, Bank of Melbourne and, later in the decade, the first of the many infrastructure stocks that came to market.

In 2000, Commonwealth Bank took over Colonial and in the process, its subsidiary Colonial First State. Two years later Perry, who served out his existing contract, left the firm and disappeared for two years. While it is not known what Perry was paid on his departure from First State, it can be assumed that he had ample money to make a comfortable living investing his own money at home. Perry is reluctant to talk about his own investing in that two-year period but he does say he beat the market comfortably, concentrating primarily on tech stocks. In that time he also decided it would be fun to spend time investing offshore in places like the US and China. Perry has always had a global fascination. In the late 1980s, he travelled through Europe seeing the incredible benefits that the fall of communism had on the US economy.

Perry was not really keen to enter the limelight again. Despite his love of media stocks and the infatuation with the people who control them, he shies away from any publicity. Eventually, his old colleague Barry Henderson coaxed him out of hiding in 2005, convincing him to join a new company called QED. Unlike the days at First State, Perry is not at the helm of QED, instead preferring to spend three days a week in the office concentrating on the group's offshore investments. The day-to-day job of running the business is left to Henderson and First State's former top-ranked analyst

Catherine Allfrey. QED is a trust for people who want to invest a minimum of $500 000.

Despite his fresh beginning, Perry made it clear that his interview in the first edition of *Masters of the Market* was his last. When approached for an update he simply said the first time around was a stressful experience and that QED was only just beginning and had no track record to talk about. We did not push him and thanked him for his first edition contribution.

We have very few doubts that any fund that relies on stockpicking and has Perry involved will be a success. He possesses the great intangible that we all would love to have — a sixth sense about whether stocks are going to go higher or lower.

16

Making a stand
Peter Morgan

Peter Morgan these days is probably one of Australia's best known fund managers, famous for his barbed comments about establishment boards. Morgan, or 'Grumpy' as he is nicknamed by many stockbrokers who have been on the end of his sometimes brusque manner, is incredibly respected because not only was he once head of equities at Perpetual Investments, one of Australia's most successful share fund managers, but in 2002 he left and created another powerful fund manager called 452 Capital.

After an unsuccessful stint in broking in the 1980s, Morgan joined Perpetual in 1990 when the company was tiny among equity fund managers, with less than $100 million under management. By the time he left twelve years later, that figure had grown by 1300 per cent to $13 billion (at the time of writing, under head of equities John Sevior, the figure has grown again to $20 billion). During his time leading the team between 1995 and 2002, Perpetual managed to deliver an average return of 14.27 per cent per annum, and Morgan and his team ran the top-ranked Australian shares fund. In comparison, the return on Australian shares averaged 9.6 per cent in the seven years to 31 August.

Morgan's decision to leave Perpetual was motivated by two factors. He wanted to get back to the good old days when he enjoyed investing, something that had waned as Perpetual's funds under management swelled. More importantly, he wanted to test himself and unleash his competitive nature. 452 was a reflection of this. Named in reference to a song about the late cricketing great Sir Don Bradman and his highest score, 452 has in short time become one of Australia's most successful boutique fund managers.

When we last spoke to Morgan, 452 was in its infancy, having only been up and running for a year. Morgan had left Perpetual as its head of equities, to the initial chagrin of loyal investors in the parent company Perpetual Trustees. Perpetual has survived his exit but 452 has become an influential fund manager in its own right, with about $4 billion in equities under management.

The creation of 452 was vindicated through the decision by one of Australia's biggest banks, the Commonwealth Bank of Australia, to take a minority stake in 452. That left Morgan and fellow staff still in control but it meant a parting of the ways with 452's co-founder, former investment banker Warwick Negus. Negus left to run the funds management business of Colonial First State, CBA's own iconic funds management arm. While there was speculation of a falling out between the pair, Morgan denied there had been any 'knockdown' fight and welcomed the shareholding as an important alliance for 452.

At the same time, the bull market (as for many other 'value' managers) hasn't quite been the right market for Morgan to perform in. A listed investment company set up by 452 has been trading at a discount to the issue price and 452's performance, as represented by the performance of a fund set up with Colonial, had lagged behind the market's robust gains.

Morgan was not keen to talk to us this time around for reasons that were not entirely clear, although it is quite apparent that little has changed in terms of Morgan's investing style.

Despite Morgan's blue-blooded upbringing — growing up in the exclusive North Shore suburb of Mosman, attending the expensive private school Scots College and then attending Sydney University to do economics — there are no pretences about him. He is incredibly direct and one is left in little doubt about where he stands on a particular issue. In something of a contradiction given his high media profile, Morgan eschews public gatherings and is no socialite.

His profile soared as he fearlessly took an active role in tackling some of the country's most powerful and entrenched boards. When boards and management stumbled, Morgan took it upon himself to voice the concerns of many small shareholders around the nation who had suffered financially. More recently, apart from being a regular media commentator, Morgan is known to write letters to the editor of *The Australian Financial Review* to register his concerns about the issue of the day. Perhaps his most famous battle was with the AMP. He stood up at the group's Melbourne annual meeting in 2000 and attacked the board for failing to put a mooted National Australia Bank takeover proposal to shareholders. Other fights Morgan has picked include his attacks on blue chips CSR and Orica, both of which he talked about at length in our first interviews, but clearly there hasn't been as much of this in the bull market of recent years.

452's investment style is similar to Perpetual's in that it is trying to identify solid and understandable companies that have been undervalued by the market. Both firms have traditionally had big holdings in building materials stocks and, like Perpetual, 452 can often take a stake of 5 per cent or more in a company — such is its confidence.

Conclusion

One of the difficulties in writing a book like this is that the prevailing disposition of the market (a rising and optimistic market in this case) partly shapes the tone of the commentary. The second edition of *Masters of the Market* was written at a time when investors were enjoying a 60 per cent rise in the Australian sharemarket in the space of two years. In an environment when everyone is making money, it can be hard for professional investors to distinguish themselves. This can cause some to question the value they add. As a result, many of the subjects interviewed for this edition were far from celebrating during this period. In the preceding two years (normally viewed as the short to medium term), some of our subjects had prospered but others felt enormous pain. A market rising on a daily basis can make even the most unsophisticated investor look like a genius. To the frustration of some, this had made the search for value in the sharemarket much more difficult.

The consistent message from the Masters this time around is that now is not the time for complacency. While some were reluctant to make a call on the market outlook, most expressed concern that at least parts of the market, if not the market as a whole, were overvalued. Despite the temptation, they believed it was not a time to be reckless in abandoning sound investment principles.

This book is not meant to be about making specific market predictions at a certain point in history. Rather, the aim has been to explore sharemarket investing techniques that have made certain investors successful over a long period of time, using contemporary examples to practically illustrate the points made.

Perhaps the biggest concern for most of the Masters in the first edition was the Australian investment community's obsession with benchmarks and relative performance on a monthly basis. In the bull market that started in March 2003, it has been difficult for some of our Masters to outperform the Australian market, an achievement most had managed to do for the previous decade. The investment styles and philosophies that we had identified as successful in the long term weren't necessarily so during this period.

Likewise, some of the Masters had been criticised for holding too much cash and missing out on the biggest bull market since the heady days of the mid-1980s. Most of these people are holding their breath waiting for better valuations to appear. How long can they hold their breath, given many of their faces are already turning a light shade of blue?

Anton Tagliaferro, Geoff Wilson, Erik Metanomski and Tim Hughes made it clear in their interviews that they would not change their investment styles to buy shares in companies just because market momentum was driving them higher. And in the long run, history tells us that they will be right. As Erik Metanomski, quoting Warren Buffett, said, 'It is only when the tide goes out that we will be able to see who is swimming nude'. Erik also made the very strong point that he is not paid to simply invest money for the sake of it — instead, his investors trust his ability to buy reasonable companies below what they are worth to reap the benefits in the years to come.

Many of the Masters this time around also believed the Australian marketplace was not pricing risk into the equation properly. With price to earnings multiples for Australia's industrial companies at a remarkable seventeen times earnings and resources in the middle of a boom (at the time of writing), some of the Masters feared investors were starting to price in good times forever. Once again, history tells us that while the Australian sharemarket rises over the long term in sync with economic progression, it never does so in a linear fashion. When will the good times come to an end? Australia is experiencing its longest ever period of uninterrupted economic growth and for many younger people in the workforce a recession is just a word conjured up by their parents.

A price to earnings (P/E) ratio contraction in some stocks would be especially painful. In good markets, if a company has an earnings shock, the stock price may only fall in line with the size of the profit revision. However, when sentiment turns, the share price not only falls by the size of the downgrade but the P/E can contract as well. Say a mining company that has been trading on twenty times earnings in buoyant conditions is suddenly forced to lower its earnings forecast by 30 per cent due to a fall in commodity prices. At the same time, the stock's P/E multiple might also fall from twenty times to ten times as result of the sudden loss of investor confidence, moving the PE much more into line with its historical average. As a result, if the share price was $1 a share before the downgrade, the price might fall to as low as 35¢. That's a loss of 65 per cent. As can be seen, the fall is made much more dramatic by investors' previous willingness to buy the stock on a higher multiple than it ever deserved.

This undercurrent of concern was a familiar theme in many of our interviews and while the conditions were not ideal, some have found a way to continue to beat the market. David Paradice and Alex Waislitz have kept ahead of the pack by listening closely to management of the companies they invest in as they search for clues about future price movements. To date that approach has been a winner.

Others like Sir Ron Brierley and Gary Weiss have largely ignored the overall market, treating the bull market as white noise while they have invested in the same types of corporate situations they always have. For others it has been a time to stay away from the market. Greg Perry has spent two years away from the market but set up his new fund early in 2005, while Robert Maple-Brown has retired and left day-to-day stockpicking at his firm to others.

The challenge for professional investors in strong markets is not only to make a return — they must make more money than everybody else. Many small investors can brag about making huge gains on individual stocks over the last two years, but achieving the same returns with billions of dollars under management and holding up to 100 stocks is a little more difficult. Even in the best bull markets, finding a lot of new investment ideas can be tough.

Our new Masters of the Market reinforced the idea that there is no single formula to success. All three are completely different in their approaches to the investment game but have each managed to achieve returns as good as anyone in the world.

Phil Mathews breaks all the old investment rules such as holding a diversified portfolio and not over-leveraging the portfolio. He backs his judgement with big bets, something many other professional investors are unable or incapable of doing. He is happy to invest up to 35 per cent of his money into one stock and often uses debt to leverage the potential return. His oil call appears to have proved a stunning success (at least at the time of writing) that could never have been contemplated by other managers.

Peter Guy, who scours the small- and micro-cap end of the market for suitable investments, has stuck to his knitting and invested in companies that have long-term growth prospects. Strongly performing stocks such as child-care group ABC Learning Centres and radiology and aged care business DCA Group have helped produce gains of more than 20 per cent a year for more than a decade. Like Mathews, he is prepared to hold a concentrated portfolio and a big exposure to his favourite stocks. However, unlike Mathews, he has to contend with outside investors and they make sure he limits his exposure to individual investments to around 15 per cent of the fund.

Andrew Sisson of Balanced Equity Management was in another league altogether. Espousing a philosophy of avoiding speculation of any kind, Sisson showed that a conservative investment philosophy of investing in only the top fifty stocks rather than trying to look at too many different stocks was another path to investing success. This approach delivered his investors a consistent return above the market over a medium- to long-term investment horizon.

While some of our Masters have found themselves in the outside lane in the bull markets of 2003, 2004 and 2005, their track records suggest they will be back in front soon enough. Perhaps in two or three years' time, they can tell us how they have fared.

Glossary

Accumulation index A total return index. This type of index measures both the price movement and the return by way of dividend or other income payments. This index produces a superior return than the price index alone, because it assumes that dividends are reinvested across the whole index portfolio. The S&P/ASX 200 Accumulation Index returned 12.48 per cent a year on average from 30 June 1990 to 30 June 2002, compared with 8.17 per cent a year for the price index alone. In the year to 30 June 2002, the price index fell 7.86 per cent, while the accumulation index fell 4.69 per cent, according to Standard & Poor's.

All Ordinaries Index, S&P/ASX 200, S&P/ASX 300 The All Ordinaries (or All Ords) is still usually quoted as the index measuring the overall performance of the Australian stock market over time. The index comprises the 500 largest companies in Australia by market capitalisation, representing about 99 per cent of the Australian sharemarket in dollar terms. In April 2000, the All Ords was changed from a benchmark index to a market indicator index, meaning some other indices provided a better representation of the highly liquid stocks in the market. For this reason, the S&P/ASX 200 Accumulation Index (or, alternatively, S&P/ASX 300) is often quoted as the benchmark. It is more often used by fund managers as the gauge from which to measure how much value they have added for investors. The S&P/ASX 200 captures the performance of the top 200 companies. There are many other indices that capture smaller samples, such as the top twenty or top fifty, or individual sectors, such as financials, utilities or telecommunications.

Amortisation/depreciation   Accounting treatments that require companies to gradually extinguish or write-off the value of an asset on the balance sheet over the life of that asset. This non-cash expense has to be watched closely as it can be applied in such a way as to over- or under-inflate reported profits. This is one reason why analysts extract these costs from their assessment of underlying value.

Analyst   Person in a stockbroking or funds management firm who undertakes research into companies, often specialising in one sector. Analysts will make the buy, sell or hold recommendations, but will not usually wear the loss (as the investor will) when they are wrong.

Arbitrage trading   Trading in such a way as to benefit from a mismatch in pricing between two different markets. The mismatch occurs because investors in different markets may have different views. Traders may be able to buy cheaply the same or similar asset in one market and sell it in another market. A common example is the typically slight difference in price of the SPI 200 Futures contract on the Sydney Futures Exchange and the level of the S&P/ASX 200 index. But there are many other scenarios as well.

Benchmarking   The services provided by asset consultants who compare the relative performance of funds in order to rank them from best to worst. Allows investors and financial planners to choose the best funds, but many believe benchmarking is a negative influence on sound stockpicking. Consultants also try to make the investing process as scientific as possible, using concepts such as 'tracking error' and the Sharpe Ratio, which respectively measure the deviation from the index and the risk/reward equation for a portfolio or fund.

Bottom-up investing   A fancy way of describing good old-fashioned stockpicking. As opposed to top-down investing, the investor does not invest with reference to overall economic themes.

Bulls and bears   A bull market is an optimistic one that is rallying. A bear market is pessimistic and falling.

Cashbox A term (often pejorative) used to describe the phenomenon of companies that have raised money from the sharemarket with little or no indication as to how the money would be invested. In late 2004–05, $2.6 billion was raised by three cashboxes, Allco Equity Partners (which subsequently used the money to bid for Baycorp Advantage), Babcock & Brown Capital (which at the time of writing had not invested the $1 billion raised) and Macquarie Capital Alliances (which has bought a European directories business Yellow Brick Road and an aged care business).

Cash flow Technically net profit and then the adding back of non-cash or accounting charges such as amortisation and depreciation and one-off items like write-offs. *See also* free cash flow.

Cyclical company A company that has earnings that go up and down with the overall economy. For example, building materials companies' earnings are highly reliant on the housing market. They will tend to trade on low PEs to reflect the risks of holding these stocks through the good times and the bad.

Dividend/distribution yield The dividend per share expressed as a percentage of the share price. Property trusts and banks have high yields because they pay big dividends.

Earnings per share A company's net profit after tax, divided by the number of shares on issue. The figure is necessary for calculating the price/earnings ratio, and can also be expressed as, 'Company X made a profit of X¢ a share'.

EBITDA Earnings before interest, tax, depreciation and amortisation. Often used by analysts for ratio analysis because it can be considered a better measure of a company's underlying profitability. EBITDA is also (in most cases) analogous to operating cash flow.

Enterprise value The value of a company expressed by adding together the value of its equity (usually its market capitalisation) plus its outstanding debt.

Financial engineering A term used to describe the sometimes complex financial structuring used by investment banks and companies to create new investment products. An example is the growing number of listed infrastructure funds, often carrying debt to equity ratios of more than 100 per cent.

Franking   An important consideration for fending off the tax office. The extent to which a company has already paid tax on any dividends paid, enabling shareholders to access credits to offset against their tax.

Free cash flow   This takes the analysis of cash flow a step further. Free cash flow is cash flow from operations (this can be seen by looking at the cash flow statement in a company's annual report) less capital expenditures and working capital. This is, in effect, the money the company has after it has reinvested sums into maintaining its business to remain competitive. Free cash flow allows companies to pay down the principal of their debt or to build cash on their balance sheets.

Fundamental analysis   Analysis that looks at the tangible drivers of a company's value and growth (and hopefully share price) including earnings, revenue and asset backing. These factors are used to arrive at a valuation to identify whether a stock is cheap or expensive.

Futures   A whole other world of products traded on the Sydney Futures Exchange. A form of derivative product whereby a trader can agree to buy (or sell) a security at a future date, potentially profiting from a more leveraged entry price. Futures are discussed at length in Brian Price's interview in the first edition of *Masters of the Market*.

Gap, gapping   A large one-off movement in the price of a security usually due to a lack of liquidity and/or the occurrence of a sudden event.

Gearing   A company's level of debt, usually measured as a proportion of equity. Same as a debt to equity ratio. Generally, it's better not to have much debt, though some companies that have steady, predictable profits (such as infrastructure companies) can carry high levels of debts and this is seen as an efficient means of maximising returns to shareholders.

Growth company   A company that is generally growing at rates greater than the overall economy. These companies usually trade on high PEs as investors price in expectation of future higher profits than these companies are earning today. The dotcoms were growth stocks — or were meant to be at least.

Hedging   Investing to minimise the risk of losses, usually by going short or using a derivative. Despite this, operators of hedge funds have been given a bad name because they are often short-term investors, can have a major bearing on movements in the price of a security to the chagrin of company management and are sometimes seen as speculators. Not true, of course.

Index funds   Funds that merely replicate an index, such as the S&P/ASX 200, and therefore achieve the average return. Not the investment strategy of any of the subjects of this book.

Investment bank   A financial institution usually offering corporate advisory, stockbroking and financial markets services to investors and companies. Large investment banks in Australia include Macquarie Bank, UBS, Goldman Sachs JBWere, Citigroup, Deutsche Bank and JP Morgan.

Leverage   Using borrowings or other instruments to magnify the returns.

Liquidity   The depth of the market, enabling an investor to trade in and out of a stock at the prevailing market price. An illiquid market might force a seller to accept a lower than market price because of a lack of buyers in the market.

Listed investment company   A stock exchange listed company generally owning a spread of sharemarket investments. LICs, popular with retail investors, enable investors to get an exposure to a portfolio of shares. Long-standing LICs include Australian Foundation Investment Company, Argo Investments and Milton Corporation, while the new breed includes Century Australia, WAM Capital, Hunter Hall Global Value and MMC Contrarian.

Long, long position or going long   Trading in the expectation that the shares will go up. As simple as that.

Margin call   Sums that must be paid by holders of options or futures contracts or other leveraged investments once the trade starts to move the wrong way and losses begin to accrue.

Market capitalisation   Also known as market value. The sharemarket value of a company calculated by multiplying the share price by the number of shares that company has issued to investors.

Mutual fund   The US term for superannuation funds or unit trusts.

Net assets per share or net asset backing   A company's net assets (assets minus liabilities) expressed in cents per share. Shares trading at a discount to net assets might be worth taking a look at, but investors need to find out what those assets are.

Options   An agreement to buy or sell a security or asset at a future point in time but without the obligation. The buyer of the option usually pays a small sum for that right, which is given up if the option is unexercised. A call option is an option to buy; a put option an option to sell. An option writer is the party that offers the option.

Placements, rights issues, floats   All different ways for companies to raise share capital. A placement is only available to sophisticated investors, although companies can't issue more than 15 per cent of their capital in this way without shareholder approval. A rights issue gives all shareholders the ability to subscribe to a share issue in proportion to their holding. A float or initial public offering usually involves a capital raising resulting in the company listing on the stock exchange.

Price/earnings ratio or multiple (PE)   The simplest of valuation tools for the private investor, which can be expressed in several ways. As the term suggests, it is the stated market price of a stock divided by its earnings per share. Usually expressed as 'A company is trading on a PE multiple of X times its historical or forecast earnings per share'. It enables an investor to look at a basket of stocks on a level playing field and evaluate which is the cheapest or most expensive. Another way of expressing it is, assuming this year's earnings are the same year in, year out, the PE represents the number of years it would take for a company's earnings to pay for the market value of the stock. Investors should determine whether they are using historical or forecast figures (most newspapers only calculate the PE on a historical basis, whereas it is better to look at future profits) and to what extent they have been adjusted (analysts try to do this) to give a true picture of the underlying earnings of the company. But the ratio should not be the only measure an investor uses before purchasing a stock.

Private equity   An increasingly important asset class giving investors an exposure to unlisted companies — usually companies that need further investment before they are suitable to be listed on the Australian Stock Exchange. A number of companies that floated on the Australian Stock Exchange in 2004 and 2005 were previously owned by private equity funds. Private equity funds use high levels of debt and target returns of 20 to 30 per cent annually while carrying the risk of potentially holding an illiquid investment.

Prospectus   A document outlining an investment opportunity. Read every page.

Scrip   A fancy way of saying shares or the certificate (or piece of paper) denoting ownership of shares. Short for subscription.

Short position   A trade whereby the investor expects to profit when the share price goes down. Good luck. Short selling was banned in 1971 but reintroduced in 1986 as the government deregulated the securities industry — just in time for the crash in October 1987. Interestingly enough, listed among the ASX's approved short selling securities back in 1988 were Adelaide Steamship, Bond Corporation, Hooker Corp, Kern Corporation and Elders IXL.

Top-down investing or analysis   Applying a reading of the broad economy or sectors of the economy to determine which stocks to invest in. For instance, investing in a retailer like Woolworths in the belief that a good economy will spur supermarket sales.

Total return   When measuring the return on an investment, this measure takes into account capital growth, the rise in the share price, plus the dividend return. Some stocks draw a higher proportion of the return from dividends, usually because they distribute a high level of their income back to shareholders in the form of dividends. Property trusts usually trade on high dividend or distribution yields, but the traded price usually doesn't rise or fall as much as that of companies that reinvest their profits in growth.

Value   An elusive concept, but something that is under-priced is value as everyone knows. A value investor applies this principle to picking stocks, usually meaning the investor places less emphasis on growth projections and is careful about the price paid for a stock.

Index